I0414430

What Strange Mystery Unites the Turkish Nations, India, Catholicism, and Mexico?

What Strange Mystery Unites the Turkish Nations, India, Catholicism, and Mexico?

✦

A Concise but Detailed History of Things Divine and Earthly

Gene D. Matlock

iUniverse, Inc.

New York Lincoln Shanghai

What Strange Mystery Unites the Turkish Nations, India, Catholicism, and Mexico?
A Concise but Detailed History of Things Divine and Earthly

Copyright © 2006 by Gene D. Matlock

All rights reserved. No part of this book may be used or reproduced by any means, graphic, electronic, or mechanical, including photocopying, recording, taping or by any information storage retrieval system without the written permission of the publisher except in the case of brief quotations embodied in critical articles and reviews.

iUniverse books may be ordered through booksellers or by contacting:

iUniverse
2021 Pine Lake Road, Suite 100
Lincoln, NE 68512
www.iuniverse.com
1-800-Authors (1-800-288-4677)

ISBN-13: 978-0-595-39446-3 (pbk)
ISBN-13: 978-0-595-83843-1 (ebk)
ISBN-10: 0-595-39446-9 (pbk)
ISBN-10: 0-595-83843-X (ebk)

Printed in the United States of America

I dedicate this book to the all the Mexican people, in the hopes that what I say will help them realize their full potential as a nation. I have lived among them for nearly 65 years and have come to admire them very much. They well deserve to be happy and prosperous in their own country.

I especially dedicate it to my great friends Hector and Micaela Abrego, her husband Fidel, my deceased Mexican wife Consuelo's fine cousins Antonio and Antonia Corona, Rita Ruvalcaba and her family, Adelberto and Guadalupe Pérez, Angel and María Perez, Consuelo's relatives in Mexico, my friends Noé and Trinidad Valencia, Anselmo and Ofelia Luviano, José and Maura Albarrán, Martín and Marta Morales, Leodegario and Amparo Luviano, Cirilo and Beda Saucedo, Francisco and Consuelo Velásquez, Pedro and Margarita Mata, Eduardo and Rebecca Felix, Eduardo's mother and sisters, Estela Talamantes, Alfredo and Carmen Beltrán, Alfredo's mother and father, Jaime and Viridiana Jorge, my great Salvadoran neighbor Mauricio Velásquez and wife Luz, Juan and Berta Villa (Let's not forget my *nietecita)*, Guadalupe and Cleo Lázaro, Ignacio and Sofía Vásquez, Alberto and Yolanda Franco, and all the other fine Mexican people who have blessed my life in so many ways. I couldn't begin to count them all. When Consuelo died, they were beside me every step of the way-in every way. And, of course, I include Consuelo in this dedication. I am almost convinced that Consuelo actually helped me write this book, for it rose up from the depths of my soul, with hardly any effort on my part. No one loved the USA more than Consuelo. She was fond of saying, "I have three priorities in my life. The first is God; the second is the USA; the third is my husband."

I know how it pained these good, hard-working people to be forced to leave their beloved country where conditions presently give them little hope for progress. I have thought hard and long about the Mexican people and want to share with them a secret that not even they may know. This is my way of saying thanks for having helped make my life so fascinating and intellectually fruitful. It is a rigorous and entirely scientific spiritual solution that will work for them as well as for us *gringuitos.* If the solution I offer in this book is applied, no longer will my fellow countrymen have to resent the influx of so many millions of them, for the Mexicans will find happiness and full stomachs in their own country.

Contents

1

The Strange Circumstances Surrounding the Writing of This Book.

Why is this book entitled, *What Strange Mystery Unites the Turkish Nations, India, Catholicism, and México?* Why did I dedicate it to the Mexican people? What does all this have to do with true spirituality? And why did I discuss in detail the cultural, spiritual, and blood links connnecting the Turks, Hindus, and Mexicans?

Several years ago, I established an online correspondence with a well-known *Sanatana Dharma* (the real name of Hinduism) holy man and devotee to the Sanatana Dharma Mother Goddess, Mr. T. L. Subash Chandra Bose, a Dravidian living in India's state of Tamil Nadu. Most of our correspondence focused on our mutual conviction that India had something to do with the pre-Columbian colonization of Mexico. Central America, and South America. I had already written several books about this matter. Mr. Bose is so convinced of this, that after his death, he wants his ashes scattered over the Nazca plains in Peru.

When I wrote him that I had finished this book and the extremely difficult circumstances leading to its conclusion, he reminded me that he had predicted all this to me just before Consuelo's death on Monday, August 15, 2004. He asked me to tell my readers this.

On Sunday, March 19, 2006, he wrote me:

> Dear Brother *Shree* Gene (Author's note: *Shree* is a term of respect.),
> Please add the below mail in your book, as my respect for your [deceased] wife Consuelo. You can correct the grammar accordingly.

Mr. Bose included the copy of the letter he wrote me a few days after Consuelo entered the hospital, critically ill of the rare human ailment called vasculitis. She was put on life support. On August 12, I decided to have this support removed and let her die as God intended. On that same day, Brother Bose wrote me as follows:

> Dear big brother *Shree* Gene,
>   No one can console you. You are a man of principle with noble thoughts. That is the reason why God blessed you with your wife Mrs. Consuelo, a Mexican woman, as a good life partner for you.
>   As a true brother, Brother Gene, let me tell you, there is but one man in a thousand who respects women. I should write this: She is a divine woman. You must treat her as the Mother Goddess in the near future.
>   You have a lot to do for the indigenous Americans. Be bold; face all the worst conditions…Again, I am insisting that you be with her [in spirit]. She wants to tell you what you have to do in your future.
>   Sorry brother, Saturday and Sunday are the crucial days and also the coming dark moon day.
>   O Mother, take care of your child. You know everything. We do not know anything; so we beg you to turn your smiling face towards your child.
>   May I request that you have a friend buy a red rose on my behalf and give it to my sister-in-law after touching her feet and telling her that her South Indian brother-in-law respects her as his mother.

On that very day, I told Consuelo's doctor to remove her from life support at 1.00 P.M. on Sunday, August 14. Friends and relatives gathered to be present when it happened. At precisely 5:00 A.M., on Monday, Consuelo died. I was with her at that moment.

As you read in his letter to me, Mr. Bose wrote that Consuelo had something to say to me for my future. He said that I should do something to help the Mexicans free themselves from the cultural chains keeping them from progressing. He said that I would be under severe duress while I did this.

Soon after Consuelo's death, I wrote my book, *The Ego-Mankind's Inner Terrorist.* By concentrating on this book, I was able to overcome my grief appreciably. Then, at the last half of August, 2005, some other depressing circumstances attacked me. I then wrote the second book, *Christianity-Mankind's First Worldwide Religion!* Writing has always been therapeutic for me. This one renewed me inwardly. After several hours of researching and writing every day, I always came away feeling refreshed and almost reborn.

During February, 2006, some extremely negative influences hit me like an avalanche. An inner urging pressured me to write a book concentrating on spiritual science. I felt as if something had taken possession of me while I was writing it. I am even partially convinced that my deceased wife Consuelo was guiding me from wherever she was. She knew of my deep interest in Mexico, the origins of its indigenous people, spirituality, and the origins of all religions. She always told me that if she went first, she'd return somehow to tell me what I needed to know and guide me.

The book you are now reading benefited me more than any other. I'd work on it for as long as 12 hours a day. Instead of getting tired, I felt refreshed and exhilarated as never before! During this time, I acted like a recluse, going out only to buy groceries and return. Sometimes the neighbors worried about me, thinking that I had died. When they called me to the door, I told them not to worry because I felt inspired to get to the root of Mexico's problems.

If anyone doubts the truth of what I am saying, there's no lack of evidence. Everything happened exactly as Brother Bose said it would, and exactly as I said it did. When Brother Bose wrote me the letter when Consuelo was dying, I read it to dozens of people before she passed away. I also read it during the Mass for Consuelo as a eulogy. The church was filled to overflowing. Many friends and relatives of Consuelo and me had to wait outside in the parking lot. Both Brother Bose and I have copies of the letter. If proof is what anyone needs to verify certain facts, he and I have it. You have already read Brother Bose's letter exactly as he wrote it to me, except for a few minor grammar corrections. The original is in my files-and his. Other strange things happened during this time also, some of which even my neighbors saw for themselves. As a result, I don't think any of my neighbors will ever become atheists!

I say this: Whoever "helped" me write this book was telling me exactly what we humans must know in order to enjoy a measure of peace and happiness in this old world.

Although I have spoken of a "spiritual" solution to mankind's problems, the term "spiritual solution" is actually inappropriate. Each human and his spirit are a dual entity. No peace or harmony on earth can come to the world if the spirit or the body must be emphasized at the expense of the other. For example, America tends to be a materialistic country. But this emphasis leads to social dissension, crime, and other injustices. Now, let's take India. It tends to concentrate on a purely "spiritual" approach to mankind's problems. For that reason, India is a hell for poor people, just as Mexico is a hell for its lower classes. Perhaps, after applying the simple "dual techniques" in this book, we humans will agree collectively that only a "dual" approach to human problems can be successful. But we must first know what "duality" really means where "spirituality" is concerned. What I have to say next and in the chapters to come may help.

If each human's real self is an eternal and subtle entity or spirit encased in a large piece of animated clay, and if this self actually exists, there must be a scientifically applicable and measurable technology for people to reconnect with it. Furthermore, scriptures, singing, preaching, conversion tactics, bible-thumping, speculation, and other bizarre behaviors we call "spiritual," may not be spiritual at all, but ineffectual and potentially destructive gropings in the dark.

Several thousand years ago, a highly civilized and cultured people lived happily and abundantly in a paradise near the northern polar regions. All the major religions on earth, of whatever nationality, state emphatically that they were the original five races of mankind. In Judaism and Christianity, we call this paradise Eden. The Hindus call it Uttara Kuru. The Tibetan Buddhists call it Khedar Khand (Country of God Shiva) and Shambala. It was also called *Sivariya* or *Sibirya* (Land of God Shiva), now called Siberia. The ancient Greek historians and myths referred to it as Hyperborea. The Chinese Taoists don't call it by a specific name, but they do describe it as a type of paradise where men lived in complete harmony with Nature.

The original five races, called Panchala (Phoenician) Krishti, Krishtaya, Krishtihan, or Kurus, were said to be able to live for hundreds of years in a state of complete bliss and harmony. They were able to maintain their enviable state through a science involving knowledge of Duality, The Holy Trinity, The Cross, and the powerful energies emanating from the sun from east to west. In those days, they knew nothing of sectarian religions. They knew only that their superior way of life was "The Krishtaya or Krishti Way of Life." Many hundreds of years later, when mankind invented names for his "gods," such as Shiva, Vishnu, Krishna, Apollo, Mithra, Dionysius, Jupiter, Zeus, Surya, Rama, Tengri, Indra, Quetzalcoatl, Kukulkan, Bochica, Agni, Kedar, Keyser, or any others, these names just hid what it really was: Krishtaya or Krishti (the original five races of mankind). You can verify what I have just said for yourself. Refer to the online Sanskrit Lexicon. Krishti or Krishtaya (spelled as Krsti in the dictionary) preceded Judaism, Hinduism, Buddhism, Jainism, or any other religious "ism." It was Krishti or Krishtaya then, and it is now-no matter what name it hides behind.

According to Hindu mythology, after approximately thirty thousand years of the existence of mankind's original fully developed civilization, a sudden shift of the earth's axis turned Kedar Khand into a frozen hell. The Kurus or The Five Krishtayas, whom we now call Turks, were forced to flee southward. In time, they united with the indigenous inhabitants of India, turning all of Central Asia and India into a single nation. Eventually, they fanned out in other directions also. Consequently, everybody on earth can trace his bloodline directly or indirectly to the Turks.

In this book, I describe much of what is presently known about the ancient Turks and their virtually infallible spiritual science. Will it work?

Some people have told me that I must be foolishly desperate to approach this riddle of mankind's spiritual nature as if it were something real. They think it is just an unreachable and vain fairy tale people yearn for during Sunday church services, on the battle field, and at the moment of their respective deaths.

They are entirely correct. I am desperate. They would be wise to get desperate as well. In his spiritual ignorance, modern Man has made a complete mess of this planet. Even some backward and barbaric theocracies are developing weapons of mass destruction-and they're not afraid to use them. I can't think of a better time to put the Turkish Krishtihans' spiritual science to the test than right now! We are seeing that the specter of Armageddon is no longer a religious scare tactic. It can be real. Which of the two do you prefer? The reality of Armageddon and the destruction of all life on Earth? Or that of a truly valid spiritual science?

2

When Are We Going to Learn the Real Meanings of Belief and Science?

In this book, I'm going to attempt to prove that the Noachide Flood was not the last time God (Creation) has tried to force mankind to live by Divine Law, which the Chinese call *Tao,* and what the Hindus call *Dharma* (The Science of Life).

God's first attempt to reform mankind was to send Adam and Eve out of Eden. If Adam and Eve were forced to work for a living, perhaps they would have insufficient time to commit evil acts. But honest work proved to be of no value. Mankind immediately began to destroy himself again, as demonstrated by Ham's attempt to perform sodomy on his own father. Both Genesis and the Hindu holy books mention Ham's unspeakable sin:

The following account, taken from the Hindu *Matsya Purana (Fish Chronicle),* is one of several versions of our Noachide Flood account:

> To Satyavarman, that sovereign of the whole earth, were born three sons: the eldest Shem; then Sham; and thirdly, Jyapeti by name.
> They were all men of good morals, excellent in virtue and virtuous deeds, skilled in the use of weapons to strike with, or to be thrown; brave men, eager for victory in battle.
> But Satyavarman, being continually delighted with devout meditation, and seeing his sons fit for dominion, laid upon them the burdens of government.
> Whilst he remained honouring and satisfying the gods, and priests, and kine, one day, by the act of destiny, the king, having drunk mead,
> Became senseless and lay asleep naked. Then, was he seen by Sham, and by him were his two brothers called:

To whom he said, 'What now has befallen? In what state is this our sire?' By these two he was hidden with clothes, and called to his senses again and again.

Having recovered his intellect, and perfectly knowing what had passed, he cursed Sham, saying, 'Thou shalt be the servant of servants.'

And since thou wast a laugher in their presence, from laughter thou shalt acquire a name. Then he gave Sham the wide domain on the south of the snowy mountains.

And to Jyapeti he gave all on the north of the snowy mountains; but he, by the power of religious contemplation, attained supreme bliss.

Compare the above account with our Genesis flood story:

The sons of Noah who came out of the ark were Shem, Ham, and Japheth-Ham being the father of Canaan. These three were the sons of Noah, and from these the whole world branched out.

Noah, the tiller of the soil, was the first to plant a vineyard. He drank of the wine and became drunk, and he uncovered himself within his tent. Ham, the brother of Canaan, saw his father's nakedness and told his brothers outside. But Shem and Japheth took a cloth, placed it against both their backs and, walking backward, they covered their father's nakedness; their faces were turned the other way, so that they did not see their father's nakedness. When Noah woke up from his wine and learned what his youngest son had done to him, he said, "Cursed be Canaan, the lowest of slaves shall he be to his brothers."

And he said, "Blessed be the Lord, the God of Shem, let Canaan be a slave to them. May God enlarge Japheth, and let him dwell in the tents of Shem. And let Canaan be a slave to them." (9:18-28.)

As you'll learn further on in this book, a great civilization called Hyperborea, the northernmost part of what is now known as Siberia or Northern Central Asia, once existed in the region we now call the Arctic Circle. Because so many Hyperboreans or Krishtayas had ceased to be Spiritual Men, devoting themselves to evil deeds, God cursed the Hyperboreans, causing the earth to tilt on its axis. Hyperborea became totally flooded. The tilting of the earth's axis turned the flooded Arctic Circle into a barren, uninhabitable wasteland of ice and snow.

According to the Bible, Noah and his family were the only survivors. In reality, the remnants of five Noachide tribes survived the flood as well as people in other parts of the world.

The Ark floated southward in Central Asia, landing on Mt. Ararat in Armenia. At that time in history, everybody in the world could have spoken only Sanskrit, according to what most of us have been taught. The inhabitants of Hyperborea, the progenitors of every nation on earth, were the people we today call Turks.

It should come as no surprise to us to note that not even the Great Flood was enough to deter mankind from evil. Ham proved that conclusively. It was then that God or Creation devised another strategy:

> Everyone on earth had the same language and the same words. And as they migrated from the east, they came upon a valley in the land of Shinar and settled there. They said to one another, "Come, let us make bricks and burn them hard." Brick served them as stone, and bitumen served them as mortar- And they said, "Come, let us build us a city, and a tower with its top in the sky, to make a name for ourselves, else we shall be scattered all over the world. The Lord came down to look at the city and tower that man had built, and the Lord said, "If as one people with one language for all, this is how they have begun to act, then nothing that they propose to do will be out of their reach. Let us, then, go down and confound their speech there, so that they shall not understand one another's speech. Thus the Lord scattered them from there over the face of the whole earth, and they stopped building the city. That is why it was called Babel, because there the Lord confounded the speech of the whole earth, and from there the Lord scattered them over the face of the whole earth. (*Genesis* 11:1-20.)

Christians and Jews have been conditioned erroneously to "believe" that the building of the Tower of Babylonia took place in Sumeria. I say that the Turks and the ancient Hindus, who founded Sumeria, brought the story with them when they migrated there from the mythical Mt. Meru, the navel, and origin of all the races of mankind. It was really the place where humankind dispersed to other parts of the world. We also know it as *Siyoni (Zion)*, the Sanskrit word for "the source or vulva of all humanity."

Tradition says that Mt. Meru was what is now Mt. Kailasa in Western Tibet. However, it could have been a mountain near Herat, Afghanistan or a similar one in Southeastern Central Asia, near what are now Afghanistan and Pakistan. (Ref: *Ancient Geography of Ayodhya,* by Dr. Shyam Narain Pande.) Many Christians and Jews think Mt. Ararat was the original Mt. Meru, but the Bible does not indicate this.

Another name of Mt. Meru is *Seneru* or *Sinaru,* meaning "Belonging to India." Linguistically, this word appears to be identical to *Shinar* or *Sinar.*

God was merciful enough to leave us with many words from the original language. Two of them are *Belief* and *Science.* These two words are similarly pronounced in most of the world's major languages. If we can recapture the spirits of those two words, we may be able to return to the source.

We humans may come to learn about and understand ourselves and the world more effectively if we learn what the ancient expressions, *Belief, Science,* and *Scientific* really mean.

The compilers of dictionaries usually state that no one knows the origin or etymology of the words *belief* and *believe. Non-Belief* and *Not-Believe* are just *believing negations.* English is an Indo-European language. Some Hindus think English and German are the closest languages to Sanskrit. They should also include Turkish because it, too, helped form our English and Germanic languages.

When the five original human races lived in Hyperborea before the Great Flood, their minds were synchronized with the Universal Mind which knew all things and was never in error. As the Chinese Taoists say, they were the Spiritual Men. However, when mankind's Ego began to take over his thought processes, giving himself false confidence in his thoughts, actions, and potentialities, he slowly lost nearly all contact with the Universal Mind and had to begin to search for truth on his own. No help from God this time around. He also discovered that he could often deceive himself further by making his ideas appear valid by forcing others to follow him.

Examining the Psychology of Religiosity.

Before going further into this chapter and my book, I must describe in detail the potentially lethal emotional state of people wanting to recruit others to suscribe to their thinking about the teachings of certain religio-political doctrines and organizations. When a person concludes that his ideas on these matters are immutable gospels, he automatically gets a feeling of omniscience and self-righteousness. He feels expanded-in tune with the Infinite. I well know this feeling. I feel it now about the subject matter I discuss in this book. It is a good feeling. However, this feeling becomes evil when we use it as justification to organize groups to pressure others to bend to our will.

When I was a child, my parents belonged to the Nazarene fundamentalist Christian church. We were taught that we were the only ones in the world who were right, and that everyone else was wrong. I remember feeling deeply sorry for people who weren't Nazarenes. My friends and I were especially sorry for a Jehovah's Witness family in our neighborhood. One day, a friend and I told the sons in that family how we pitied them and were praying for the salvation of their "poor lost souls." The boys answered that they, too, were as worried about us as we were about them.

When the Iraqi conflict against dictator Saddam Hussein began, thousands of anti-war political activists here in Southern California congregated on the streets, keeping people from going to work or doing other business. They justified their criminal activities by saying they were "just trying to make people aware and wanted them to convert to their way of right thinking." They were convinced that only they were "thinking right." They refused to admit that the innocent people they were harrassing were already aware. They also wanted to go to work, get home from work, or take their children to school and back.

On the day I was reworking this chapter, the legal authorities of Afghanistan were about to condemn a man to death for having converted to Christianity. The Afghan judges wanted to find a way out of the situation by declaring him insane. However, the clerics of Afghanistan's state religion declared that if the courts freed the man, they and their followers would kill him anyway. For this reason, no country should ever be governed indirectly or directly by a theocracy.

But the religious people of Afghanistan aren't the only ones who think that they know what God wants of mankind. A prominent Democratic politician here in the USA said that Jesus wants the United States to liberalize its immigration laws.

As I have already said, I feel as strongly and "omniscient" about what I teach in this book as politicians and religionists feel about their "gospels." In order to keep my "religious ardor" in the right perspective, I undertook a study of all the major religions on earth. I found out that that the seed teachings of all these religions except one (I don't need to mention its name), were exactly what I describe in this book. Therefore, I concluded that all religions except one teach the basic science of spirituality. No one should be encouraged to leave his religion and join another. He is "right" where he is.

I want to warn any religious organization who accepts what I say in this book, not to impose it on members by any sort of pressure. Neither should anyone create an organization to keep members in line. If such happened, Nature would automatically and surely render the teachings totally useless and irrelevant for them. No religion can excommunicate anyone-but Nature certainly can. We call mankind's inalienable and natural right to decide for himself whether or not he is to be saved, Buddhism or Christianity (*Krishtaya*).

We call mankind's ignorant, barbaric, and impossible quest to make people march to the same music, *belief* or *infancy of the human thought processes*. Actually, *belief* is a strange emotion forcing humans to sacrifice their lives to prove or disprove any of their theories, ideas and convictions. They use words to convert prospective followers.

Of course, in order to survive, infant mankind had to take some risks, or he would never have survived. You've heard the trite old expressions, *If you are not with me, you are against me,* and *I don't accept your beliefs, but I'd die for your right to believe them.* I can't think of any more efficient way to die miserable and surely than falling into the mire of *Belief/Not-Belief.*

The Turks and Hindus bequeathed to mankind all his religions. But they did not just sit down someplace and dream up ways to worship God (Creation). Man's religions exist in the innermost depths of the souls of all humans. They are as much a part of us as our own bodies, spirits, behaviors, and minds. In fact, they *are* our own bodies, spirits, behaviors, and minds.

The word *Belief* derives from the name of an ancient Turkic-Hindu God called *Bali, Baliu,* and *Bel.* In ancient Sumeria, God Bel was depicted as a man with a bull's head and horns. He represents the second mystery of the Holy Trinity-The Son-as completely cut off from the Father and the Holy Spirit. His sacred direction was North and South. When cut off from the sacred direction of the Father, East and West, Bel can offer mankind only blood, tribulations, and unending tragedy on earth. That is why Bel was commonly called "Lord Second." (See *The World's Sixteen Crucified Saviors,* by Kersey Graves, p. 128.)

In Orissa, India, *Bali* is a large sect, having hundreds of thousands of followers. Even in the Catholic Church to which I belong, I have seen grotesque images of a blood-spattered Christ in Latin-American communities, minus the Cross, lying in a coffin. In Mexico, thieves, cutthroats, and sinners in general worship Bel as a skeleton named Saint Death. It is especially revered by drug smugglers and cut-throats seeking illegal entry into the United States. The image is commonly seen along the border between Mexico and the United States.

Bel worshipers are often flagellants who torture their bodies in various ways. In the Phillipine Islands, New Mexico, and Mexico, *Penitentes,* as they are so-called, will allow themselves to be nailed to crosses. Supposedly, Eve, the wife of Adam, introduced Adam to the religion of sin and degradation. That is how "Belief got its name: *Baleva/Beleva.* The Hindus also share in common with Christians, Jews, Moslems, Turks, and others the myth of Adam and Eve. It was this myth that gave rise to the now outlawed Hindu custom of *Suttee* (widow burning) on the pyres of their dead husbands.

In Sanskrit, *Bala*="explain, describe, force, against one's will, without being able to help or change things, militarily, troops, young, childish, infantile, not full-grown or developed, newly, rising early, ignorant, simple, foolish, fit for sacrifice, child, fool, simpleton, or any immature living creature,"

Eva means earth, world, conduct, habit, usage, custom. We derived the word Eve from the Sanskrit *Eva*.

The connotation of *Baleva* is, "forcing one's childish, foolish, ignorant, infantile, underdeveloped, sacrifice worthy, earthly habits, conduct, and customs on oneself and others" (preferably on others).

The Turkish *Bela*="calamity; misfortune; evil; trouble."

In Kashmir, India, one of the places to which the Turks emigrated after the flood, *Balava* (believe or belief) means "tumult; disturbance; insurrection; rebellion; mutiny." *Balavayi* (True Believer) means "rioter; one who stars an insurrection; a mob of rioters."

The Spanish *palabra,* meaning "word," derives also from *Belaba*. When we depend on *palabras* or our English *palaver* to teach us the fundamental truths, we're always going to be refugees from Mt. Meru, The Beginning or Source of All Mankind.

We seem to invoke God Bel unconsciously when our baser passions are aroused, such as hate and violence. A warlike, violent-prone person is called "bellicose." In Spanish, he is *bélico*. A person rising up against established authority is a "rebel. When a person loses control of himself, becoming temporarily insane, we may say he has gone "ballistic." It seems that any word in which the syllable *bal/bel* is found implies some undesirable trait, thing, or behavior. For example, a "ball" is at the mercy of ballplayers. A "bull" is either ferocious or meat for dinner. A "balance" or scale implies measuring one thing against another. A "bullet" is a murderous projectile.

For the Phoenicians, *Bel* was the Devil, God of the Underworld.

In India, the members of the Baleva sect observe a special holiday held every mid-August, in which people exchange gifts to show their willingness to sacrifice themselves for the things in which they believe (*Baleva*). According to their myths, a certain king, *Bali Raja,* offered devotion to the God *Narayan,* by giving up his kingdom and his own life. In some parts of India, it is customary for people to celebrate *Baleva* by drawing pictures on the walls of their homes and then worshipping them. They will also place the imprints of their palms on either side of the entrances, hoping that demons will get stuck on them.

Not only was the Ancient Egyptian culture readily assimilated by the Phoenicians, so, too, was that of Sumeria. The result was not only a fusion of cultural beliefs, but also confusion, which resulted in the loss of the original meaning of the Baal Myth.

The god Bel, from whom the Beltane Festival derives its name, was the Ancient Babylonian counterpart of the Syrian Baal.

"Bel" is translated with the titles "Lord" and "Baal". "Baal" is sometimes represented as "Ba-al". Babylon was a village in c2230 BCE when Ur was a city. "Babylon", is the Greek rendition of the Hebrew word "Babel", and is translated as both "Confusion" and "Gate of Bel".

The "Confusion" aspect is recalled in the story associated with the Tower of Babel and the confusion of languages…(*Ancient Egyptians and the Constellations,* by Audrey Fletcher, Adelaide, South Australia; part 15.)

In Sumerian, *Ba*="Father." "*Bel*"=Confusion." *Iva*=Eve. Therefore, when someone says, "I believe," he is really saying, "I, the Father/Mother of Confusion."

It is indeed strange that so many people hallow this hideous Bel or "The Second Son," admitting that they dearly love to be cut off from The Holy Trinity. As Audrey Adelaide said, it means "Confusion" or "Belief."

Basically, all I have said so far renders down to this: Mankind is so confused and lost by the Babel of human languages, scriptures, preaching and words, all governed by his Ego or limited perceptions of life, that he can never attain wisdom by trying to make some true sense of them. He can attain spiritual salvation only by looking inwardly to himself, through the entirely scientific spiritual technology called The Holy Trinity.

Of course, we know that "The Second Son" signifies some good in human existence. But there are always two sides to every question and equation. And there is sacrifice in all three components of the Holy Trinity.

There are also two aspects of the Holy Trinity:

1. *Buddhism* or the efforts of each individual to be his own priest and savior.

2. *Brahmanism* or collective control of human society by the priests and clergy. This is the type of social control leading to horrors like *Suttee,* actual blood sacrifice, arguments, squabbles, all manner of wars, and tragic human lives. In no way should clerics be able to govern human societies, for when and if it happens, the consequences are always dire. No individual, if he has his choice of "druthers," would subject himself to Bel's wrath.

Skeptics often tell me that the Turkic-Sanskrit *Baleva/Balava* doesn't indicate any similarity to our own god *Belief.* When I research the etymology of any word, the word itself must match, or become the mental and physical representation of, its effect. For example, if I find a word in a language that expresses "have," such as the English "got," I realize that it is unrelated to the "God" that means "Creation." If it has the name, it must also have the game. And if it has the game, it must be linked with the name. Ask yourself what, more often than not, is the effect of "believing." I did. "Belief" is the type of behavior and mentation that we humans must employ when we choose to cut ourselves off from the Father and the Holy Ghost. Religious, sectarian, secular, agnostic, skeptic, atheist or not, we immediately revert to worshipping God Bel when we tell someone, "I believe," or "I don't believe." When we utter that word, even when joking, we are automatically saying publicly and privately: "I am ignorant of Divine Truth. I have no knowledge of that which is real. I have no desire to reconnect with the Father and the Holy Ghost. I know only blood, turmoil, and confusion."

No matter how ignorant and/or disdainful of The Holy Trinity he may be, no matter whether he admits it or denies it, the atheist, just by saying he's an atheist, is announcing to the world that he is a card-carrying, wild-eyed, and fanatical worshiper of Bel (The Second Religion). Nature insists that all of us must announce to the world what religion or combination of religions we belong to. She won't have it any other way. No one can fool Mother Nature. Nature doesn't know anything about sects, such as the myriad sects of Hinduism, the 24,000 Christian sects, those of Buddhism, etc., or who is right and who is wrong. But she knows this: By your thoughts and works alone, she can tell you what imbalances of the Holy Trinity exist within your soul.

If you are a beginning student of the entirely scientific and verifiable science of The Holy Trinity, you should know that this book concentrates mainly on the Triune Religion. I must do all in my power to keep your mind riveted on my main objective.

There are many ways for us humans to make sacrifice. Only one requires blood and even violence: *Bel!* Do you want all this confusion to control your every waking and sleeping moment? If you do, sleep in a North-South direction every night. Make sure that unscrupulous politicians, businessmen, criminals and prisoners do it also. Do that, and you'll never be "disappointed." I'll explain this mystery of the "Holy Directions" in the latter part of this book.

When mankind was cast out of Eden (the primordial human environment), he had to make the slow, millenniums-long struggle to return to the source. He soon found out that unlike before, God would never again hand it to him on a silver platter. He had to learn about truth the hard way. Mankind came to forget that he was inexorably connected to the source. He became convinced that his way of thinking and acting as an individual (Ego), or the collective mind of his respective culture, as normal and legitimate. But normal and legitimate it is not! For this reason, Nature puts every conceivable and inconceivable obstacle in Man's way, to keep him from becoming a master of the universe. Most of the trouble we have in the world, and that which is to come, stems from mankind's stubborn, malicious, and conceited insistence on taking his mind and thoughts seriously. Many people will die for their beliefs. We know for sure that they did in ancient Turkey and India. Guess what engendered such folly.

I know without making proper inquiry that more than a few people will read what I have written here, declaring conceitedly and confidently, "I don't believe it!" That is Nature's way of keeping them from finding out what Universal Truth is until they are ready. It represents their reverential devotion to causing wars, civil unrest, and social fragmentation. When will we accept the truth about that word?

I realize that mankind, being a baby in this old world, has not acquired enough knowledge to confront it with solid truths dealing with what and what not to do. Therefore, we are all crushed in the reptilian worship of "The Second God," who is none other than Bel himself.

As much as I cringe in shame and disgust with that expression, I am as much imprisoned in it as anyone else. I cannot open my mouth without using the term. When I'm talking to people, they often wonder why I scorn The Second God. But I can't help myself. I, too, am deplorably ignorant. Listen to the politicians and the pundits on the TV newscasts. They are fanatically generous in imparting their "beliefs" to the world. But the fact that *God Beleva* is our jailor does not give us any excuse to hallow and worship it any longer. We must accelerate human progress and find some way to extricate ourselves from this filthy mire. We must link ourselves tightly with the Father and the Holy Ghost. We must adhere faithfully to the full significance of the Holy Trinity.

If, by now, you are willing to accept the possibility, as I do, that Belief/Not-Belief is an inappropriate and dangerous state of mind in this world, what can we substitute in its stead? I recommend that we live by the spirit of *Cabala*. It means "acceptance." At all times, when we suspect that someone or something is seeking to capture our respective minds, we must train them to affirm this possibility by substituting such expressions as the following:

> I accept the possibility that little green men come here from Outer Space.
> I accept the possibility that the suspect may have commited that crime.
> I accept the possibility that you may not be guilty.
> I suspect that this new political ideology may not be good for humanity.
> I suspect that this automobile salesman wants to cheat me.

Remember: In all cases, never put the negative dependent clause first. Always begin with "accept" or "suspect," placing negative possibilities in the second clause. If we practice using such expressions as these, we may someday bury "The Father of Confusion," mankind's Second God, in a deep grave.

Although this book describes an actual science of spirituality, I want you to study books about and cultivate friendships with atheists in order to further your knowledge and deepen your wisdom. Where books are concerned, I can recommend none better than Kersey Graves' *The World's Sixteen Crucified Saviors.* He was one of the most famous atheists in American history. Study closely everything he says in the book. Read other books about atheism, also. Attend atheist gatherings-not to be converted, but to know more about the mental processes making atheists what they are. Listen to what they say. Where atheist friends are concerned, cultivate friendships only with the most cultured and erudite. Then, and only then, if you consider both sides of the equation, you will surely know whether or not The Triumvirate Religion is in every way a science.

The next Sanskrit-originated words I want to tackle are *Science* and *Scientific.* This word is also of Sanskrit Origin: *Siyoni/Suyoni.* It crept into English as *Zion.*

Si/Su = "bound or fettered to, procreated or brought forth from."

Yoni = "womb, uterus, vulva, vagina, female organs of generation, place of birth, source, origin, spring, fountain."

Siyoni/Suyoni = "Bound to or brought forth from the Source."

Siyoni or Suyoni is an epithet of India's Mt. Meru, the original home of all the races of mankind. When the Jesuit priests entered India, they noted that Northern India was often referred to as *Seunadesa,* meaning "Land of Zion."

Right now, the nations of the world are slowly becoming embroiled in a violent, bloody squabble over Israel, erroneously thinking it is the original Zion or Mt. Meru. The Hindus say that Mt. Meru is Kailasa in Western Tibet. And even if it is not, it at least represents the holy directions in which one must sleep and direct his spiritual energies. Hopefully, the Christians, Jews, and Moslems will come to see that they are all fighting for domination of the wrong location of Mt. Zion. They, too, worship *God Baleva!* A long as people keep refusing to recognize their Turkish roots, and the truth that the True Zion is Mt. Meru in India, we're going to keep on killing and drawing blood in honor of Baleva.

There is only one, and only one, solution to the ghastly horrors now taking place in Israel. It is a spiritual solution. But what is a spiritual solution? Does it mean we must all drop our weapons and lather each other's faces with dirty, slobbery, disease-laden spit kisses? Is it possible for us to love people we despise? Should we scapegoat our leaders for all the bad in this world? Should we read our respective holy books and then decide who is right and who is wrong? Of course not. If such were true, even God Himself might be tempted to turn atheist against himself. God may be incomprehensible, but stupid He is not!

A true spiritual solution is the application of simple principles working for everyone. Political solutions and blood-shedding won't work in this case. Did you know that if all the Christians, Jews, and Moslems would just go to bed at night, with their heads facing east and their feet pointing west, most of the participants' thirst for blood would eventually weaken? Not overnight of course, but we'd surely come to see light at the end of the tunnel. You'll find out in this book why changing the position of your bed is an ideal spiritual solution to many political troubles making mankind drown in blood, pain, and sorrow. But I can't say whether you'll accept it, for politics and politicians are the Trojan Horses of human history:

> Do politicians need so much to have history told the way they want? Really, they have their own, twisted view of history. They loathe the truth. They only want to see politics everywhere, in their own light at that. (Murad Adji, *A Story Told By The Rocks.*)

Thousands of years after the races of mankind left Turkey and Northern India, *Siyoni/Suyoni* became *Science*, connoting "penetrating certain fields of knowledge to the source."

Since my early youth, I have been searching for the origins of mankind and religion, including the riddle of whether we humans have a spiritual side of our beings. Naturally, I delve into spirits, guardian angels, miracles, and other similar creatures and phenomena. Along the way, I met many other people engaged in the same endeavors. All of us felt and feel that we are penetrating our field of interest to the source. But what happened? Certain people claiming to be "scientific," knowing nothing of what we are doing, whose interests involve penetrating mathematics, geology, biology, physics, astronomy, medicine and other specialized fields to their source, came along and told us that they, not we, are the real authorities in our specialized field of interest. Yet, we do not claim to be experts in their respective fields of knowledge. How did all this confusion *(Baleva)* come about?

As you'll find out in this book, no one can say I haven't discovered some valid and verifiable information. Could it be that mankind has forgotten the true meaning of Science? Why is it that I, who tirelessly investigate my field of specialization, must regard myself as unscientific?

I want to warn you beforehand that I will not discuss the problems of mankind, using the tools and theories of mathematicians, physicists and others. I'm going to use spiritual investigators' scientific theories and approaches. Essentially,

I present the world's most ancient spiritual axioms for people wanting to return to their inner selves: *Jacob's Ladder,* knowing what and where the Source is, the Holy Directions, and the true science of *The Holy Trinity.*

So what is best for us? The Mountain of Babel? Or that of Zion?

3

People of the World-Do You Know You Are All Turkish? Your DNA Can Prove it!

I extracted the following quotes from a free online book, *The Kipchaks-An Ancient History of the Turkic People and the Great Steppe;* Introduction, by Murad Adji. Published by St. George International Charity Foundation (Jargan), 2002. Westerners have read a lot about the Mongol hordes, led by Atilla the Hun, and how they struck fear in the hearts of Europeans. He almost defeated Rome itself. But rarely do we get a lucid historical perspective from the other side of the fence, about the Huns and Turks who once overran Europe. Murad Adji will enlighten us all. I will quote him abundantly in this book. I recommend that everyone read his free online books and those that are for sale. They won't be disappointed, for in learning about the Turks, we at last finding out who we are. Murad Adji's words are crying for a receptive audience.

Note: Mr. Adji is a Russian citizen of Turkish descent. The person who translated his book has a laudatory command of English, but it is still faulty and not edited well. I did not edit the quotes in any part of my book, but left them exactly as I found them in Mr. Adji' website. Even so, Mr. Adji's important message to mankind gets through powerfully and clearly.

Many people, in fact billions of them around the Earth, speak Turkic languages today, and have done so since the beginnings of history, from snow-swept Yakutia in Northeast Asia to temperate Central Europe, from chilly Siberia to torrid India, and even in a good many villages in Africa.

The Turkic world is vast and diverse. Turks are its largest tribe. They are the title nation of Turkey, a big country in West Asia and a long-familiar name for the rest of the world for its distinct identity, ancient customs and traditions, and high and unique culture, a subject of a myriad of books and features.

At the other end of the Turkic world, the Tofalars, numbering only a few hundred, are not someone you can tell much about. It's a sure bet they are hardly known to anyone beyond their dense Siberian forests and the couple of villages they call home town. But then, the Tofalars, perhaps, still speak the original, ancient Turkic tongue after many centuries of only occasional contacts with outside cultures that could distill their speech with borrowings.

The Turkic world is great indeed, and thoroughly enigmatic, too. It is like a cut diamond, its every facet a nation-Azerbaijanis, Altaians, Balkarians, Bashkirs, Gagauzes, Kazakhs, Karaims, Karachais, Kyrgyz, Crimean Tatars, Kumyks, Volga Tatars, Tuvans, Turkmen, Uighurs, Uzbeks, Khakass, Chuvash, Shorians, Yakut-too many names to reel off in the same breath.

Dozens [of millions] of peoples live in the Turkic world—all alike and different at the same time. You can always tell where they belong, from the special sounds and undertones of their speech. Which means a word that is one thing in one place may be a completely different thing in another. This diversity of meaning makes the Turkic languages fathomless, on top of their simplicity and ancient heritage.

They were not always that different, though. There was a time, too long ago, when all members of the Turkic race spoke one tongue that everyone understood in every corner of the Turkic world. Around two thousand years ago, they started for various reasons to move away from one another, geographically and linguistically, from their next of kin and their common tongue, developing their endemic dialects that were a closed book to outsiders. For a while, they were keenly aware of their common ancestry and remembered their shared language that they could still speak at bazaars and fairs drawing merchants from far away.

Their common primeval language provided a framework for belles-lettres. Poets and story-tellers honed every word of their writings, so they could then caress the ear of the Turkic world at large. Besides, the common language was spoken by government officials mustering the troops or collecting taxes from their subjects. Large empires, from end to end, spoke and wrote Turkic.

Is it only the language that makes one Turkic nation different from another? Is it the linguistic diversity that gives brilliance to the diamond we call the Turkic world?

Everything is much more complex than it looks on the surface at times.

Can you imagine, some communities on Earth are ignorant of their Turkic origins and will never believe you if you tell them who they are…. They were conquered, at one time or another, and forbidden, on pain of death, to speak their native tongue. They just forgot it clean, out of fear of reprisal. And with it their forefathers and all that had come before…. They were now people without memory or knowledge of their real past.

This is the kind of thing that happened to people on our planet, though.

Of course, these people have visages that look exactly like the faces of their ancestors (what the genes would then be good for?). Take the Austrians or Bavarians, Bulgarians or Bosnians, Magyars or Lithuanians, Poles or Saxons,

Serbs or Ukrainians, Czechs or Croats, Burgundians or Catalans.... Nearly all of them blue-eyed and fair-haired (exact replicas of the ancient Turkic men and women), and all blissfully oblivious of their common roots. Doesn't that strike you?

Many unsuspicious Americans, Britons, Armenians, Georgians, Spaniards, and Italians have Turkic blood flowing in their veins. And especially Iranians, Russians and French. They, too, wear the unspoiled faces of their ancient Turkic forerunners, and they, too, are dead sure they are anything but....

A sad enough story. It has been made that way, though-sad, or more accurately, broken before it could be written to the end.

The Cossacks are what you can label an exception: a nation-yes and no, a tribe-depends on the way you look at it. If you will understand it, of course. Their true story lurks somewhere behind a veil of cock-and-bull stories. What we have then, in the end, is that the Cossacks have contrived somehow to get lost on the crossroads of Time-they style themselves Slavs, and still remember much of their native Turkic tongue. Indeed, Turkic is palavered informally in some Cossack villages. True, they call it, with tongue in cheek, their kitchen-speak, not native language.

I have pondered for many long years why the Turkic world is so little known to so many people on Earth. Was it by fluke or design? You will hardly find another language with as many nuances and dialects as the Turkic-really, people of common blood, common ancestors, common history speaking different languages and thinking differently of themselves. Why, indeed?

The next quote is from one of Mr. Adji's books, that hasn't yet been translated from Russian to English:

Geographical map is a serious historical document bearing information not less than a heavy book. But we should be able to read it: The Great Movement of Peoples left their trace on the map. Then, in the 2nd-5th centuries AD, appeared a huge steppe country, the Desht-i-Kipchak, with the settlements, cities, villages, and road stations.

The Türkic culture dominated from the Baikal to the Alps. In all of the steppe zone. Europe then "began" in Siberia! Centuries passed, seems that it all disappeared. But nothing was forgotten. The map remembers what people forgot.

For example, the borders of the Desht-i-Kipchak. They are intact! In Russian, the word "kurgan", as writes the most prominent toponymician E.M.Murzaev, previously meant "border", "boundary". Why? Because first of all kurgans distinguished the Türkic lands. Beyond the kurgans began the other's land.

The border of the Desht-i-Kipchak in the north passed by the Moscow River, the northern bank belonged to the Finns and Ugrs, and the southern to the Türks. Only within the limits of Moscow are known quite a few kurgan groups, the majority of them are on the southern (right) bank. They are also in the former "Türkic" Moscow suburbs where there were settlements of Türks, the toponyms witness to it. For example, Kolomenskoe, its old name is Kolloma, in Türkic "Guardian", "Providence". Kopotnya is from "Tall Settlement" (or "Tall Grass"), Kuntsevo from "Shelter" or "Inn"…These words are obviously not of the Slavic origin…And to the north of the Moscow River, there are no kurgans, there lived other people, with other culture, and the toponymy there have other root and also not Slavic.

(Note: wherever you see notes in parenthesis, either by Mr. Adji or the translator, they are not my comments.)

Authors Note. Seems, we need to clarify. Say, in the 12th century the border was not a line, as nowadays. It was a wide zone in which neighbors were interested in equal measure (a zone of a dialogue, of exchange and the peace). The Moscow River, Oka and adjoining lands were such territories before the arrival here of the Slavs, therefore the Türkic monuments are alongside the Finno-Ugric monuments. It is natural. For example, the Nizhni Novgorod initially was called in Türkic, Bulgar, and since the old times was famous for its fairs. To the Bulgar fair were coming merchants from the Europe, from Persia.

In the south the country of Türks reached Iran, the kurgans bear witness to that. The border remains almost without changes, Türks still live there, and they are called the Iranian Azerbaijanis.

Between the northern and the southern border of the Desht-i-Kipchak also nowadays remain thousands of Türkic place names, it is presently a real treasure for the toponymy! For example, opposite the Moscow Kremlin, on the right bank, is Balchug. In Russian there is no such word, and in Türkic it is "bog", "mud". Clearly it's a Türkic toponym.

There is a multitude of similar examples. As a rule, the names of the many old cities of steppe Russia are from the Türkic root: Orel is "Road Upward", Tula is "Full", Bryansk (Birinchi, Bryanechsk) is "First", "Main", Saratov (Sarytau) is "Yellow Mountain", Simbirsk (Simbir) is "Lonely Tomb"…Kashira, Kolomna, Kaluga, Voronezh, Penza, Chelyabinsk, Kurgan…There are a lot of names, and everyone tells the forgetful Kipchaks about their native land.

The geographical maps captured the traces of the aggressive wars of Ivan the Terrible and Peter I. They show how Rus grew at the expence of the neighbors. The map keeps the very dark history which is being tried to wash off the re-written chronicles. And it becomes understandable, why the ancient Türkic city of Kipenzaj, shown on the European maps, became the Russian Penza, Shapashkar became Cheboksary, Buruninej became Vironej, Sarytau became Saratov, Chelyaba became Chelyabinsk, Birinchi became Bryansk…

In Atilla's time the lands farthest from the Altai were called "Aleman", in Türkic "Distant". From here comes the nowadays toponym Alemania, present day Germany. Many of the "Germanic tribes" were blue-eyed, with wide chick bones, with the obvious Kipchak appearance, and they spoke in Türkic, which shows in their runic writing, ancient customs and folk memory. They are comers from the far-away Altai!

The part of the population of the France and Italy, England and Austria, Yugoslavia and Czechia have a similar early history. Judging by the archives, almost to the end of the 16th century there was in use the Türkic language. In fact, later, during the time of the inquisition, the Roman Catholic church carried a great purge" of the archives, but, fortunately, some documents survived. It is these documents that allow to assert the unconventional, that the Türks lived in Central Europe...A detailed discussion about it follows later.

Certainly, the Türkic place names remained on the maps of the Europe. In them the history of some countries and peoples is clearly read.

Are You Getting Mr. Adji's Message?

Most of us know that in the latter days of Rome's greatness, hordes of Central Asian Turks, whom we call Goths, Ostrogoths, Visigoths, Alans, Alemans, Franks, and other tribes, gradually began to infiltrate Europe. The so-called "native Europeans" felt a cultural and linguistic kinship with them. After all, at one time or another, all of us have been Turks and Ramanakas (Hindus).

We can compare those times with our present relationship with England. We are the same people living in other parts of the world. But five hundred or one thousand years from now, we may find it difficult to accept that we Americans and the English were at one time the same people. Even now, Europoids living in this country, though of Dutch, German, Swedish, Norwegian, and other descendancies, "feel" closer to England culturally and linguistically than they do with the homelands of their immigrant ancestors. Here's an example for people to ponder. The Spanish-speaking people in this country and Anglo-Americans feel that each group is different. However, England was settled by Spanish Goths or Iberians (ancient Turkish Georgians). Mr. Adji is just trying to refresh our memories of who and what all of us are: Turks and Hindus!

When I was traveling in Central America, during the 1950s, the Salvadorans complained about the large population of wealthy Turks (*Turcos*) living there. Yet, they and the Amerindian tribes there are also descendants of Turks, as we all are.

Here is the path of the Burgund clan. The <u>Ulus</u> Burgund came to the Europe from the spurs of the Baikal Ridge, the eastern-most toponym "Burgund" is known there. Then they lived in the Caspian steppes, then a part of them settled in the foothills of the Caucasus in Karachai, where is a settlement Burgund. And in the 435 AD their ulus, led by the <u>Attila's father</u>, reached the present France, creating the Burgundy, the Burgund-yurt...The French-Burgundians preserved the dishes of the Türkic national cuisine, elements from the dress and utensils, and have not forgotten the traditions and the customs. They lost the native language.

It is possible to trace the Ulus Savoi. This toponym also stretches by a thin chain on the geographical map from the Altai...It also coincides in time with the Great Movement of the Peoples.

And the word "Tering" may also serve as a compass in a similar historical travel.

"Tering" in Türkic is "Plentiful". So was called, for example, an extensive, fertile valley. From Balkhash (also Balkash-*Translator's Note*) (this lake was previously called Tering-Kül-*Author*) to the Central Europe this toponym is clearly marked. Coincidence? Certainly not. Attila's cohorts, judging from the West-European literature, were Terings (Türings, Tyurings), Burgunds and others "Germanic tribes". All of them were fine horsemen, they fought under the banners with a cross...Not surprising is a line of the historian Jordanes about Terings, about their skill in the horse breeding...The native Europeans did not breed horses then! And did not drink koumiss. That was a favorite Türkish occupation.

Looking at the map of Danube gives a plethora of the Kipchak names. By the way, "Balkan" in Türkic is "Wooded Mountain". So is called one of the areas Azerbaijan, with surprisingly beautiful wooded mountains.

The Chernogorets (Black Mountaineers—*Translator's Note*) in the Balkans are teased "Karaties", why is that? Without knowing the Türkic language, there is no answer. But the answer is simple. "Kara" is black, "Tau" is mountain. So, "Karaties" and "Chernogorets" is the same.

There are as many Türkic toponyms on the map of Eurasia as there are stars in the sky. However to learn about them is impossible (for peoples in Russia—*Translator's Note*). The books on this thematic were published, but only beyond the Russian borders. Only a narrow circle of scientists knows about them. One of them is a prominent geographer Edward Makarovich Murzaev. He wrote his own book, maybe the main in his life, "Türkic geographical names"...The book, mockingly, was published with a measly print (only five hundred copies).

The borders of the Great Steppe can also be clearly discerned in England. There they are a memory of Anglo-Saxon campaigns which in the 5th-6th centuries AD were lead by the Türks (Saks or Saxes?).

Defeating the natives, Kipchaks established their "island" state, starting the city of Kent, which gave the name to the Yurt, later to the kingdom. "Kent" in Türkic is a "Stone Fortress" (Compare Tashkent—"Stone Fortress"—*Translator's Note*). That was a foothold for the advance deeper into the island. Across the gulf, on the continent was built the city of Calais, from here, we know, began the Anglo-Saxon campaigns, here was prepared the fording of the gulf...The map confirms this story.

Authors Note. "Kala" is also Türkic, "Fortress", with not a stone, but with an earthen rampart.

And, maybe, the most fascinating, what the toponymy shows, is right on the surface. "Ing" in the Old Türkic expression means "Booty". Is this the source for "Ingland", the "Captured Land"? Before the arrival of the Türks the island was called Albion.

One more fact, at first for reflection, and then and for the disputes: the Church in Ingland did not recognized the Pope, only the Pope St. Gregory I the Great (590-604—*Translator's Note*). managed to win the trust. At first the Englishmen followed the traditions of the eastern rites. Why? Where it came to the island from? They were called Arians, why? The very first abbot had the Türkic name Aidan (it means "Light" in Türkic), he taught the natives to believe in the Heavenly God. The missionary went along with a translator. Again, why was that?

By the way, who come that in the far England there are kurgans, which became the long-standing attractions? Precisely the same kurgans are also in the other lands of the Great Steppe. There are none in Scotland…And do the Englishmen know, what their favorite polo game (on horses and with sticks) was popular in Altai before the Great Movement of Peoples? They drove not a wooden ball, but a head of the enemy bound in a leather bag. Türks have not forgotten this game, as well as many other ancient games.

The Kipchak Blood did not freeze in the veins of some Englishmen. Their appearance and behavior give out their roots…The English Kipchaks, seemingly, have forgotten the proverb of their ancestors long before Anglo-Saxon campaigns: "Do not get in another's trousers". They will not hide you.

Having conquered half of the world, the Kipchaks seem to have left the history. After each large intercene conflict an ulus after another ulus left—the Desht-i-Kipchak, becoming either a "new" people, or merging with another peoples. The Türks melted away, as snow under the sun.

My readers wanting to penetrate and research further what I have said here will notice that Murad Adji's detractors call him a fanatical nationalist who will stop at nothing to put the Turks on top of the world again. But he is anything but. All he wants is for us humans to know exactly who we are and exactly where we came from. They not only gave us our blood and physical visages, they even gave us our religions. They, along with the ancient Hindus, are truly the fathers and mothers of the world. How can anyone who finds out what Mr. Adji said, and what I shall say in this book, get the courage to declare war against his own blood brothers? Our own Jesus Christ was called *David Koresh. Korush, Kurash, Kurush, Kurios,* were titles of the Turkish leadership and priestly class. Even Mohammed was a member of the Arab leadership and priestly clan called *Quyresh.*

Anyone doubting the truth of what author Murad Adj said has only to pick up the Torah, the first five books of the Christian Old Testament, to confirm that nearly every word Mr. Adj has said is true. In fact, the word Torah itself derives from the Turkic *Terai*. It means "History."

Noah and his sons, Shem, Ham, and Japhet, were Turks. The fact that the Ark settled on the border between Armenia and Turkey indicates this. Abraham was a Chaldean, for even the Iraqis, as well as the Kurds, along with their Sumerian, Hittite (Khatti, Hatti, (*Keder*), and Kassite Kish, Kashi, Kaiser (*Keser*), were Turks. The Syrian Catholic church of Turkey calls itself "Chaldean."

If you've read the Torah, the story of mankind's early beginnings, you've surely noticed that Genesis and the other books of the Torah mention such place names as Kabul, Havilah, Sophir, Khaiber, Gozan, Thibet, Lhasa, Kophen River, the tribe of Dan, etc. These biblical place names were and still are scattered throughout Afghanistan, Pakistan, Kashmir, Rajasthan, Gujarat, and several other Turkic-populated areas in Northwestern India and Central Asia.

Indirectly, even this book is a miniature *Torah* or *Cabala*, for it presents the truths about mankind's exodus from Eden (Siberia or Hyperborea), and the wanderings of the post-diluvian Turkish nomads to the far reaches of the earth. Never again should we forget our holy beginnings.

4

Jesus Christ-For Atheists, Unbelievers, and Everyone Else!

It is not unusual for a person to be born and raised in the religious faith of his parents, only to reject it later on in life. He may either leave the religion or sect, converting to another one, or he may retain his religious convictions without joining other religious philosophies. We call such people "secular."

There is another group of people who become agnostics, admitting honestly that they don't know whether divine forces exist in the world. Many individuals become atheists, denying outright, hotly, and even violently, that no divine forces exist in the universe and that when we humans die physically, our individual awareness disappears completely, never to appear again in any form. In nearly all cases, the agnostics and atheists will openly renew their faith in God and religion, just before or at the hour of their demise. Before dying, some pretend to stay true to their apostasies while inwardly confessing that there is a God in the universe, regardless how they rejected the idea in their youth. Better to be safe than sorry. Or is their another reason?

I was such a person. As a child, I was deeply religious. By the time I was twelve, I left the Nazarene Church to which my parents belonged, trying other Christian sects on for size: Baptist, Methodist, Christian, and other churches. When I was a young university student in Mexico, I joined the Roman Catholic Church, not out of conviction, but just to make myself culturally palatable to the Mexicans. That was nearly 60 years before I began this book. I never regretted that decision. However, while still remaining in the Catholic Church, I often gorged myself abundantly and lengthily on Buddhism, Hinduism, Rosicrucianism, Mental Physics, and a variety of other religious persuasions. I'm happy to say that in all that time, I held fast to the conviction that I wasn't an atheist; that I was more than just an animated piece of earth.

Like nearly every skeptic and atheist who quits "doubting" when he nears the grave, I did the same thing, but in another way. I am the type of person who loathes the mortal sin of "believing" ideas and teachings for which no proofs exist. I must know (*gnosis*), just as surely as I know the sun rises and sets. Instead of ending my life as a "believer," I hope to end it as a "knower."

"Knowing" is infinitely more satisfying and reassuring than holding fast to stubborn "beliefs." Another beautiful aspect of "knowing" is that no one needs to convert to the Catholicism to which I belong. He can be a Jew, Buddhist, Hindu, Jainist, or whatever. Jesus has truly existed since the beginning of time. In many cases and in many other incarnations, he was crucified, dying on the cross or tree to which he was appended, coming back to the physical world. His martyrdom didn't always happen in "Christianity" alone. And he wasn't always called Jesus Christ. I hope that the facts I've put in this book will have great meaning and significance for you as well.

In 1964, my family and I left Kansas and went to California where I applied for and received a position as Spanish instructor in a Southern California high school. A young American-educated Pakistani history teacher was also a new faculty member there. He often marveled that most Christians are convinced that Jesus Christ died on the cross and arose from the dead three days later. He told us that Jesus had survived the cross ordeal and that he, his mother Mary, and St. Thomas had escaped to Northern India. Predictably, none of the teachers at our school would accept this "pagan heresy" on his part. However, I decided to be open-minded about what he said and began investigating for myself. My investigations bore no appreciable fruit until 1973. I read an illustrated article in a Mexican magazine, corroborating everything my Pakistani colleague had said. It even provided pictures of Jesus' descendants, his tomb, and an impression of his scarred feet, imbedded in concrete beside his sarcophagus.

The Mexican article about Jesus' tomb and living descendants was a translation from the German magazine *Stern*. *Stern* commissioned some writers to go to India and investigate this matter. When Cardinal Valerian Gracias, Archbishop of Bombay at the time, got word of their investigations, he begged them: "For the love of God, don't write anything about this!"

In 1989, when my now deceased wife Consuelo and I were enjoying a weekend in Tijuana, Mexico, I bought a book entitled, *Jesús Vivió y Murió en India (Jesus Lived and Died in India)*, written by the German researcher and writer, Andreas Faber-Kaiser. It's one of the most enlightening books I've ever read. One of the illustrations in the book shows a stone relief of St. Thomas, that archeologists found in the ruins of Taxila, Pakistan. An inscription below the relief identified Thomas and his mission to India. In Jesus' time, Taxila was one of the leading cultural centers of the ancient Turkic world. The book also shows pictures of Moses' Kashmiri tomb on Mt. Nebo, just as the Torah states. Yes, Moses was also a Turk.

Those who don't want the world to know Jesus is buried in India state that the stories of his escape to India are deceitful fabrications of the Ahmadiya Moslem sect who care for an ancient tomb which they say contains Jesus. That just isn't so. Many ancient books describe Jesus' flight to and mission in India. Place names attributed to Jesus are found all over Kashmir. A Hindu holy book, *Bhavishya Purana,* gives a lucid account of why Jesus fled to India. It was written in A.D. 115. Read a partial translation, as follows:

> On a certain day, (King) Salivahana went to the Himalayan mountains, and there, in the center of the country of the Huns, the powerful king saw a distinguished personage seated near a mountain. The saint was of a light complexion and wore white clothing. Salivahana asked who he was. He replied amiably: "I am known as Ishvara Putaram or 'The Son of God' and Kanaya Garbam or 'Issue of a Virgin.' Being given to truth and penances, I preach the truth to the Amalekites and follow their true principles.
>
> Astonished by this answer, the king asked him about his religion, and he answered, "Oh, King, I come from a distant country where truth doesn't exist, and where wickedness knows no bounds. I appeared there in the country of the Amalekites as the Messiah. I made the sinners and lawbreakers suffer, and I also suffered at their hands.'
>
> I appeared as Issah Masiah (Jesus the Messiah). I received the Messiahhood (Christhood)...etc., etc.

The *Bavishya Purana* mentions that Jesus and Salivahana first met each other in the land of the Huns. The Huns were and still are Mongoloid Turks.

Are you skeptical that the story of Jesus' escape to India exists in a Hindu holy book? It has been translated into English.

The enemies of truth in religious teachings claim that the document is fraudulent. I've read several Christian condemnations of the *Bavishya Purana.* It was written just after Jesus' death, in about 115 AD. He was 120 years old when he passed away.

In the *Bavishya Purana's* account of Jesus' Christ's flight to his new home in India, I deliberately left out something he said to King Salivahana, that I'll quote in another chapter. What he told Salivahana may truly amaze you, giving you deep insight into the Divine Nature of Jesus Christ.

At this point, you may be tempted to think I'm trying to convert you to accept and "believe" all that I say about Christ in this book-or that I'm some kind of Anti-Christ. However, neither those of us who accept Christ's escape to India as truth, nor Christ, nor God, nor hopefully, anyone else, should care one whit whether anyone accepts or believes Jesus escaped to India. If this book should destroy his so-called faith, he probably didn't have any to start with. Why? Christ did not come to earth to give us history lessons and a biography of his life which we must be frightened into "believing" in order to avoid eternal hell. As for the rules (Ten Commandments or The Noachide Laws) for behaving in a civilized, altruistic, and civilized manner, they were no different than those that also existed in Israel and the rest of the ancient world.

Christ came here to guide all mankind and keep us aware that we are really not our physical bodies, but something else. It's not even imperative that we accept and "believe" *that*. We can still remain atheists, agnostics, unbelievers, skeptics or non-churchgoers. We can even refuse to accept the reality of God and Jesus. However, there is one reality that not even atheists and skeptics can afford to reject. At the end of this book, I'll tell how atheists and skeptics can lose their souls-if they are brave enough to accept wholeheartedly the consequences of their respective anti-spiritual mindsets.

In a book about the history of ancient Turkic Afghanistan, I found such biblical personages as King David, Saul, Adam and Eve, Goliath, and even Solomon. However, in the Afghan account, Goliath was riding on an elephant when David knocked him off the elephant. The Afghan account mentioned that after being banished from Eden, Adam went to Ceylon or what is now Sri Lanka (Serendipity). Eve went to Jiddah, in Arabia. (Ref: *History of The Afghans,* by Khwaja Neamat Ullah.)

It was painfully difficult for me to challenge, weaken and anesthetize my previous religious conditionings. After all, I was born Christian and still am. But I remained strong and resolute in my quest. I did not overlook any kind of anomaly, such as the strange similarities between Brahm-Abraham, Sarah-Saraisvati, and Hakra (Hagar?). I also found other Noahs and several Moseses in Hindu myths, but the Hindus say that many of the myths in their holy books occurred in Central Asia, especially in Siberia, ancestral home of all the Turkish peoples. Even the biblical Hindu Hittites and Amorites, the fathers and mothers of Jerusalem, also Abraham and Sarah, were Turks. If one cannot accept that the Hittites and Amorites were Turkish *Krishtayas,* he'll never get any sense out of the Bible. But they were also Hebrews and Phoenicians, as you'll find out later on. Basically this book centers around the fathers of all humanity and all religions: the Greeks,

Turks, and Hindus. When you close the last page of this document, the *Torah* and the *Kristos* may cease to be a mystery to you.

In 1989, I naively and incorrectly assumed that I had found out all that was humanly possibly about these matters. I decided to put what I had learned up to that point in a book entitled, *Jesus and Moses Are Buried in India, Birthplace of Abraham and the Jews.* No sooner had the book gone into print, I then came upon literal avalanches of equally pertinent information. I realized that I hadn't appreciated adequately the part that the Phoenicians and Jews, simultaneously the Indo-Turks, had played in the ancient world. It was difficult for me to accept the truth that ancient India once extended from Siberia down to what is now Sri Lanka and in what are now Palestine and Israel. In saying this, I am being conservative, At one time, Turkic-Hindu (Kuru-Ramanaka) influence encompassed every inch of this globe. The influence stretched even to Britain and the Americas.

Another mistake I made in my investigations was my concentration on the "forest" called India and not enough on its "trees," such as the Greeks, Turks, Armenians, and the sub-continent Hindus themselves. I also fell into a trap that some Hindu activists set for me. They claim that the so-called "Aryan invasion" was a concoction of white racists. They insist that the Aryans were lily-white. But later on, I found out that the Aryans were of all races. I finally had to conclude that the Turks (Kurus or Aryans) were the most numerous and influential of the "trees" in giving India and Greece mankind's first fully developed civilizations and religions. Hitler tried to make the world think the Germans, not the Turks, were the true Aryans. Fortunately, he failed to convince the world. But that is not to say that the Germans are not Turks. In truth, we all are!

Even with all *Jesus and Moses etal's* shortcomings, some occasional sloppy scholarship, and gross errors caused by my previous iron-clad mental conditionings and biases, I'm proud of it. It will give any sincere researcher a wealth of material in order to unravel many of the riddles and mysteries of ancient history, as well as to prepare his mind for greater insights and adventures.

After the book was published, I felt that I had deprogrammed myself sufficiently to know that Christ never died on the cross but escaped from his enemies back in Jerusalem. But the information I kept accumulating, almost non-stop, made me realize that I had just perverted my mind to blind me to the reality that *Jesus had, indeed, died physically on the Cross.* Christ would never have lied to us. His spirit really re-entered his body, bringing him back to physical life. As a precaution, in order not to continue being crucified time after time and then returning to his physical body as often, he went to India with his mother Mary and St. Thomas. He was able to live out his life peacefully.

After returning to his earthly form, Christ took up his staff and limped painfully to Central Asia and Northern India, the home of his ancestors and all mankind, to reassure the people there, who knew him in his youth. As Christ said, he came to earth to show us how to live abundantly. By "abundance," he meant a long earthly life and infinite returns to earthly life in the future.

I have also realized that those who made us think Jesus rose to a Heaven in the sky unintentionally led us astray. Had Jesus left this world after his crucifixion, he could not have convinced us that we continue living here after death. The Turkish peoples from Siberia to Northern India, who knew about him soon after his birth and met him as a youth, thanks to three Turkish kings or wise men, had also heard about his crucifixion and death. Although there were no technologically advanced communication media in those days, news still moved fast throughout the ancient world. It is a historical fact that Anatolia or Kurustan (Turkey) and parts of India as far down the western coast as Kerala were the first people to accept Christ's Messiah-hood. After that, Christ's simple but all-powerful message bounced back to the Middle East and Europe.

You may be surprised to learn that when I started my research, I was interested mainly in enlightening myself. I published the results of my research in case anyone else was equally interested.

Jesus and Moses, etal, inspired me to look within myself and the minds of all humans, to find out why we insist on falling into the venomous trap of Belief/ Non-Belief, causing us to treat unproven facts and fictions as gospel truth.

When I was a teacher, I discovered that if one wants to really learn any subject in depth, he should start "cold," with what little he has at hand, and try to teach it to someone else. Long before I began my career as a teacher, I found out that I could learn better if I imagined that I was teaching what I was learning to others. Therefore, I started doing research on beliefs and non-beliefs, putting what I was learning in book form, pretending that I was back in the classroom. Only in this case, I *was* the classroom. In this way, I was able to become my own teacher of whatever I wanted to learn. After finishing one book, I'd start another, trying to make it easier, simpler, and more instructive than the prior one. I published several books in this fashion. These books represent my step by step struggles to find out what God, Jesus, and mankind are all about, for they are inseparable. They may help you in your own struggles. Here's why:

After finishing my last two books, *The Ego-Mankind's Inner Terrorist* and *Christianity-the World's First Worldwide Religion,* I realized joyfully that my mind was about to make a complete circuit of personal and collective human existence. I realized this when I reviewed *Jesus and Christ are Buried in India, etal.* Not only had I unconsciously alluded to the Turkish Krishtaya. I even stated, "Christayas roots extend back to the dawn of human reasoning." In short, I had known it all along! This circle, strange as it may seem, became at one and the same time, my own search to return to myself, as well as a history of mankind's struggles to do the same thing. The former was inextricably linked to the latter. We humans, without realizing it, "have always known it all along." In my case, and I suspect in that of nearly all humans, we are too ignorant of ourselves and history to know that mankind indeed remembers his individual and collective past. We just need to open our minds sufficiently to admit this to ourselves. Therefore, I realized that my two previous books were just self-realization on my part. As for anyone reading those two books, plus this one, atheists and non-atheists alike will bene-fit. They are actually the first rungs of the cabalistic *Jacob's Ladder.* You see, man-kind has presently fallen almost to the bottom of human existence. Don't be blinded by our technological development. If we don't know about the dual sides of our selves, we know nothing, no matter how technologically advanced we have become. To save himself, Man must remember what and where he's been and climb back up the ladder. After the publication of this book, and if I'm still alive, I will take this circle you are now reading and attempt to keep on reducing its cir-cumference to singularity-if such is humanly possible. In short, it will point out clearly what the remaining rungs up the ladder are.

I fail to understand why the early Church never told us that Christ has been with and among us since the beginning of time, and not necessarily in our brand of Christianity. Why have we never found out that the original Phoenicians were Turkish Christians? Why did our historians, both secular and sectarian, keep us from knowing about the wonders of the primogenitor Turks of ancient Siberia, Hyperborea, and Central Asia? Many Christs, each bearing the same honorific title, were crucified before our "Christ" suffered the same indignity. Other "Christs" still appear to us as great leaders. thinkers, or just average humans. And not all of them are martyred. Many of them appear to be normal humans like ourselves. Beings like Christ and guardian angels appear to us almost daily, but we're unaware of their presence.

I am reminded of a poor black couple, with a teenage daughter, who told me how they once received help from a divine being or guardian angel. Unable to afford a home, they lived in an RV. One day, as they were walking downtown, here in Victorville, California, the daughter fell in love with a certain pair of shoes she saw in a shoe store. The girl begged her parents to buy them for her. The father said he would buy the shoes if they didn't cost too much. When they entered the store, a pleasant mannered and well-dressed man offered to serve them. The girl said she wanted to try on those shoes. He removed the shoes from the display window and brought them to her. The girl was desperate to own them. The father asked the salesman how much they cost. The salesman quoted a high price that this family couldn't afford to pay. Seeing that the girl was so crest-fallen, the salesman said, "I have an idea. Take the shoes with you; pay me when you get enough money."

The mother and father gratefully accepted his generosity and trust in them. Before leaving the store, they asked him: "Who are you? We want to know, so that we can tell the personnel about our arrangement, just in case you won't be here when we return."

The salesman said, "I'm the owner of this store. My name is _____."

A few weeks later, the father and mother had saved enough money to pay for the shoes. They returned, asking for him. The employers working there said that they had never heard of the man.

There are more poor people on earth than prosperous ones. And there may also be more dishonest people than honest ones, according to my life experiences. It would be foolish and impoverishing for businessmen to give unknowns merchandise without demanding immediate payment or some other kind of security. How did that strange man know he could trust this honest couple?

Had the employees known all about the all-encompassing spiritual nature of that gentleman, even they would have known that he was, indeed, the *real owner.*

My next door neighbor, a Salvadoran man, told me how some invisible bene-factor saved his life when he was living back in Central America. One day, when Mauricio was crossing a street in downtown San Salvador, a speeding car rushed toward him. He realized that he had no time to get out of its way. At the moment of impact, some invisible being grabbed his shoulders, lifted him out of the way, and placed him back on the street. Who-and what-did such a marvelous thing?

Such encounters with spiritual beings happen to virtually all of us, many times in our lives. I insist that each and every one of us interacts with them occasion-ally, perhaps even frequently-or every day. However, they generally set up special scenarios, so that we won't realize they exist among us.

In my previous book, *Christianity, Mankind's First Worldwide Religion,* I relate how "something" used me to warn an elderly friend about his young wife's intended infidelity. But I didn't know she intended to be unfaithful. She never communicated anything to me, for we mutually disliked each other; neither did I know I was the tattletale-not even when the words were supposedly coming out of my mouth. "Something else" set me up as the fall guy. Unseen beings have intervened in your life also-more times than you know. I guarantee it. If such has happened, why don't spirits aid and advise us more frequently? I can't answer that question.

If I, a mere mortal, can have such experiences, who am I to say confidently that spirits, guardian angels, and demi-gods like Jesus Christ are just figments of our imagination?

Jesus Christ truly exists among us and within us, but we are rarely aware of his presence. For what reasons, I don't know.

Testimonies are virtually worthless as evidence of divine beings existing among us. We are not generally aware of their presence and interactions with humanity. We tend to regard such stories as lies.

I personally tend to take testimonies of encounters with spiritual beings seriously because I have had many paranormal experiences in which certain mysterious beings living among humans neglected to hide their presence from me. This is another reason why I'm sure that Christ in no way lied to us. *He really did die*, leave his body, and return to it. But my opinions need not become yours as well. As I have already said, do what you want with what I have told you. What we call God does not require of you any sort of acceptance of mystical history stories, biographies of divinely inspired men, gospels and scriptures which nobody will ever truly understand, divine powers. miracles, and divine intervention. No conversions to any religion, either. All you have to know is the route "home," described in kindergarten-simple terms. If you obtain and read my well-researched account of the life of Jesus and his ministry in India, you'll get a fine beginning to initiate your own search for yourself.

I've heard the admonitions of blindly religious people who say that Christ's principal teachings won't save us-just a simple, naïve belief that he lived and died two thousand years ago. They say that people who rely on good works can never be saved. I've also noticed that many of those same people would sell their mothers' souls for a dollar bill and commit other crimes against humanity with impunity.

I will occasionally quote in this book from the Apocryphal *Gospel of Thomas*. The *Gospel of Thomas* is really not a gospel but a *Cabala*. It guarantees at the beginning that he who comes to understand the 114 sayings attributed to Jesus Christ in this Cabala "will not experience death." I see nothing wrong with reassuring myself that I'll always be eternally alive and aware of my eternal life.

Welcome aboard, atheists, agnostics, skeptics, unbelievers, and infidels! Religious folks of whatever creed or denomination are also welcome. However, if you are skeptical of what I'll say in this book, intending to trash it after finishing it, or giving it to the Salvation Army, the Divine asks only one simple favor from you-one that most atheists, skeptics, unbelievers, and infidels can easily accept. You'll read about it in the last chapter.

5

Why Scriptures and Gospels Can't Save Anybody!

Figure 1. I'itoi's Maze. It is one of the most powerfully revealing religious symbols in the world.

The Arizona O'odham Indians' "I'itoi's Maze," a powerful religious symbol and archetype of the human mind, is one of the most amazing natural archetypes that Creation (God) can send us. Notice that the image of I'toi or Sewa (none other than the Turkic-Hindu God Shiva or *Kedar*) has no eyes, face, ears, or nose. He must get through life that way. In front of him lies a nearly straight path to the Ultimate Reality. It just veers or curves slightly to one side, to throw him off track. Nature doesn't have any regard for persons whose minds and spirits are deaf, dumb, stupid, and blind. We can be nearly sure he'll choose the wrong paths in the maze. I'itoi's Maze demonstrates that Man can choose infinite paths in the universe to find out about his true nature, each of them leading him deeper and deeper into the mire. He can change religions, visit hundreds of gurus, read all the "Babel" in holy scriptures, or whatever. Nothing will work. The sad thing about these "paths" is that they are too infinite. None of them will lead him anywhere. For example, what do we do if we get lost on a journey, in a jungle, in a cave, or whatever? Do we keep on going? Or do we retrace our steps back from where we came? I'itoi's Maze tells us that regardless of whatever road we choose, we're going to remain hopelessly lost. The only hope for mankind is for him to reject all the choices, teachers, dogmas, and con jobs tempting him. What he looks for has been within him all along. Just find the road back home. Jacob's Ladder is the only way. As you'll discover in this book. God, or whatever else you want to call It/Him/Her/Them, according to your respective religious persuasion, has given us all a familiar natural archetype that anyone, of any religion, of any nationality, of any region on this earth, of any level of education, and of any age, will immediately understand. History has shown us that anyone who stubbornly insists that this archetype is exclusive of his cultural and religious upbringing, is the True Anti-Christ. He will allow devastating wars and calamities capable of destroying nearly all living beings, as happened in the Noachide Flood. He will conceitedly and foolishly declare that anyone who doesn't share his exclusiveness is the Anti-Christ. I sometimes think that God has used this archetype as some kind of practical joke, in order to cull out those who have the sense to understand it from those who don't.

Those who have read my previous books doubtlessly observed that I harangue mercilessly the sins of Belief/Not-Belief-even in this one. After I was mustered out of the Marine Corps in 1954, I bought Eric Hoffer's book, *The True Believer*. The book electrified me and vindicated my dislike for that despicable emotion, for it is not a way of thinking as we are erroneously taught. In Mexico, where I graduated from college, I noted that the Mexicans at that time in history idolized "Belief/Not-Belief." They often asked me: "What are your most deeply held and cherished beliefs?"

They became shocked and even insulting when I answered, "What does having to believe a lot of mularkey have to do with my character as a person? I'm always striving to become better and better, in every way."

When I first began writing my books about Belief/Not-Belief, I naively thought that what I had to say would awaken people, freeing them of its enslavement of their minds, just as Eric Hoffer's book had given me a measure of enlightenment. But I was wrong. Americans are generally as crazy about God Bel as the Mexicans are. It was then that I decided to just concentrate on the subject matter in this book, which deals with the progenitors of all mankind (the Turks), Jacob's Ladder, the Holy Directions, and the Holy Trinity (Kristos or Logos). They can never be intelligently refuted or contradicted-at least, not by people who truly love God (Creation).

The wonderful aspect about Jacob's Ladder, the Holy Directions, and the Holy Trinity is that we can still keep on studying and progressing scientifically, socially, and economically. No need to return to ignorance, for ignorance is what got all us humans lost in the first place.

A great difficulty I will have, in spite of this book, is that not one of my readers will understand it fully as I want it to be understood. In every way, each human being is an entity unto himself. Our ways of understanding are just as individual as our finger prints, eye prints, physical and facial features, ways of walking, emissions of life energies, and the like. Most of us allow ourselves to think that some people are "like" others. In truth, there are only approximations. Jesus himself said that his teachings would not unite any of us. All words, even scriptures, are just Babel-even my own writings. All beings, things, and phenomena on earth, such as all animals, birds, fish, one-celled bacteria, even earth, air, fire, and water, are in eternal competition against one another. If you doubt this truth, explain such things as earthquakes, tsunamis, hurricanes, tornados, floods, droughts, and forest fires. Do you really think they occur "by accident?" We aren't even safe from being bombarded from Outer Space. Life on this earth has been destroyed more than once. We don't need holy books to convince us of that reality. Science has proven it. And when we travel to Outer Space, we'll still be fighting for dominance over all organic and inorganic matter there. Even the planet we presently live on, and those remaining for us to inhabit, are giving us a run for our money. Who can prove that this isn't so?

> I am come to send fire on the earth; and what better wish can I have than that it should be kindled? There is a baptism I must needs be baptized with, and how distressed I am for its accomplishment! Do you think that I have come to bring peace on the earth? No, believe me, I have come to bring dissension. (Luke 12:49-53.)

Simply put, Jesus came to earth to give us, free of charge, the one and only way we can survive the eternal holocaust going on everywhere in the universe.

6

The Turks Gave Us Our God, Our Holy Cross, the Name of Jesus, and the Holy Trinity!

Before discussing the way Creation (God) keeps us from competing successfully with Him/Her/It/They, I must define what the word God really means. The Turks' primal religion, Tengri, known in early post-Christian Europe as *Arianism* or *Aryanism* (*Ari* in Turkic), allowed a person to use a Divine Word that best expressed and revealed his Inner Self.

The following is a partial list of the spiritual and mental states (Gods) that best met the spiritual requirements of the ancient Turkic worshippers:

Hodai/Khodai. The ancient Turks often regarded "H" and "K' as fundamentally the same sounds because in many languages, "H" is guttural. This is our word for "God," the unseen archetype of all Creation. It originally meant "vulva" or "vagina," meaning "The Source of All Things," or "Creation." It was the choice of Divine Manifestation of the *Kara Turks* or those whom we now call Jews and Christians (*Panchala Krishtaya*) or Catholics (*Ketylika*.) The Kashmiri language, derived from Turkic and Sanskrit, reveals "God's essential Nature:" God, meaning "the beginning, commencement, of anything." (Reference: *George A. Grierson's Dictionary of The Kashmiri Language*. It is of interest to note that many of the ancient Turks who worshiped "God" or "Bogh," many hundreds of years before Christ, had the Torah as their primary holy book. This, along with the fact that they were all also Panchala Kristaya, was the primary reason why Catholic Christianity spread like a prairie fire throughout Central Asia and deep into India in a short time.

Bogh. A word identical in meaning and function to "God." The Sanskrit word *Bagha* or *Bakh* means the same thing, but in an androgynous sense. It is still used in the Turkish-influenced nations.

Hz/Khz. This is the word that the ancient Turks used to refer to our Jesus, the reincarnated son of the Archetype of All Mankind: *Kristos.* It is really a synonym of the next God on my list.

Apollo. An epithet of Apollo is *Ie* or *Yah.* He was also *Hrist, Kristos, Hz,* and *Khz.* For the *Khristayas* (Way of Life of the Phoenicians or Turks). the physical encarnation of The Archetypical Father was *Kristis.* Siberia (*Shivarya*) was named after the God *Shiva* (The Archetypical Father of The Original Five Human Tribes, the Panchala Krishtaya). Shiva was *Japhet,* a son of Noah, *Jyapeti* in Sanskrit, *Jupiter,* derived from Sanskrit *Dyupitar, Dyaus* (Zeus), *Dyu* (Jew or Sun God) and more, were all names that the ancient Turks used to define the nature of *Tengri,* their primordial concept of God.

Buda. Those who were devoted to *Buda* or *Hz/Khz* were determined to search out their own souls and achieve spiritual superiority through their own efforts, without the intercession of priests, preacher, rabbis, and imans to force them how to live and think. In India, religious leaders imposing a spiritual police state on people were called *Brahman.*

Dini, another epithet of Buddha and Jesus. It is interesting to note that the religion of the Navajos, derived from the Sanskrit word for sailor, *Navaja,* call themselves *Diné,* meaning "People of Religion." They, too, are Buddhists or Christians. This word leaves no doubt as to their origins.

Gospodi or *Gozbodi.* This name was so sacred and hallowed, that not even the priests of Tengri dared to utter it. However, linguistically it reveals itself as "Christ the Buddha," having the Holy Trinity or "Cross" as its symbol of True Scientific Divinity.

Bel. Those who were masochistic, liked violence, and felt that blood sacrifice and reading scriptures made one "right" with God. For us, it symbolizes Christ nailed to the horizontal beam of the Cross as completely disconnected from the vertical beam symbolizing *Kristi,* the archetypical father of mankind's five races. Because World Civilization first began in the Arctic Circle, and because it afterwards extended southward as far as what is now Sri Lanka, the Bel followers decided that the Sacred Directions were North and South. At night, their bodies aligned themselves with the North and South. Using terror and brute force, their theocratic leaders forced everyone to do this. They surrendered their bodies and souls to *Baleva* or *Ab-Babel,* "Father of Confusion."

Allah/Ollo. The devotees to Allah or Ollo felt that only a strong theocratic government, with the dictatorial priests and preachers directing their lives and telling them how to think and act, could lead mankind to salvation, because on his own he could not do it. It was a form of Hindu Brahmanism.

Not-Gods, Highly Developed Individuals, Masters, Lords, or Semi-Deities. These had names similar to the Gods themselves: *Hrist, Kristos, Rab, Allah, Tenri,* and *Isa.* Jesus Christ was called *Mesih* (Messiah) and *Isa.*

The Tengri worshippers had a number of deities from which to choose. I have just named a few, in order not to confuse my readers too much.

The ancient Turks, no matter what "inner God" they worshipped, attended religious services in the same Tengri (Aryan) temples. No one was made to conform to any particular religious persuasion.

Author Murad Adji confirms much of the above:

> Who was...that Great Tengri, the heart of Turkic culture?
>
> Tengri was an invisible spirit inhabiting the Heaven, as vast as the Heaven itself and as wide as the whole world. The Turkis reverently called Him the Eternal Blue Sky or Tengri Khan, the latter name emphasizing His supremacy in the Universe.
>
> He was the Only God, the Creator of the world and all forms of life on Earth, the Lord. So much was said in ancient legends, which are still remembered in our time. To understand the wisdom and depth of faith in Tengri, people were to embrace one simple truth—God is one and He sees everything. You cannot conceal anything from Him. He is the Lord and Judge.
>
> The Turkic people developed a habit of looking forward to Judgment Day. Not in helpless fear, though, for people were sure that supreme justice existed in the world. It was the Judgment of God, to be passed on to everybody, king or slave.
>
> God is protection and punishment, all in one. This was what the Turkis' faith in the Only God was based on.
>
> Religion was the supreme achievement of the Turkic people's spiritual culture. The Turkis threw out their pagan gods and turned to Tengri-each in one's own tongue, Bogh (Bogdo or Boje); Hodai (or Kodai); Allah or Ollo, Gospodi or Gozbodi.

Note: Hodee is the Hebrew word for Hindu. We must keep in mind that the Turks and the Hindus are the same people.

> These words resounded in the Altai Mountains as long as two and a half thousand years ago. And, of course, many other words were addressed to Tengri as well.
>
> Bogh was the most frequent word on people's lips, though. It invoked peace, calm and perfection. The Turkis now went into battle with Bogh in their hearts and minds. And took up every challenge with Bogh at their side.
>
> Another form of address to God, Hodai (literally, Be Happy), emphasised the unique qualities of Tengri—the Almighty in this world, its Creator. All-

powerful and Benevolent. Allah (or Ala) was the least frequent word used by ancient Turkis. It only came to their minds in moments of desperation when they wanted to ask the Great Tengri Khan for something very important in their lives. The word derived from the Turkic al (hand), suggesting "giving and taking". In its original sense, Allah could only be uttered while saying a prayer with hands held out in front of you and palms up to face the Great Blue Sky. Gospodi was the rarest of all-it could only be spoken by priests. Literally, the word means "seeing the light" or "eye opener". It was an address one could say in a moment of truth, and it was full of philosophical wisdom. A truly righteous man could ask for guidance in penetrating the inner sense of things. The rules to be followed in prayer, celebration or fasting, were polished over the centuries, to develop into a code of behavior or rites, performed by priests. Turkic priests could be told from laymen by the way they dressed and behaved. Their clothing consisted of long robes (caftans or mantles) and peaked hoods, which were white for senior clergy and black for the rest of the priesthood. You can guess all right that ancient artists cut images of priests on Altai rocks. So we now know what those "white wanderers" (a popular phrase for them) were-preachers of the faith.

The Turkis chose a simple equal-armed cross, *aji,* for a symbol of Tengri Khan. The cross was not new to Turkic culture, though-it had been an important element in Turkis' lives, along with a "skew" cross that was a sign of the underworld and old, underground gods.

As can be expected, aji crosses were very crude and simple, gradually evolving into real works of art crafted by jewelers, who used to give them a gold coat and adorn them with gems to please the eye and heart.

Skew crosses appeared in the Altai between three and four thousand years ago. In actual fact, those were not crosses and were named so by Europeans when they first learned about Tengri religion.

Semantically, the cross is an intersection of two lines. The Tengri sign shows no intersection, and is, in fact, a solar circle with four equally spaced rays radiating from it. Get the difference?

Sun rays, otherwise interpreted as grace of God emanating from a single centre. They are a Heavenly sign that marks off Turkic culture, the culture of a people that had profound faith in the power of the Eternal Blue Sky.

Occasionally, a crescent was added to the Tengri sign (or cross, if you like), to convey a different message-a reminder of time and perpetuity. The Sun and Moon were closely related to ancient Turkis (hence their twelve-year calendar).

The Tengri sign was embroidered on battle banners and worn on a chain on the chest. It was tattooed on foreheads and woven into designs and ornaments by artists. It was all in the spirit of strong national tradition.

I asked my friend, Dravidian holy man Shri Subash Bose, whether he knew what the word Tengri really meant.

Question:

Dear Brother Bose,

By now, you've probably seen that online book I sent you, written by the Turkish historian, Murad Adji. He speaks of the ancient Turkish God Tengri. I have been trying to find the true meaning of that word. Most generally, one has only to go to the Sanskrit dictionary to find out anything he wants. But this time I can't find it. Never in my studies of Hinduism have I found that word. But Mr. Adji says that when the Turks emigrated to India, the Ramanas or Indians accepted Tengri as one of their principal gods. I notice that the word *Giri* means "mountain and the eight mountains surrounding Mt. Meru." But I cannot find the meaning of the word *Ten.* Linguistically it is close to the word Danu. One of the Turkish republics in Russia is Tannu, also named Tuva or Tiva. It is very strange that some of our Southwestern American Indian tribes also call themselves Tanu and Tewa. Brother Bose, which Hindu god would you say that Tengri is? I have suspected that he may be Kubera. And then again, he may be Shiva. The reason why I thought he may be Kubera is that he discovered iron. Also, another name of Kubera is Danu, meaning "Conqueror." What do you say? You don't have to agree with me, for I want your opinion which I will take seriously.

Answer:

Dear brother Gene,

Also there is a name for Lord Kubera called "Tanathan."

The word Tengri, appears as Thengri in Tamil. Then or Ten means (South). The shortened version of the word Therku is Ten. Gri or Kri means mountain, the mountain (Gri) in the southern (Then or Ten) part of Mount Himalayan-Immayam). The name of mountain Pothigaimalai is called Tengri, from which pleasant (Tendral) wind comes to many parts of Tamil Nadu, in particular to Madurai city and around. Saint Agasthiya said remain Pothigaimalai (Tengri). You must know that Malai means Hills or mountain.

Tanam-means Gold, if we add Gri or Kri it will show that Tangri means Golden Mountain, known as Mount Meru. There is a name of mother goddess as Dhan+vandari or Tan+vandri.

By comparing the above two, possibly the word Tengri may be referring to Mount Meru, where the mother goddess abides.

Since I claim that Jesus Christ is a spiritual and blood descendant of the ancient Krishtayas (Aryans), I will let the word "God" predominate in my discussion of the original human concept of Jesus Christ. Naturally, there are many words for "God" in the world. Perhaps the most common word of God in the pre- and post-diluvial world was and is the Turkish Tengri or Tenri. The name isn't important. It's the game that counts.

The original meaning of "God" implies that Creation is feminine. I have no explanation of this. Perhaps none is necessary, according to what Brother Bose told me.

7

Could the Ancient Hyperboreans Live a Thousand Years?

The holy books of the world's major religions state that at one time, humans could easily live for a thousand years. Moreover, they state in what part of the world people could live that long: ancient Siberia, Hyperborea, which are really all the Turkish peoples from Northwestern Canada, Alaska, Siberia, including the countries down to and including Northern India. In short, the whole of Central Asia. The Hebrew Torah, the Hindu Vedas, The Greek myths, the Koran, the Mayans of Mexico, and the ancient Chinese history books all mention this anomaly. I have drawn from all those sources.

Nei Ching, The Yellow Emperor Classic of Internal Medicine, was supposed to have been written more than five thousand years ago. It is a Taoist document. The book describes a conversation about human health and healing between the Yellow Emperor and a divinely inspired teacher named Chi'Po. I will just quote from a few passages.

> Huang Ti said: "I have heard that in ancient times there were the so-called Spiritual Men. They mastered the Universe and controlled Yin and Yang, the two principles in nature. They breathed the essence of life, they were independent in preserving their spirit, and their muscles and flesh remained unchanged. Therefore, they could enjoy a long life, just as there is no end for Heaven and Earth, All this was the result of their life in accordance with Tao, the Right Way.
>
> "In medieval times there existed the Sapients; their virtue was preserved and they unfailingly upheld Tao, the Right Way. They lived in accord with Yin and Yang, and in harmony with the four seasons. They departed from this world and retired from mundane affairs; they saved their energies, and preserved their spirits completely. They roamed and traveled all over the universe and could see and hear beyond the eight distant places. By all these means

they increased their life and strengthened it; and at last they attained the position of the Spiritual Man.

As the Nei Ching says, the Sapients and the Spiritual Men could choose to leave their bodies and explore the universe, or they could choose to remain in their bodies and enjoy the physical and material world. There were no limits put upon them. Naturally, such a life would make most of us happy.

The Nei Ching continues to say:

> "They were succeeded by the Sages, The Sages attained harmony with Heaven and Earth and followed closely the laws of the eight winds. They were able to adjust their desires to worldly affairs, and within their hearts there was neither hatred nor anger. They did not wish to separate their activities from the world; they could be indifferent to custom. They did not over-exert their bodies at physical labour and they did not over-exert their minds by strenuous meditation. They were not concerned about any thing, they regarded inner happiness and peace as fundamental, and contentment as highest achievement. Their bodies could never be harmed and their mental faculties never be dissipated. Thus they could reach the age of one hundred years or more.
>
> "They were succeeded by the Men of Excellent Virtue who followed the rules of the universe and emulated the sun and the moon, and they also discovered the arrangement of the stars; they could foresee the works of Yin and Yang and obey them; and they could distinguish the four seasons. They followed the ancient times and tried to maintain their harmony with Tao. In doing so they increased their age toward a long life." *The Yellow Emperor's Classic of Internal Medicine,* translated by Ilza Veith. Published by University of California Press, Berkeley, Los Angeles, London 1972.

Notice that all humans fell five steps to degradation. The cabalistic idea of "Jacob's Ladder" means that if we want to again become Spiritual Men, we must climb back to where we originated.

As Chi'Po said, in the beginning of mankind's existence on earth, humans unconsciously and naturally obeyed the *Tao. Tao* was the original name of The Fundamental Laws of Nature. The term was once used by all the peoples of the ancient world, included the Americas. The Greeks called it *Theo, Zeus,* and *Jupiter.* For the ancient Mexican Toltecs and Aztecs, it was *Teo, Teotl,* and *Tonatiu* (Sun God). Some of our North American Indian tribes used the term *Manitou* (God of Mankind). The Romans called it *Dio, Deus* and *Zeus.* In Sanskrit, it was known as *Dyu, Dyaus,* and *Dyaus Pitar.* The Jews call it *Tau.* Notice the nearly exact linguistic similarities between the Greek and Sanskrit names. The Phoenicians called it *Taut, Taus, Taut, Tash.* For the Egyptians, It was *Thoth.* The

O'odham Indians of Southern Arizona and Northern Mexico called and call it *Josh* and *Ju* (The Sun). It was also named after what was an ancient post-deluvial king of Siberia: *Shiva*. Shiva was really Dyaus-Pitar, Jupiter, or Japhet. In Sanskrit, he was called Jyapeti. Siberia was named after him: *Shivarya* (The Noble One). Shiva is not only a God of the world, and with his names and epithets, but he was and is the first God worshiped In India. As I stated in the previous chapter, God's Turkish name was *Tengri* or *Tenri*. The Tengri symbol was a cross. In fact, our Christian cross was derived from the Tengri religion. Nearly every past and present religion in the world had and has a Cross as a symbol of veneration. It was carried to the world by the Phoenician Krishtayanis or "Catholics," for the Krishtayanis, who were really Turks, also called their powerful religion *Katylika* in Turkish, and *Ketuloka* in Sanskrit. Both terms mean the Universal Religion of Mankind.

Like most of the other major holy books of the world, the Mayan *Popol-Vuh* states that until mankind rids himself of the temptation to play God, the creative forces will keep him bound in ignorance and sexual slavery:

> They were endowed with intelligence; they saw and instantly they could see far, they succeeded in seeing, they succeeded in knowing all that there is in the world. When they looked, instantly they saw all around them, and they contemplated in turn the arch of heaven and the round face of the earth.
>
> The things hidden [in the distance] they saw all, without first having to move; at once they saw the world, and so, too, from where they were, they saw it.
>
> Great was their wisdom; their sight reached to the forests, the rocks, the lakes, the seas, the mountains, and the valleys. In truth, they were admirable men. Balam-Quitzé, Balam-Acab, Mahucutah, and Iqui-Balam.
>
> Then the Creator and the Maker asked them: "What do you think of your condition? Do you not see? Do you not hear? Are not your speech and manner of walking good? Look, then! Contemplate the world, look [and see] if the mountains and the valleys appear! Try, then, to see!" they said to [the four first men].
>
> And immediately they [the four first men] began to see all that was in the world. Then they gave thanks to the Creator and the Maker: "We really give you thanks, two and three times! We have been created, we have been given a mouth and a face, we speak, we hear, we think, and walk; we feel perfectly, and we know what is far and what is near. We also see the large and the small in the sky and on earth. We give you thanks, then, for having created us, oh, Creator and Maker, for having given us being, oh, our Grandmother! Oh, our Grandfather!" they said, giving thanks for their creation and formation.
>
> They were able to know all, and they examined the four comers, the four points of the arch of the sky and the round face of the earth.

But the Creator and the Maker did not hear this with pleasure. "It is not well what our creatures, our works say; they know all, the large and the small," they said. And so the Forefathers held counsel again. "What shall we do with them now? Let their sight reach only to that which is near; let them see only a little of the face of the earth! It is not well what they say. Perchance, are they not by nature simple creatures of our making? Must they also be gods? And if they do not reproduce and multiply when it will dawn, when the sun rises? And what if they do not multiply?" So they spoke.

"Let us check a little their desires, because it is not well what we see. Must they perchance be the equals of ourselves, their Makers, who can see afar, who know all and see all?"

Thus spoke the Heart of Heaven, Huracán, Chipi-Caculhá, Raxa-Caculhá, Tepeu, Gucumatz, the Forefathers, Xpiyacoc, Xmucané, the Creator and the Maker. Thus they spoke, and immediately they changed the nature of their works, of their creatures.

Then the Heart of Heaven blew mist into their eyes, which clouded their sight as when a mirror is breathed upon. Their eyes were covered and they could see only what was close, only that was clear to them.

In this way the wisdom and all the knowledge of the four men, the origin and beginning [of the Quiché race], were destroyed.

In this way were created and formed our grandfathers, our fathers, by the Heart of Heaven, the Heart of Earth.

Genesis tells us that Nature will not give Man effective control over her secrets until he rids himself of his animal-like propensity to exploit, harm, murder, accept, reject, classify, and judge innocent human beings. Those with the greatest knowledge, money, fame, and power must be especially virtuous and humanitarian. Man will not be allowed to have more than a tiny amount of control over natural phenomena. First, Man must submit himself totally and honestly to the reality of a Higher Power, just as he must now render obeisance to man-created governments. This is the fundamental reason why most educated and powerful men think that lack of spirituality is "scientific" and that simple, uneducated people are "superstitious".

And the Lord God said, 'Now that the man has become one of us, knowing good and bad, what if he should stretch out his hand and take also from the tree of life and eat, and live forever!' So the Lord God banished him from the Garden of Eden, to till the soil from which he was taken. He drove the man out, and stationed east of the garden of Eden the cherubim and the fiery ever-turning sword, to guard the way of the tree of life. (*Genesis* 4:20-24.)

The Bible mentions the ages of the patriarchs of old. In the following list, note that after the flood, the longevity of human kind began to decrease dramatically:

Pre-diluvial Period

Adam 930; Seth 912; Enoch 905; Kenan 910; Mahaleel 895; Jared 862; Methuselah 969; Lamech 777.

Post-diluvial Period

Noah 950; Shem 602; Sala 433; Eber 464; Peleg 239; Serug 230; Nahor 148; Terah 205; Abraham 175; Isaac 180; Jacob 147; Job 140; Levi 137; Kohath 133; Amaran 137; Moses; 120; Joshua 110; Eli 98; David 70.

The following ancient historians confirm that pre-historical mankind lived for up to hundreds of years until just after the Great Flood:

Hecataus; Hellenicus; Acusilaus; Manetho; Berosus; Machu; Hestiaeus; Hieronymus; Hesios; Ephorus; Nicolaus; Josephus.

The Hindus share most of our own Old Testament or Torah traditions also. The five original tribes of mankind were collectively called *Panchala Krishtaya* (Phoenician Christians) or *Panchala Kristihan* (Phoenician Christian Conquerors), also called *Arya* (*Ari* in Turkic). Each brought with them an oral history of their pre- and post-diluvial past, which in the Turkic language was called *Tarih*. Unlike many other languages, the Turkish language remains fundamentally stable. And no wonder! Many of the words in that strange language are incredibly short. Such short words don't easily change perceptibly.

When I was a youngster, my teachers said that the word "history" means "his story." Its real meaning is History of the Hittites (*Keder*) or Kassites (*Keser/Kaiser*)-the Turks. We *Homo-Sapiens-Sapiens* all descend from the mysterious Turkish tribes who, even today, remain a mystery to us. We can now clearly see that "history" really means *Torah of the Kassites* (Turks). From where did we get the words Kassites and Hittites? Naturally, from the Turks.

When the Five Panchala Kristihan or Aryan descendants of Noah entered India, they brought them their their science of the Cross, The Holy Trinity, Universal Life Energy, and the reasons for mankind's deprivation of a long life on this earth.

Bavishya Purana, an ancient Hindu holy book, says:

There is a couple named Adama and his wife Havyavati. They are born from Vishnu-kardama and will increase the generations of mlecchas...In the eastern side of Pradan city where there is a big God-given forest, which is 16 square yojanas in size. The man named Adama was staying there under a Papa-Vriksha or a sinful tree and was eager to see his wife Havyavati. The Kali Purusha quickly came there assuming the form of a serpent. He cheated them and they disobeyed Lord Vishnu. The husband ate the forbidden fruit of the sinful tree. They lived by eating air with the leaves called udumbara. After that, they had sons and all of them became mlecchas. Adama's duration of life was nine-hundred and thirty years. He offered oblations with fruits and went to heaven with his wife...The son of Hamuka was Matocchila. He ruled for 970 years. His son Lomaka ruled 777 years and went to heaven. His son Nyuha (Noah) ruled for 500 years. He had three sons named Sima, Sama and Bhava. Nyuha was a devotee of Lord Vishnu.

Once the Lord appeared in his dream and said: "My dear Nyuha, please listen, there will be devastation on the seventh day. Therefore, you have to be very quick that you make a big boat and ride in it. O chief of the devotees, you will be celebrated as a great king".

Then he made a strong boat which was 300 feet long, 50 feet wide and 30 feet high. It was beautiful and all the living entities could take shelter in it. He then himself rode in it, engaged in meditating on Lord Vishnu.

Lord Indra called the devastating cloud named Sambartaka and poured heavy rain continuously for 40 days. The whole earth, Bharat-varsa, had merged in the water and four oceans came up together. Only Visala or Badarikasrama was not submerged. There were 80,000 great transcendental-ists in Visala who joined with king Nyuha and his family. All of them were saved and everything else was destroyed.

Note: *Mleccha* (M'Lekkha) is an ancient Sanskrit word, meaning "Foreigner." The Hebrew word for "Sailor" is Malakh. Bharat-varsa is India itself. Note also that this story implies that India had once conquered the whole world.

The Turks and the Hindus share the same history because when the Five Pan-chala or Ari Krishtayas entered India, they merged their own traditions with those of India. But all that has changed. India has since been cut down to what is now the Indian sub-continent. Even now, parts of it are being hacked away. Therefore, just as most of today's modern Christians don't know about the Aryan Turks, neither do the Hindus know anything about that part of them which was amputated so many centuries in the past. I think this is the reason why the Hindus see Adam and Noah as the same person, for that was the period when the Aryans or Krishtaya first showed up in their part of the world.

The Roman natural philosopher, Gaius Plinius Secundus (23-79 AD, better known a Pliny the Elder, wrote that the Hyperboreans lived beyond the Ripaean mountains (Central Asia) that the Hyperboreans were a happy race and no discord or sorrow ever occurred there. He said that they lived for as long as they desired, up to a thousand years. When they got tired of living, they would leap off a certain rock into the sea. (*Pliny Book IV*, see 89.)

The Greeks also knew about Hyperborea, claiming that it was the birthplace of Apollo. The Bulgarians say that Apollo was born in Pataya, Bulgaria.

Herodotus affirmed that they were connected with the cult of Apollo, the sun-god, and their nation was a paradise. He stated that they lived "beyond the North Wind, which certainly indicates some region near the Arctic Circle. These Hyperboreans were said to be able to leave their bodies at will, traveling to any part of the earth. They did this by astral projection and bilocation.

I extracted the following article from the online encyclopedia *Wikipedia:*

> Jean-Sylvain Bailly (1736-1793), who was an astronomer and a mystic, comments that "it is a very remarkable thing that enlightenment appears to have come from the North, against the common prejudice that the Earth was enlightened, as it was populated, from the South..." He then goes on to point out that, according to all the legends and ancient wisdom, "as humanity began to reconstitute itself after the Noahic Deluge, the purest stream of civilization descended from Northern Asia into India, which to this day carries "evidence of having the most ancient astronomical system on Earth". He continues on to point out that, in most of the ancient mythologies of the world, there appears to be a race-memory of a racial origin in the far North and a subsequent gradual migration southward.
>
> Another great scientific mind of the same era, the Comte de Buffon, placed the first civilizations in northern and central Asia, east of the Caspian Sea, but he seemed to be in general agreement with Bailly about a northern origin for mankind, rather than a Middle Eastern or Southern one. Rev. Dr. W.F. Warren, who was president of Boston University and belonged to several learned societies, revived the polar origin theory for mankind in a book published in 1885: "Paradise Found", of which the thesis was "That the cradle of the human race...was situated at the North Pole, in a country submerged at the time of the Deluge."
>
> His theory compared very well with all the relevant sciences and comparative mythology—especially that of Germany. Warren was a Christian and an avowed anti-Darwinist, and he utterly rejected the concept of man having evolved from the ape, through a period of primitive savagery. He believed that the earliest men were the noblest and the longest-lived, "and it was only after the Deluge, that humanity began to take on the feeble lineaments of ourselves." At least, in his work he reveals some amazing insight into what could have caused the Deluge, through God's Hand, by pointing out that, after the survivors of the polar flood settled in their north Asian exile, "they found the

skies (or heavens) tilted in respect to the way they had known them: the North Star was no longer overhead", and he mentions that "they perfectly understood why this was so...but their rude descendants, unfavoured with the treasures of antediluvian science, and born only to a savage, nomadic life...might easily have forgotten the explanation"—which was that, "instead of the human horizon, it was the Earth that had shifted". Here, at long last, we get the first oblique mention of a polar shift.

Support from India

Bal Gangadhar Tilak (1856-1920), a renowned pioneer protagonist of Indian Independence at the turn of the century, was also a scholar in astronomy and Vedic antiquities, who among other feats, was able to place the oldest Indian Vedic civilization at around 4500 BC.

Tilak was jailed by the British for his anti-British writings for several years, and this time he put to good use in studying the Veda scripts, in relation to known astronomical and geological events. He published his findings in a work: "The Arctic Home of The Vedas", in 1903. In this he stated that, according to his readings of the Vedas, the original Arctic home of humanity was destroyed around 10,000 to 8,000 BC by the last Ice Age, and that from 8,000 to 3,000 BC, was the Age of Wandering, before the Vedic people finally settled in India between 5,000 and 3,000 BC. By then, he went on to add, they had already begun to forget their Arctic origins, and their traditions had begun to go rapidly downhill.

As we have seen in earlier accounts, his timing of this cataclysm fits in very closely with what we know of the destruction of Atlantis and Mu, so we can attribute it to the same cause-a sudden polar shift, resulting in both tidal waves and tectonic upheavals followed by a very rapid relocation of the polar icecaps: the so-called "Ice Age". So, we have the destruction of Mu, dated very approximately at 12,000 years ago, that of Atlantis around 10,000 to 12,000 years ago, and, according to best estimates, the destruction of Hyperborea also at around the same time-frame of 10,000 to 12,000 years ago. Could this then, be also the time of the Biblical "Flood" one wonders?

As far as I'm able to determine by reading sundry authorities, this would seem to be the case. So it's up to my readers to resolve for themselves whether this is a pure coincidental matter, or whether God chose to bring about the cleansing of an evil and disobedient world by means of a purely natural catastrophic event—which would seem to be a perfectly logical thing to do if One were the Supreme Intellect, who created the entire Universe along purely logical lines.

Wanting to know more about what the Hindus think of the existence of Hyperborea, which they call Uttara Kuru (Northernmost Turkey), I again wrote to my friend Mr. Subash Bose about these matters:

Question:

Dear Brother Bose,

Nearly all the major groups of people on earth discuss Uttara Kuru. The Chinese, Turks, Greeks, the Old Testament of the Jews and Christians, and the Mayan holy books state that at one time the people of Uttara Kuru lived up to a thousand years and could enter, leave, and re-enter their bodies at will. Do the Indian books state that? Please let me know.

Answer:

Uttara Kuru: Let me assume it as a Tamil or Sanskrit word.

Uttara—means North.

Kuru—I am spelling it as, Guru—means Teacher.

Uttara Kuru—may also mean the Himalayan mountains. Parvathi, the consort of Lord Siva, is the daughter of Mount Himalayas).

North direction is for the Mother Goddess. She can bless all beings to get wisdom or Gnana Sakthi, to attain the liberation from the cycle of birth and death.

Oh Mother! You are the one the glorious bright light, hidden in a shape having head, two wings, tail and body and which is covered with five sheaths such as Food sheath, Breath sheath, Mind sheath, Intelligence sheath and Bliss sheath. Those who realize and understand shall become knowers of Brahma Vidya or Brahma Gnani. (Sakthi Mahimna Sosthiram-24—An extract from our book "The Divine Light of Soul and the Goats and Tiger Game".)

Yes, it is a fact that those who know the Brahma Vidya shall attain Jiva Mukthi.

They can travel to any far distance and reach the feet of Paramatma (Supreme Lord), can have direct communication with him/her and shall return to earth to live as human beings.

In the term of metaphysics, those who have attained Jiva mukthi are similar to dead persons because they do not have any attachment to the material world. They find happiness in each and every thing, there is no misery or sorrow for them. It is in so many ancient manuscripts…

Such Jiva Mukthas (liberated man while living) lived in this earth thousands of year on this mother earth, their souls are capable to leave the body, reach the Supreme soul and re-enter into their body again. Those who traveled in Tamil Nadu, can practically see such Jivamuktha's just living even like a beggar, sleeping on the road and look like a mad person. But they are the real

Jivamukthas, The Great Purusas, it is the blessings of mother Goddess to us to see such divine personalizes. Hope the above may fulfill your requirements.

The Tibetans call Uttara Kuru *Kedar Khand* (Country of God Shiva). There is also an area of India's state of Uttaranchel called *Panch Kedar Khand,* The Abode of Phoenician Shiva.

Unlike our present concept of Christianity, the Hindus and Buddhists teach that Heaven and Hell are in no other place but this earth. Therefore, some earthly humans are living in hell, others in purgatory, some are composed of various states of heaven, hell, purgatory, etc., because not all of us progress uniformly. We are illustrious in some areas of development, mediocre in others, and abysmal in other ways. Regarding conduct and spiritual progress, we are checkerboards. As Brother Bose said, we even have spiritual humans among us, such as Jesus Christ. They don't always make themselves known, and they don't always have to be crucified. So everything boils down to this: We have people and beings among us who are in various states of development. Some are at the bottom, others somewhere near the middle, and others have reached the supreme state.

8

Were the Original Five Races of Humanity from Outer Space?

We who presently call ourselves Christians and Jews, having forgotten all about our Turkish Aryan roots, recognize our *Torah* (meaning *History of the Turks*) as *Genesis, Exodus, Leviticus, Numbers,* and *Deuteronomy.* All the mysteries which mankind must solve for his own salvation and survival we inherited from the original five races of mankind: *Yadu, Turvasa, Druhyus, Anu,* and *Puru.* Each and all of those races known also as Aryans, were, and still are, Turks (Ari or Kuru).

Genesis 6 tells us that in remotest times, a people called *Nephilim* appeared on earth:

> When men began to increase on earth and daughters were born to them, the divine beings saw how beautiful the daughters of men were and took wives from among them that pleased. The Lord said, "My breath shall not abide in man forever, since he too is flesh; let the days allowed him be one hundred twenty years." It was then, and later too, that the Nephilim appeared on earth-when the divine beings cohabited with the daughters of men, who bore them offspring. They were the heroes of old, the men of renown.

Notice that the Bible implies that the Nephilim arrived in successive waves. Most people who've read Genesis naturally intuit that they came from Outer Space. From where else could they have come?

Did they arrive in Space Ships? Who can tell for sure? The Phoenicians themselves said that before the Great Flood, their civilization was 30,000 years old. (*The Rg Veda-a History,* by Rajesvar Gupta; p. 16.) In that amount of time, they could have developed an outstandingly high state of civilization, both societal and technological. Even scientists are saying that Man may never venture too far into

Outer Space if he cannot travel at the speed of light. I remember a TV series called *Star Trek.* Whenever any of the crew members in the space ship wanted to see a certain planet, they were turned into light and beamed down.

In the *Thomas Gospel,* which is really a Christian Cabala, Jesus tells his admirers and enemies that he and his disciples came from light. If mankind is ever to accomplish such an incredible feat, a basic pattern must also be beamed down, so that his bodily atoms and molecules can restructure themselves within their original form which is the Holy Ghost of each human.

> If they say to you, 'Where did you come from?' say to them, 'We came from the light, the place where the light came into being on its own accord and established itself and became manifest through their image.' If they say to you, 'Is it you,' say, 'We are its children, and we see the elect of the living father.' If they ask you, 'What is the sign of your father in you?' say to them, 'It is movement and repose.' (Thomas Saying 50)

Christ said virtually the same thing to his disciples in *Ephesians* 5-8: "…now you are light in the Lord; walk as children of light…"

You are all children of light, and the children of the day; we are not of night, nor of darkness." If "light" does not mean what is says, day-light, then what is it?

The ancients, those of all religions, held sunlight to be holy. The Bible associates it with God. "He not only lives in light (Ex:24-10:1; Tim: 1-10:16;) is clothed with it (Ps. 104-2); but he is light (1 John 1:5; Hence when God becomes Incarnate, He is called "The Light of the World" (John 1;1-18; 18:12; To walk to the light brings salvation (John 8:12; 12:36; 1 John 1:12; 12:36; 1 John 1:7; 2 Cor. 4:6, etc); a life lived without God is darkness (John 3:19; 12:46, etc.) In my researches, I counted so many Old and New Testament statements that God is Light, that I couldn't even begin to count them all. People who disagree with me say that Christ was referring to "accuracy in interpreting the scriptures." But no one ever understands the scriptures correctly, if at all; not even I, a researcher of the world's scriptures. Everyone interprets in his own way.

Nearly everyone in Jesus' time was illiterate and unsophisticated. They understood "light" as being from the sun and in no other way. For this reason, most people who heard him preach intuited that he was really an incarnation of Apollo. Therefore, his fame extended rapidly from The Holy Land, throughout Central Asia, and deep into West Central India. Had people understood light to be anything else than what it was, the Jesus Christ that we know would be unheard of today.

Christ made it abundantly clear that he, his disciples, and all men are basically formed from the "breath of God," which is pure light. Not the "light of understanding" but flashing, brilliant light. The sun. Nothing on this earth, plant or animal, can exist without light. Of course, the necessary conditions on a planet must make it possible for something to be created from light-The Breath of God."

In the *Bavishya Purana,* the ancient Hindu account of the meeting between Jesus and King Salivahana, the good king asked Jesus to describe his religious teachings. Jesus answered: "In truth, oh King, all power rests with the Lord, who is in the center of the sun…"

We know that the Nephilim and "those who followed" didn't see these "aboriginal earthlings" as undesirable and inferior, for they intermarried with them, producing progeny. The Torah tells us no lies. Those humans who preceded the Nephilim were just forerunners of one of the five original races known as the Nephilim. They, too, could have once arrived here in the form of light waves.

At first, things went well for the Nephilim: the five Krishtaya or Aryan tribes, the Yadus, Druhyus, Tarvasa, Anus and Purus. The earthly environment so greatly benefited them that they were able to live nearly ten centuries beyond the lifespan that God had allotted to them. They were not limited in any way, either. They could enter and leave their bodies at will. If they got bored with just whiling away the centuries in physical form, they could go on vacation to other parts of the universe as pure light energy.

If any of them ever became ill for one reason or another, they could become healed immediately with a dose or two of extra light energy. The Chinese *Nei Ching,* The Yellow Emperor's Canon of Internal Medicine, confirms this:

> The Yellow Emperor said, "From earliest times the communication with Heaven has been the very foundation of life; this foundation exists between Yin and Yang and between Heaven and Earth and within the six points.

Notice how the *Nei Ching,* which explains the nature of the *Tao,* concords with the *Torah.* Therefore, we can conclude that the *Nei Ching* may be the Torah of the race of Anu.

Again I quote from the Nei Ching:

> The Atmosphere of Yang is similar to Heaven and to the Sun. Those who lose this atmosphere shorten their lives and do not prolong it. The movements

of Heaven are illuminated by the sun. Yang rises up to protect man's body externally.

Again and again, the Torahs of the world insist that all life comes from the light of the sun.

The Nei Ching says that before mankind started falling into spiritual and moral decay, all his diseases were healed by "the Gods." From then on, he had to resort to medicines, manipulations, operations, and the like. "The Gods' are nothing more, nothing less, than the basic elements and energies coming from light.

As I said, our five post-diluvial progenitors healed themselves with concentrated light energy which they kept in a box. The Torah (The *Five Books of Moses,* states that this radiant energy, which we call The Ark of the Covenant, could kill or cure. When Moses was conferring with God atop the Turkic Mt. Taurus or Sinai, God gave him directions for making his own light energy box. This energy locked within this box was capable of giving life or of destroying it. It could even destroy cities and entire nations.

In Sanskrit, *Arka* means "belonging or relating to the sun; the sun; copper; fire."

The Hindu holy books also speak of this all-powerful light energy. According to the myths, the invading Krishtayas brought it into India.

The Aryan Bulgarian, King Kubera, leader of the Turkic Nagas, and his army of Yakshas or Yakhus (Yehudas) led his subjects to the Hindu Gangetic plains. This could have happened after the Great Flood. They brought along with them a long line of horses or oxen which pulled in their "holy temple." It was a wooden, fortress-like coach. Indian Orientalist, Malati J. Shendge describes it as follows:

It was "an eight-wheeled, nine-doored, impregnable fortress..." Inside this wheeled sanctuary was a golden casket called *Swarga* (Heavenly Light) or *Hiranyaya Kosa* (God's Treasure House), with three spokes and with three supports." Within the casket lay a strange piece of igneous rock. The ancestors of the Jewish people called it *Yaksa.* Although the casket was kept closed most of the time, a mysterious bright light always radiated from it. Over the millenniums, the word *Swarga* changed to the Hebrew *Zarkor* (Searchlight). The Hebrew word *Zohar,* a document explaining the Caballah, derives from *Swarga.*

The energy from the *Yaksa* (Guardian Angel) element could rejuvenate the mind of any person who was devoted to the Holy Trinity. It could even make plants grow in bone-dry deserts. It also radiated a powerful kinetic energy. However, if an evil person touched the "Guardian Angel" (*Yaksha*) stone, he was either burned to a crisp or tossed about like a bouncing rubber ball. Only the purest of priests could enclose themselves in the Ark, and even then for just a brief moment or two.

Author Murad Adj hinted in his book that for some reason, priests could never enter into the temples honoring *Hodai* (God) or *Tengri* for more than a few minutes.

> Prayers were said outside a temple, under the open sky of Tengri. Like it was back in the Altai when people congregated for prayer at the feet of sacred mountains. Judging by their remains, temples were not large. In the beginning, they were built as reminders of those sacred mountains back home, eventually evolving into architectural features.
>
> No one could enter a temple, except for the clergy, who were qualified, and only for a few brief moments. They wouldn't hang back more than that anyway, for they were not allowed to breathe inside the sanctuary.

There must be a deeper reason why the priests of God or Tengri could not even breathe in a temple. Did the ancient Turcic temples house Arks? Or were they just being superstitious? I would say that they were more rational than all the humans who came after them. They learned how to smelt all base and precious metals. They invented nearly all the world's alphabets. They traveled everywhere in their ships. They were accomplished astronomers. They were poets, scientists, and philosophers.

Would people such as those actually be afraid to even breathe in their temples because of some irrational superstition? They had good reasons to be nervous when they entered those temples devoted to sun worship.

We've been conditioned to "believe" that only Moses found a "Yaksa" stone. But tradition holds it that Kubera did, also. Moses found his "Yaksa" in the Taurus Mountains. Kubera found his in Bulgaria. It could be true that enough "Yaksa" was found for all the Tengri or Hodai (God) temples. The Turks say that Mt. Sinai was a Taurus mountain. I decided to study the names of mountains in Bulgaria, to see if I could find Kubera's Mount Sinai. I found a mountain there called *Sinanica.* I went to my Sanskrit Dictionary and discovered a *Senanikha,* meaning "Body belonging to Lord Brahma (or Heaven)." Could there be more Yaksa stones on top of Mt. Sinanica? Could there be any still available on that elusive peak in the Taurus mountain chain? It would be good to find out.

The Ethiopians say the original Ark is kept in a Coptic temple in the town of Axum. They keep it covered so that it won't endanger people's lives. When are we going to persuade the guardians of that Ark to let our scientists get a peep at it?

Why were Kubera's subjects called Yaksas? The powers in the light radiating from the Ark could turn people into supermen, capable of overcoming any obstacle and giving them everlasting life and health. Kubera was a king whom anyone would be fortunate to have! If a person advanced in the science of The Holy Trinity let the radiations coming from the Yaksa penetrate his being, then he was immediately converted into a mental giant and Spiritual Man.

Orientalist Shendge wrote:

> Yaksa "seems to be intimately related to something that is related to the body but is not the body. There are indications that it can leave one body and enter another. This transferable quality points to spirit or something like the spirit, a kind of essence of the whole personality, the moving force behind it, which was believed to migrate from one body to another. (p. 116.)...A short passage in *Brhhadarnyaakopanishad* (5.4) may serve as a comment on this: "Whoever knows this *mahad yaksa* with Brahma and the association with Brahma may point to the primal force." (p. 117.) Author Shendge further states, "Primarily Yaksa may have been a godhead, a supreme deity which was conceived to be the essence of the universe as well a of the individual..." (*The Civilized Demons-The Harappans in Rgveda;* p. 120,)

Over and over again, we get assurances from the world's holy books that the Kristos or Holy Trinity is a reality on which everyone can depend.

9

Did the Ancient Turks and Hindus Have Airships?

Early in the 16th century, a brilliant Turkish admiral, Piri Reis, obtained some of the charts that Columbus had used to cross the Atlantic to the Americas. After examining Columbus' maps, Piri Reis noted that they were precise. The admiral had an impressive collection of copies of ancient charts, some of them thousands of years old. Being a Turk, he could have had access to documents still held in secret in some Turkish nation. Each time that he dropped anchor in whatever port, he sent his sailors out to find people who owned ancient maps and were willing to sell them. Using the other ancient copies in his collection, the admiral made his own world map in 1513. In 1929, some historians rummaging around in the harem section of the Topkapi Palace, in Istanbul, Turkey, found this old chart buried under a pile of trash.

Upon examining the Piri Reis map, the historians were astonished to note that it presented a detailed and precise outline of the east coast of Southern Mexico, Central America, and South America, as well as the western coast of Africa. But this part didn't surprise them because Columbus' charts had been used to draw this map. What shocked them was a huge island off the coast of what is now Vera Cruz and an exact outline of the mountains, valleys, islands, rivers, and plains of the North Pole and Antarctica before those polar regions became buried under the thousands of feet of ice covering them today. Supposedly, no one knew that Antarctica ever existed until 1818. Scientists have always maintained that the Antarctic ice cap is millions of years old. They say that this ice cap has existed for tens of thousands of years. As for that large island, Plato said that one just like it had sunk under the sea in about 9,000 BC! The Piri Reis map shows Greenland as two islands. A French expedition made seismic soundings proving that ice covers the space between the two Greenland islands. Army engineers and the U.S. Navy Hydrographic bureau, as well as other scientific organizations, have proven beyond doubt that the Piri Reis map shows the landforms under the Northern and Southern ice caps exactly as they existed before becoming covered by snow and ice. I invite my readers to examine this anomaly themselves on the many websites discussing the map and those ancient polar landforms.

What is even more unbelievable and shocking is that all the scientists and experts who have examined this map are in total agreement that these polar land forms could have been charted only from extremely high altitudes above the earth! Some ancient nation, as early as 12,000 years ago, had airships. A number of people would like for us to think that the pilots of those airships were really little green men from Mars. I'm far from ready to accept such declarations without confirming evidence. However, documents like the Piri Reis map point directly toward the only ancient nations that had mechanized land and air vehicles: Turkey and India.

Recent underwater archeological explorations prove that large portions of India were civilized thousands of years before Egypt and Sumeria became a gleam in the eyes of their Turkish and Hindu forefathers. Also, Hindu myths talk frequently of their ancient land and air vehicles, atomic weapons, and the like. Most of us know about the Biblical story of Ezekiel being saved by an ancient airship. That incident took place in a Turkish nation: Afghanistan.

Piri Reis himself stated that he had copied much of the information on his map from maps dating back to Alexander the Great:

> I have used twenty maps and mappae mundi dating from the time of Alexander the Great showing the islands inhabited by men. The Arab people refer to these maps as caferiye. As well as eight caferiye of that kind, I have made use of one Arabic map of India and four modern Portuguese maps, some of which delineate the lands of Sind, India and China according to geometrical methods, and one map drawn by Columbus in the western lands. By reducing all these maps to one scale this form was arrived at. So that the present map is as correct and reliable for the seven seas as the map of our countries is considered correct and reliable by seamen.

Piri Reis' map is not the only map showing the polar landforms and other landforms of the world as it appeared more than ten thousand years before the birth of Christ. Three other maps, made at approximately the same time that Admiral Reis made his, those of Oroneus Fineaus, Mercator, and Phillipe Buache, show pre-glacial Antartica before it was supposedly "discovered" in 1818. These maps were also included information from copies of ancient charts made thousands of years ago. Estimates are made that the original charts were made as far back as 12,000 to 14,000 BC.

Wanting to get some hard scientific evidence that the Piri Reis map shows the pre-glacial Antarctica correctly, Professor Charles H. Hapgood, of Keene College, NH, sent pictures and details of the map to the Reconnaissance Technical squadron (SAC) of the United States Air Force Westover Air Force base, in Massachusetts. He asked the officials there to give him their opinion of the Reis map. The following was their reply:

> 6, July, 1960
> Subject: Admiral Piri Reis Map
> TO: Prof. Charles H. Hapgood
> Keene College
> Keene, New Hampshire
> Dear Professor Hapgood,
> Your request of evaluation of certain unusual features of the Piri Reis map of 1513 by this organization has been reviewed. The claim that the lower part of the map portrays the Princess Martha Coast of Queen Maud Land, Antarctic, and the Palmer Peninsular, is reasonable. We find that this is the most logical and in all probability the correct interpretation of the map. The geographical detail shown in the lower part of the map agrees very remarkably with the results of the seismic profile made across the top of the ice-cap by the Swedish-British Antarctic Expedition of 1949.
> This indicates the coastline had been mapped before it was covered by the ice-cap.
> The ice-cap in this region is now about a mile thick. We have no idea how the data on this map can be reconciled with the supposed state of geographical knowledge in 1513.
> Harold Z. Ohlmeyer
> Lt.Colonel,USAF,Commander

Note: The worldwide web has changed the way we corroborate the statements of writers and researchers. Before the advent of PCs, authors had to provide their readers with abundant references for them to search for in libraries. This is no longer necessary. To corroborate what I have written thus far, you'll find innumerable references to the Piri Reis map on many websites. You should also read all you can find under the headings of Cattigara and Trikuta. I will discuss this further in Chapter 14, with some astonishing maps.

If, as I say, The Aryan Krishtayas and Ramanakas had flying ships and other technological marvels, why can't archeologists find any of them? Why can't some proofs be brought to light? I am confident that this will happen someday. Surely, when archeologists start penetrating the ancient ruins at the bottom of the sea near the coast of Gujarat, India, they will confirm many statements made in Hindu myths, which right now seem bizarre and unbelievable to most of us.

A famous Hindu historian, P. N. Oak, author of *World Vedic Heritage,* claims that millions of thousands-of-years-old documents, an estimated 90 million, are rotting away in a depository in Poona, India, waiting for the Turks and Indians to quit bragging about having an illustrious past—and prove it. I know they can do it. A Turkish gentleman, who has read my books and articles, tells me that the archives of the Chaldean Christian community in Turkey contain thousands of ancient documents, many of which were saved from the fire that burned down the library of Alexandria.

Perhaps what I have just stated will clear up the mysteries of Mexico's Teotihuacan, The Peruvian ruins of Tihuanaco, and those of Karal, Peru, for all three of these ruins have Turkish names. Teotihuacan derives from *Teo* (God) plus *Tiwa* (one of the names of the Turkish republic of Tannu, Tewa, or Tiwa) plus *Khan* (Turkish name for king; kingdom.) The Tannu or Tiwa/Tewa people were so highly advanced that in India, the word came to be *Deva* (Demi-God). Tihuanaco is estimated to be around 20,000 years old. Its name may derive from *Tiwa* plus *Naga.* The old pyramids and ruins at Karal are older than the pyramids of Egypt. Karal derives from the Turkish word *Kral,* meaning "Royal Domain."

Taking into consideration all that I have said so far about the ancient Turks, I know that my Christian, Jewish, Turkic, Buddhist, Shinto, Confucian, Taoist and Hindu readers may be wanting to ask me:

> If what you say about the Turks is true, what happened to make them sink into ignominy? Why are the Turkish republics the most mysterious and unknown countries in today's modern world? Why do they no longer demonstrate the traits that their Kedar Khand, Nephylim, Aryan, or Krishtaya ancestors once had in such abundance, that they were even able to live up to one thousand years, bilocate to any part of the universe at the speed of light, and heal themselves with certain elements contained in sunlight?

I must apologize for not being able to answer such important questions. As a Christian. I have never abandoned entirely the science of the Cross and the Holy Trinity that the Turks gave to your forefathers and mine. Perhaps you should ask those who, at sword point, ripped the Aryan God Tengri and his son Keder/Keser out of the hearts, minds, and souls of the Turks. *They do have the answer!*

10

The Post Noachide Migrations

Although the Great Flood destroyed millions of people, it didn't drown all the bad guys. If Ham, a son of Noah, sodomized his own father, one can just imagine how much evil existed in the world at that time. In desperation, the five Krishtaya tribes decided to send Tengri missionaries to teach mankind this God's message of the Cross and the Holy Trinity, mankind might reform.

Murad Adj says that they first concentrated on China:

> ...China sent back Turkic preachers from its borders. With a vengeance, literally. It was shortly overrun by Turkic horsemen who put China to its knees by force, the defensive Great Wall regardless. Eventually, however, people in the country that styled itself the Celestial Empire learned about Tengri. The Chinese probably had their own ideas about the cult of the Heaven and tried to uphold them.
>
> ...It was all different in India, however. Interest in Tengri caught on immediately, and an Indian page opened in Turkic history two thousand and a half years ago, or even slightly earlier.
>
> The Altai and India now shared a common spirituality. They certainly had solid backgrounds for that communion, faith in the first place. (In truth, the Hindus interpreted their Buddha in a way different from what Turkis made out their Tengri, and still they felt free to search for an eternal truth and have spiritual dialogues with one another.) Indian legends of nagas are a reminder of that distant past.
>
> In Hindu mythology, nagas were semidivine beings, half human and half serpentine, who had the Serpent as their forbear. They lived in a country far north of India, in a land where incalculable treasures and an iron cross lay buried in the ground. That distant land was known to Hindus as Shambhu (Benevolent), or Shambhkala (Shining Fortress in Turkic).
>
> According to legend, nagas had human faces and long snake bodies. They could assume either human or wholly serpentine form. They were very gentle and musical creatures who loved poetry, and their women were of striking beauty.
>
> An ancient Hindu holy book, Mahabharata, tells of the origins of religion and the evolution of spiritual culture. The book is really a chronicle of Ancient

India, with some of its pages devoted to the nagas and their mysterious northern land. No, this is not a fairytale. It is an account of real events which is told, in a long-standing Indian tradition, in legend form. (Indian scholars approach their legends in all earnest, calling them absolutely reliable sources.)

The Hindus, for example, made no secret of the fact that they had borrowed their sacred texts, Prajnyaparamita, from the nagas, or Turkis. This body of wisdom could only be read by the wisest of proselytizers, who alone were capable of absorbing the message of text.

In this way, the Hindus did a great honour to Turkic culture-they have preserved for the Turkic race a sacred treasure that the Turkis have managed to forget.

The land of Shambhkala lay at the foot of Mount Sambyl-Taskhyl, in the catchment area of the Khan Tengri River. There, a wall of icy mist concealed cities, monasteries and blossoming forests. Legends abounded about that enigmatic land. It was rumoured that monastics in possession of consummate knowledge lived in that land.

Many people failed in their attempts to reach that land. No one came anywhere near it. It was commonly held that it was hidden in an inaccessible valley somewhere in Tibet, where earthly life touches the ultimate heavenly reason.

This view was voiced by some major Orientalists in the 19th century, and was strongly endorsed by, among other leading public figures, Nikolai Przhevalsky, the famous Russian traveller and ethnographer, Nikolai Roerich, a philosopher, and Elena Blavatskaya, an educationist. For all their high stature, we cannot share their view. It's human to err, especially if you look for something in a wrong place.

Theirs was certainly this case. Actually, scientists knew almost nothing about the Altai and its ancient culture, while many of them were not even aware of much there was to know in the 19th century. By suppressing and distorting the Turkic nation's history, the Russian authorities drove Russian historical science into a corner, where recognized celebrities, let alone commoners, could be misguided.

No one was aware at the time that belief in the God of Heaven had been brought to Tibet and India from the Altai, of all places, and struck deep root there. Modern Tibetan Buddhism (or less formal, Lamaism), the core religion of Tibet, Mongolia and Buriatia, a republic in Russia, originated among the Turkis.

The name of Tengri was certainly known in India. How else could you explain the Buddha's blue Turkic-slit eyes? Was it a reflection of a long-forgotten epic? Such as one that unfolded two and half thousand years ago when strange horsemen rode into India from the North? They settled in India, to become a new nation, the Shak. In fact, they were Sacae of the Turkic race.

And more, Hindus called Buddha (his teaching was disseminated at exactly that time) Shakyamuni or the Turkic god. It is highly probable, we assume, that Buddha's teaching could be spread by the Turkis. This is abundant evidence, you will agree. Besides, Buddha, Indian tradition goes, could turn into a naga. Finally, at least fifty million of India's inhabitants profess faith in the God of Heaven. They are neither Buddhists nor Moslems. They are called Christians in India, but they are not like any other Christians around the world-they have distinct religious rites and symbols. They will accept no other sign but the Tengri cross, which they wear on their chests and say their distinct prayers in front of it. This is probably the only place in the world where the Turkis' creed survives in its undistilled form. Indeed, nothing goes without leaving a trace.

Traces of past events may at times surface suddenly in the least expected place.

Here is a good example. According to Indian legends, none other than Turkis taught Hindus how to plough their fields with iron ploughshares and reap their harvests with iron sickles. Hindus always praised the nagas for their fertile lands and copious crops. The old ploughs unearthed in the Altai and Indian and Pakistani legends appear to bring together the fragmented knowledge about ancient Turkis and fit in place many missing pieces of the jigsaw puzzle left by history.

While we are on the subject of borrowings, the famous Indian cavalry, too, traces its beginnings from the coming of the Altaians. It will not be out of place here to emphasise again that Turkic influence on Indian culture was enormous at that time. Convincing evidencr of this has been unearthed by archaeologists. More proof is, of course, available elsewhere.

Altaic tribes came to India to stay forever there rather than just hit and run. About one in ten Indians or Pakistanis today has a family tree rooted in Turkic soil. A significant proportion, you will agree.

India was ruled for a long time by the famous Sun Dynasty, one of its two major ruling families founded by King Ikshwaku, a nephew of the Sun, who migrated from the Altai, where he lived in the Aksu River Valley, to India in the 5th century BC. Once installed in power, Ikshwaku started building a city, Ayodhya, to be the capital city of the Koshala (or Koshkala?) Kingdom. The city, which still stands today, has a museum dedicated to the Sun Dynasty, with enough evidence about the Turkis who had arrived from the Altai.

Ayodhya alternated between prominence and decline, and at one time it was regarded as the capital city of Northern India, an indication of the great influence Koshala had on that region. Eventually, the city fell into decay and neglect, only to experience an upsurge again. With the arrival of Turkis, life was no longer calm or smooth in India.

Ayodhya stood on the banks of the Sarayu (modern Ghaghara) River. It looks like another Turkic place name, with an undisguised connotation of palace. Why not? The city was the capital city of a powerful kingdom, with splendid palaces, temples and beautiful residential houses. The river takes its name from the royal palace.

In fact, the map of India shows a lot of Turkic place names. Take Hindustan, the vast region in Northern India. The name sends a Turkic message, with its typically Turkic stan ending (Tatarstan, Kazakhstan, Bashkortostan or Daghestan), which means "country" in Turkic.

Nothing stands alone in life. Nothing comes from nowhere and goes without a trace. During the rule of Sun Dynasty kings, numberless families resettled from the Altai to India. Migration continued for many centuries. You could see Altaic families among the Indian nobility, their members going on to become great generals, poets, scholars or clerics. But all of them spoke Turkic. The destinies are now part of Indian legends and in genealogies of some Indian aristocrats. To give an example, the celebrated dynasties of maharajas of Udaipur, Jodhpur and Jaipur rose from their Turkic roots in the Ancient Altai.

Little surprise, though, for India and the Altai were, in all but in fact, a huge single country, both parts of which were linked by roads that can still be used today-the Biisk and Nerchinsk routes.

The earliest road the Turkis built to reach India was the legendary Suspension Pass, a mysterious road no one knows of today. No parts of it have survived, save for folklore and suspension bridges, its replicas continue to be built in the Pamir Mountains and Tibet to this day.

Turkic cavalry used suspension bridges to cross mountain streams and deep gorges on its way to India. It took a very brave man to ride a horse over soaring cloud-high cliffs.

Pilgrims, too, followed this road to see their relations or pray at sacred Mount Kailasa, or visit the city of Kashmir.

It was a cherished dream come true for a Turki to see Mount Kailasa, as also India itself. It was broadly held that a man who happened to see Mount Kailasa would be happy for the rest of his life. According to legend, it was a place where Tengri Khan himself rested from his chores, from time to time. A sacred place indeed.

The Illustrious Khan Erke

The world first learned about the mighty Kushan Khanate in the 1st century AD, when the famous King Kanishka elevated the Turkic race to glory. Happily, we know his real name-Khan Erke (or Kanerka, which was stamped on his coins).

More than anyone else before or after him, Khan Erke, a born philosopher and poet, a sagacious ruler and brilliant warlord, contributed to the high glory of Turkic culture. He made it unchallenged in the East. To their friends and foes alike, Turkis appeared to be endowed with unnatural talents and powers.

Erke ascended to the Kushan throne in 78 AD and ruled for twenty-three years. Word, not sword, nor spear, nor iron shirt of mail, was his main weapon, and above all the word of God. To Him alone Erke and the Turkic world owe a debt of gratitude for their spectacular victories.

Khan Erke's principal gift to the East was faith in Tengri.

His mission was made the easier thanks to his thorough knowledge of the rites, prayers and the teaching itself. He could speak for hours, using fine words and polished style that kept his listeners alert and thirsting for more. The khan's nice speech and wise policies showed the indigenous population that the Turkic settlers valued kindness and generosity more than they did gold, perfidy or power over non-Turkic people. Their ruler was the true spokesman for his people. And the locals accepted him on faith, and his people as well.

Khan Erke was convinced that every human being could, by controlling his own behaviour, build paradise or hell for himself and his near and dear. No one, he said, could blame anyone but himself for his misery and woes. God gives everyone his deserves—no less no more.

This is really the only just Judgment-you alone are accountable to God for your good and evil actions-under the Eternal Blue Sky. Only this matters, and nothing else. The message of the new religion was simple enough-do good wherever you can for the world to be kind to you.

This truth being as simple as that, people embraced it without hesitation. Their new faith was simple and wise, unlike any other on Earth. The most attractive side of the new creed was that you have your future in your own hands. Remember this and don't miss your chance.

Turkis, for example, believed in the eternity of human soul and in their reincarnation after death. Everyone knew that even a hardened sinner could atone for all of his sins. He was given a chance and hope to cleanse himself any time in his life on Earth. Faith in Tengri reinforced people's spirit and encouraged them to excel.

"Seek salvation in your deeds," Khan Erke exhorted his subjects.

Strangers were bewildered by the rite Turkis performed in the name of Tengri. It was a grand occasion, and very festive, too. They never said the name of the God of Heaven in haste. The rite was ceremonious and leisurely. No one in the pagan world had ever witnessed so much grandeur and splendour or imagined it could be that way.

Pagans took the Turkis for what we now call extraterrestrials-people from a world completely unfamiliar to them. The Turkis had everything neat and tidy, so little wonder their Altai was paradise come true for other Oriental races and its inhabitants got the name of Aryans. Not unlike Shambhkala in India, this birthplace of the Turkic race themselves were the stuff of endless legends.

During the reign of Khan Erke, cities awoke to the melodious peels of bells summoning the congregation to morning prayer. We can only guess what it felt like in those thrilling moments.

Actually, very little is known about them. What kind of bells were they? How did the bell towers look? No one can give the answers after so many centuries. We certainly know, though, that bells really existed (some evidence of them has been unearthed). The Turkic word for bell (kolokol) probably comes from that remote age-in ancient Turkic, it meant "facing the Heaven", or more specifically, "praying to the Heaven". And pray people did.

Prayers were said outside a temple, under the open sky of Tengri. Like it was back in the Altai when people congregated for prayer at the feet of sacred mountains. Judging by their remains, temples were not large. In the beginning, they were built as reminders of those sacred mountains back home, eventually evolving into architectural features.

No one could enter a temple, except for the clergy, who were qualified, and only for a few brief moments. They wouldn't hang back more than that anyway, for they were not allowed to breathe inside the sanctuary.

Things were different with other peoples. Their congregations swarmed their temples. Later on, however, the Turkis adopted this practice, too. (To our regret again, very little is known as yet about the destinies of various cultural traditions or why some were superseded by others.)

It was general custom to burn incense before prayer. Incense burners (censers) were used for this purpose. According to an ancient Altaic legend, evil forces could not abide by the smell of incense (the incense-burning ritual was called qadyt in ancient Turkic, from the root verb "repel" or "scare off").

The Turkis prayed to subdued singing. The choir fervently intoned a sacred melody, Yirmaz (literally, "our songs"), in praise of the God of Heaven.

Whatever side of Turkic culture you take, you always see the equal-armed cross of Tengri, called vajra in the East.

Khan Erke did not spare himself to propagate his faith. His reign is deeply impressed on the memory of Oriental nations. It was a great reign indeed. Happily, we know fairly much, from the archaeologists' digs, about Tengri crosses and ruined Turkic cities and temples that existed in the Kushan period.

We can only guess about the confusion that overwhelmed people who refused to accept Tengri. They were lost in doubt and depressed, tormented by their own powerlessness.

After all, iron tools and weapons, an excellent army and general affluence in the country were strong indications of the high mission of Turkic culture, in a way completely different from divine services. For these reasons the Altai and, by implication, the Kushan Khanate were, therefore, regarded as the key spiritual centres in the East, a promised land sought out by people in other lands. (Incidentally, some later geographical maps label the Altai as Paradise-really.) People came here from afar to find out more about Turkic culture. A school of arts was opened in Gandhara for foreigners, along with several theological centres across the Kushan Khanate.

At one time, a Jew by the name of Joshua (Jesus Christ) studied in the Altai, following the example of Moses (Moshe or Mousa). An indirect reference to this is contained in the Koran. On his return to Palestine, then a province of the Roman Empire, Joshua brought news of horsemen in the service of the God of Heaven. His words are recorded in the Apocalypse, the Christians' earliest religious book. For this he was called Jesus Christ (Isa), or "God Blessed", that is, a "Divine Witness".

Priests from India and Tibet were frequent guests at the Kushan khan's court. Appropriately enough, for Khan Erke transformed Kashmir into a holy city and a centre of pilgrimage.

Altaic pilgrims, too, had a temple in Kashmir to worship their own god, and Turkic was heard there day and night, all year round. Could it probably be the Golden Temple that is still a major attraction in Kashmir?

Khan Erke devoted much of his time and effort to the promotion of his creed and culture, benefiting enormously the Turkic world as a whole. Buddhists held their Fourth Assembly in Kashmir, which drew many theologians from around the East. They gave recognition to Tengri and His teaching that expanded the content of Buddhism (which evolved into the well-known version of Buddhism, Mahayana).

The text of Mahayana was engraved on copper plates that immediately became (and still are) a sacred dogma of Buddhism in China, Tibet and Mongolia, among other places. These plates, or more correctly the Fourth Assembly, signaled the birth of a new school of Buddhism, which was later named "Tibet Buddhism" or "Lamaism".

The East's greatest enlightener, the sagacious Khan Erke knew how to make friends and allies. He has been consecrated as a saint by the Buddhists, and his name is cited in a prayer. The Turkis are, however, fully oblivious of their illustrious khan.

Fortunately, some other peoples have fond memories of him.

About God Kubera, India's Regent of the North, King of the Yakshas or Yakhus, God of Wealth, Miners, Farmers, and Good Fortune.

Most Hindu scholars are willing to admit that the Krishtayas a.k.a. Aryans were the fathers of Indian civilization. In his book, *Ancient Geography of Ayodhya,* Dr. Shyam Narain Pande states:

Ancient Ayodhya, near Meru mountain, identified with the Pamir plateau is the ancient common home not only of Indians but of mankind…Indians and Iranians claim their common home towards the Asian Steppes, the 'Ariyana-Vaego' of the ancient Iranians, the country between Oxus and Xaxartes, north of Pamir plateau. The Western origin of the Chinese civilization proves that people from the steppes and lake regions of Asia, from time immemorial, have settled down in the Yellow River basin. The date is believed to be C. 2145 B.C. on the authority of Shu-chiang and Confucius. Those who followed agriculture in China must have been Rama.

According to Dr. Dandekar, the earliest common habitat of the speakers of proto Indo-Europeans [languages] is the steppes between the Urals and Altai. In view of the fact that the proto Hellenes can be shown to have entered in Greece in C. 200 B.C., that the Hittites migrated in C. 2800 BC. towards the

Caucasus mountains and the Caspian sea and the proto Aryans must be assumed to have separated from the main stock in C. 2500 B.C., the proto Indo-European unity must be, with reasonable certainty, dated from 3500 B.C. (pp. 45-46.)

Several hundred years after the Great Flood, the Turkic country now called Bulgaria appears to have been the leader of all Central Asia. They were a horde called Kubera. Their leaders were Khagans (kings) of the Bulgarians and often called *Kubrat,* derived from the Sanskrit *Kuber-Ratha,* meaning, "Hero of the Kuberas." Kubera appears to have been a large group; not a single individual.

Kubera's followers were called Yakshas or Yakhus. These had to be today's partially mongoloid Siberian group called Yakhuts. They are associated also with similar peoples in the area called Buryats and Saka. When I was going through a list of Nomads of the Steppes, I was surprised to find many other tribes whose names are also common today in India Proper. In India, we have the Yadu (also known as Yayati, Yakhuda, Japeth, etc.), whose name derived from Yakhut, the Bharats (India's true name) and the Sakas or Scythians.

Indian thinker and historian Kuttikhat Purushothama Chon wrote in *Remedy the Frauds in Hinduism:*

> In December, 1988, the Soviet scientists have found to their surprise that the Yakutian nationality living in remote Siberia have in their blood the HLA-b70 antigen, which is possessed only by the Hindus of North India…Archeological evidences in Indus valley, and skull and bone measurements of some people of South India indicate the Siberian origin. Philologists have found a common origin for Sanskrit, Persian, and European languages. Literary Russian language has 30 to 40 percent of words with Sanskrit origin…The original Siberian home of our Vedic ancestors has been conclusively shown in our Vedas in many places. Rig Veda mentions existence of large Aryan kingdoms in Roosam (Russia) and Hariyupia (Eastern Europe). (p. 116.)

It is no coincidence that Yakuts, Buryats, and Saka of Siberia have similar names to the Yadu or Yakhuda, Bharats and Saka of Northern India.

Kubera, also known as Khyber, Kheever, etc., being a Naga, was leader of the Aryan Phoenician and Juddhi maritime caste (Hebrews), with several thousand ships. The legends state that he even had airships. The Great Flood changed the geography of Central Asia so drastically, that today we can not find much, if any, indication that any kind of maritime civilization ever existed in Siberia.

The Torah or Old Testament lists Kubera or Khyber's name as Eber or Heber:

> Sons were also born to Shem, ancestor of all the descendants of Eber…Two sons were born to Eber: the name of the first was Peleg, for in his days was the earth divided; and the name of his brother was Joktan…*(Genesis 10:25.)*

In other words, the dispersal of humanity from Mt. Meru occurred with the progeny of Kubera or Khyber. Flavius Josephus confirms this:

> Heber begot Joctan and Phaleg. He was called Phaleg, because he was born at the dispersion of the nations to their several countries…*(Antiquities of the Jews:1.6.4)*

The Hindu epic *Ramayana* confirms what the Torah and Joseph stated, but going into much more mythical detail.

During Kubera's time the Huns (Mongoloids) of the plains and mountains were not as highly civilized as they are now. Their own lands were almost uninhabitable. Therefore, they decided to invade and conquer the Scythian or Aryan nations. Jordanes, in his story about the origins of his Kipchak or Turkish ancestors, the Goths, Ostrogoths (Eastern Goths), Visigoths (Western Goths), etc., describes them in unpleasant and unflattering terms:

> …after a short space of time, as Orosius relates, the race of the Huns, fiercer than ferocity itself, flamed forth against the Goths. We learn from old traditions that their origin was as follows: Filimer, king of the Goths, son of Gadaric the Great, who was the fifth in succession to hold the rule of the Getae after their departure from the island of Scandza,—and who, as we have said, entered the land of Scythia with his tribe,—found among his people certain witches, whom he called in his native tongue Haliurunnae. Suspecting these women, he expelled them from the midst of his race and compelled them to wander in solitary exile afar from his army. There the unclean spirits, who beheld them as they wandered through the wilderness, bestowed their embraces upon them and begat this savage race, which dwelt at first in the swamps,—a stunted, foul and puny tribe, scarcely human, and having no language save one which bore but slight resemblance to human speech. Such was the descent of the Huns who came to the country of the Goths.
>
> This cruel tribe, as Priscus the historian relates, settled on the farther bank of the Maeotic swamp. They were fond of hunting and had no skill in any other art. After they had grown to a nation, they disturbed the peace of neighboring races by theft and rapine. At one time, while hunters of their tribe were as usual seeking for game on the farthest edge of Maeotis, they saw a doe unexpectedly appear to their sight and enter the swamp, acting as guide of the way; now advancing and again standing still. The hunters followed and crossed on

foot the Maeotic swamp, which they had supposed was impassable as the sea. Presently the unknown land of Scythia disclosed itself and the doe disappeared. Now in my opinion the evil spirits, from whom the Huns are descended, did this from envy of the Scythians. And the Huns, who had been wholly ignorant that there was another world beyond Maeotis, were now filled with admiration for the Scythian land. As they were quick of mind, they believed that this path, utterly unknown to any age of the past, had been divinely revealed to them. They returned to their tribe, told them what had happened, praised Scythia and persuaded the people to hasten thither along the way they had found by the guidance of the doe. As many as they captured, when they thus entered Scythia for the first time, they sacrificed to Victory. The remainder they conquered and made subject to themselves. Like a whirlwind of nations they swept across the great swamp and at once fell upon the Alpidzuri, Alcildzuri, Itimari, Tuncarsi and Boisci, who bordered on that part of Scythia. The Alani also, who were their equals in battle, but unlike them in civilization, manners and appearance, they exhausted by their incessant attacks and subdued. For by the terror of their features they inspired great fear in those whom perhaps they did not really surpass in war. They made their foes flee in horror because their swarthy aspect was fearful, and they had, if I may call it so, a sort of shapeless lump, not a head, with pin-holes rather than eyes. Their hardihood is evident in their wild appearance, and they are beings who are cruel to their children on the very day they are born. For they cut the cheeks of the males with a sword, so that before they receive the nourishment of milk they must learn to endure wounds. Hence they grow old beardless and their young men are without comeliness, because a face furrowed by the sword spoils by its scars the natural beauty of a beard. They are short in stature, quick in bodily movement, alert horsemen, broad shouldered, ready in the use of bow and arrow, and have firm-set necks which are ever erect in pride. Though they live in the form of men, they have the cruelty of wild beasts.

When the Getae beheld this active race that had invaded many nations, they took fright and consulted with their king how they might escape from such a foe. Now although Hermanaric, king of the Goths, was the conqueror of many tribes, as we have said above, yet while he was deliberating on this invasion of the Huns, the treacherous tribe of the Rosomoni, who at that time were among those who owed him their homage, took this chance to catch him unawares. For when the king had given orders that a certain woman of the tribe I have mentioned, Sunilda by name, should be bound to wild horses and torn apart by driving them at full speed in opposite directions (for he was roused to fury by her husband's treachery to him), her brothers Sarus and Ammius came to avenge their sister's death and plunged a sword into Hermanaric's side. Enfeebled by this blow, he dragged out a miserable existence in bodily weakness. Balamber, king of the Huns, took advantage of his ill health to move an army into the country of the Ostrogoths, from whom the Visigoths had already separated because of some dispute. Meanwhile Hermanaric, who was unable to endure either the pain of his wound or the inroads of the

Huns, died full of days at the great age of one hundred and ten years. The fact of his death enabled the Huns to prevail over those Goths who, as we have said, dwelt in the East and were called Ostrogoths.... (*The Origins and Deeds of the Goths,* by Jordanes. Translated by Charles C. Mierow.)

Disastrous changes of climate and the savagery of the Rakshasas and Pisacas (the Sanskrit names of the early Huns) became so unbearable that Kubera and his Yaksha subjects, in order to avoid total annihilation as a people, decided to flee to India. But the Huns followed them, nipping at their heels every step of the way. It was there that Kubera decided to capture most of the Rakshasas (Steppe Huns) and Pisacas (Mountain Huns) and deport them to what is now Sri Lanka. *[Author's note: Since the history of the Aryan Turks and that of the Hindus merged, I cannot guarantee that this dispersion to Lanka started in India itself. It could have begun back in Bulgaria. I am just doing the best I can with the information I have gleaned from Hindu mythology and history. Even Murad Adji acknowledges that the Hindus have preserved what little the Turks know of their own ancient history.]*

In those days, Lanka was much larger than it is now-perhaps twice the size of all of India. The land was tropical, fertile, and lush. He thought that if he took them there, they would settle down to more civilized and benign behaviors.

The progeny of Adam populated the world by way of *Serendipity* or Ceylon. *Serendipity* was also known as Lanka. Even the Moslem Koran states this. Tens of thousands of low-lying islands literally circled the southern part of the globe, making ocean travel easy in those days. Little by little, these islands began to wear away, leaving mainly the Maldives, the Seychelles, and the Malayan Archipelago. Scientists say that within the next fifty years, the sandbar nation of Maldives will ultimately succumb to the sea.

In his book, *Outlines of Ceylon History,* author Donald Obeyesekere states:

Both the *Skanda Purana* and the *Ramayana* represent Ceylon as a huge Continent, a tradition not unsupported by science. The geology and fauna of the Island point clearly to a time when Ceylon was part of an Oriental Continent, which stretched from an unbroken land from Madagascar to the Malay Archipelago and northward to the present valley of the Ganges. The valley was then occupied by a spreading westward across Persia, Arabia and the Sahara Desert and forming the southern limit of the Palaearctic Continent which embraced Europe, North Africa, and North Asia. In the course of ages the greater part of the Oriental Continent was submerged in the sea, leaving Ceylon as a fragment in the centre, with, on one side, the Maldives, Laccadives, Seychelles, Mauritius, and Madagascar, themselves separated from one another by hundreds of miles of sea, and, on the other, the Malay Islands;

while the Ganges valley was upheaved, making North and South India one land, and, later Ceylon itself was separated from South India by a narrow sea. The greater part of Ceylon is said in the *Ramayana* to have been submerged in the sea in punishment of Ravana's misdeeds, and the Greater Basses light-house, which stands on a solitary rock in the south-east sea of Ceylon, is still called Rawana's fort. The meridian of Lanka of the Indian astronomers which was reputed to pass through Rawana's capital passes through the Maldive Islands at 75° 53' 15 East Greenwich, quite four hundred miles from the present limit of Ceylon. On this coast the Sinhalese chronicles record extensive submersion by the sea in the reigns of Panduwasa (*circa* 500 B.C.) and Kelani Tissa (200 B.C.). At this latter period Kelaniya is said to have been a distance of "seven gows" (28 miles) from the sea. "The guardian deities of Lanka having become indignant with Tissa, king of Kelaniya (for the unjust execution of a Bhuddist Elder), the sea began to encroach. 100,000 towns (Patunugam), 970 fishers' villages and 470 villages of pearl fisheries, making altogether eleven-twelfths of Lanka, were submerged by the great sea. Mannar escaped destruction of sea-port towns Katupati Madampe." (P. 1.)

The exiled Rakshasas and Pisacas did not take advantage of their tropical, Eden-like home in Lanka. The Ramayana gives the details about Kubera and his decision to transport these Tartars to Patala or America. In Sanskrit, *Pa-Tala* means "Protector of the Upper World" or Eastern Hemisphere." *Atala* was the Western Hemisphere or "Under World." Patala was similar to the Greek Atlas who supported the world on his shoulders. The following is what the Ramayana says about Kubera's difficulties with the Tartars:

> Kubera performed penance for ten thousand years in water with his head submerged, to please Brahma. Then he performed penance standing on one foot in the center of Pancagni. Brahma appeared and asked him to choose any boon. Kubera requested that he might be made a lokapalaka (protector of the universe, known biblically as Peleg or Phaleg)) and the custodian of wealth, and Brahma responded by supplying Kubera the treasures Sankanidhi and Padmannidhi and also the Puspaka Vimana as his vehicle. He was also appointed one of the Astadikpalakas (Indra, Agni, Yama, Niirti, Varuna, Vayu, Kubera and Isa are the eight protectors of the eight regions). Kubera's city is called Mahodaya.
>
> Kubera really felt happy and told his father Visravas about his new status and dignity. The father also blessed the son. Kubera requested his father to get a city built for him to live in, and his father told him to settle down in Lanka built by Maya on top of the mountain Trikuta in the middle of the South Sea. From that day onwards, Kubera took his abode in Lanka. (It was originally built for Indra.) (*The Puranic Encyclopedia*, by Vettam Mani; pp 434-435).

Trikuta ia the Sanskrit name of the now submerged large island near Mexico's state of Veracruz, shown on the Piri Reis map. Today, we call the remaining vestiges of that island nation, The West Indies. Was Trikuta ancient Atlantis? (Ref: My book, *The Last Atlantis Book-You'll Ever Have to Read.*) In my special map in Chapter 14, I'm going to provide you with an astonishing proof, which nobody can refute effectively, that the Ramayana and the Piri Reis map are telling us truths that may force us to rewrite our history books!

The expression, "Kubera performed penance for ten thousand years with his head under water," just means that the Kuberas were well acquainted with the world, having visited various part of the world in their ocean-going vessels and air-borne ships for around ten thousand years. As the world's maritime nation caste, they were convinced that they owned by divine right all the waterways and coasts of the entire world, as well as the exclusive monopoly to exploit its natural resources.

Finally, the Khyberis began to see that the incorrigible Rakshasas were increasing in such numbers that most of them would have to be transported elsewhere. If not, Hindu civilization in Ceylon would be doomed just as it had nearly wiped out that of the Aryan Krishtayas. Since America was, for all practical reasons, almost totally uninhabited, the Phoenicians and Jews decided to take as many Rakshasas as possible to what are now Southern Mexico and Central America where, hopefully, they could be trained and raised in the arts of civilization and culture—as well as to mine gold, copper, and silver for them. The story of Kubera is the same as our Biblical story of the dispersal from The Tower of Babylon, presided over by Heber and his son Phaleg/Peleg.

> When the harassments of the Raksasas became unbearable, the Devas sought protection from Siva, and Indra detailed to him about the unrighteous actions of Malyavan, Somali, and Mali. Siva directed the Devas to Visnu, who set out to fight against the Raksasas, Mali cut at Garuda, and Visnu killed him (Mali) with this Sudarsana Cakra. The other Raksasas retreated to Lanka. As their presence in Lanka was dangerous to the Devas, Visnu directed the Sudarsana Cakra to go to Lanka every day and kill the Raksasas in groups. The Cakra began its work, and the remaining Raksas escaped to Patala. Lanka became thus deserted and Kubera took his abode there. The Yaksas, born from the hunger of Brahma, roamed about without a leader and ultimately settled down in Lanka under the leadership of Kubera. (Uttara Ramayana). (*The Puranic Encyclopedia;* p. 435.)

The *Cakra* (pronounced as "Chakra") was a type of mechanized scythe that could mow down dozens of men at a time, just as if they were blades of tall grass.

The Hindu books speak of a number of persons and groups being deported to Patala, especially "Nagas." These "Nagas" were actually Phoenician groups who had snake emblems for totems. "...Patala is the abode of serpents." (*The Puranic Encyclopedia;* p. 581.)

> ...the legend told in the Mahabharata that Arjuna, the companion and *Chela* of Krishna, it said to have descended into Patala, the 'antipodes,' and there to have married Ulipi, the daughter of the king of the Nagas. Apparently Patala is America, and the Nagas were initiates. The above is said to have happened some five thousand years ago. (*The Encircled Serpent,* by M. Oldfield Howey, pp. 297-298,)
>
> Originally the Asuras or Nagas were not only a civilized people, but a maritime power, and in the Mahabharata, where the ocean is described as their habitation, an ancient legend is preserved of how Kadru, the mother of serpents, compelled Garuda (the Eagle or Hawk) to serve her sons by transporting them across the sea to a beautiful country in a distant land, which was inhabited by Nagas...The Asuras (Nagas) were expert navigators, possessed of very considerable naval resources, and had founded colonies upon distant coasts. (*Ibid;* p. 47.)

One Hindu myth states that God Vishnu once went to *Patala-Loka* (The Underworld or America) to help the people recover from a huge flood. In the Americas, Vishnu, also known as Dionysius, became the Toltec Quetzalcoatl, the Mayan Kukulcan, and the Inca Bochica.

The Collation of Theosophical Glossaries, compiled by Scott J. Osterhage, says the following about Nagas:

> Naga (Sk). Literally "Serpent". The name in the Indian Pantheon of the Serpent or Dragon Spirits, and of the inhabitants of Patala, hell. But as Patala means the antipodes, and was the name given to America by the ancients, who knew and visited that continent before Europe had ever heard of it, the term is probably akin to the Mexican Nagals the (now) sorcerers and medicine men. The Nagas are the Burmese Nats, serpent-gods, or "dragon demons". In Esotericism, however, and as already stated, this is a nick-name for the "wise men" or adepts. In China and Tibet, the "Dragons" are regarded as the titulary deities of the world, and of various spots on the earth, and the word is explained as meaning adepts, yogis, and narjols. The term has simply reference to their great knowledge and wisdom. This is also proven in the ancient Sutras and Buddha's biographies. The Naga is ever a wise (wo)man, endowed with extraordinary magic powers, in South and Central America as in India, in Chaldea as also in ancient Egypt. In China the "worship" of the Nagas was widespread, and it has become still more pronounced since Nagarjuna (the

"great Naga", the "great adept" literally), the fourteenth Buddhist patriarch, visited China. The "Nagas" are regarded by the Celestials as "the tutelary Spirits or gods of the five regions or the four points of the compass and the centre, as the guardians of the five lakes and four oceans" (Eitel). This, traced to its origin and translated esoterically, means that the five continents and their five root-races had always been under the guardianship of "terrestrial deities", i.e., Wise Adepts. The tradition that Nagas washed Gautama Buddha at his birth, protected him and guarded the relics of his body when dead, points again to the Nagas being only wise men, Arhats, and no monsters or Dragons. This is also corroborated by the innumerable stories of the conversion of Nagas to Buddhism. The Naga of a lake in a forest near Rajagriha and many other "Dragons" were thus converted by Buddha to the good Law.

Naga, a serpent; a tree; a mountain; the sun; the number *seven*; a symbol of wisdom; an Initiate. Naga The word means a snake, especially a cobra; but in the Mahabharata it refers to a race of beings inhabiting Patala, the daughter of whose king, Ulupi married Arjuna. "But as Patala means the antipodes, and was the name given to America by the ancients, who knew and visited that continent before Europe had ever heard of it, the term is probably akin to the Mexican Nagals the (now) sorcerers and medicine men." (Theosophical Glossary, H. P. Blavatsky, p. 222) One myth relates that the Nagas were the offspring of the Rishi Kasyapa (the son of Marichi q.v.). Regarding this H. P. Blavatsky wrote: "What is the fable, the genealogy and origin of Kasyapa, with his twelve wives, by whom he had a numerous and diversified progeny of nagas (serpents), reptiles, birds, and all kinds of living things, and who was thus the father of all kinds of animals, but a veiled record of the order of evolution in this round?" (Secret Doctrine, II, p. 253) Another tale represents the Nagas as a semi-divine race (the race of Kadru) inhabiting the waters, or the city of Bhogavati situated under the earth: they are fabled to possess a human face with serpent-like lower extremities. Ananta (q.v.) is king of the Nagas. In The Secret Doctrine, the word Naga stands for a Serpent of Wisdom, a full Initiate—the serpent has ever been used in Occultism as the symbol of immortality and wisdom. "In the Secret Doctrine, the first Nagas—beings wiser than Serpents—are the 'Sons of Will and Yoga,'" (Secret Doctrine, II, p. 181). "Some of the descendants of the primitive Nagas, the Serpents of Wisdom, peopled America, when its continent arose during the balmy days of the great Atlantis," (Secret Doctrine, II, p. 182). (Bhagavad-Gita, W. Q. Judge, p. 75)

A number of Hindus have told me that back in India, their teachers proved that Patala is Mexico and Central America by folding a world map and running a pin through India. The point comes out in the vicinity of Patala or Meso-America. According to the ancient Hindu myths, evidently these Phoenicians and Jews *(Khyberi)*, were universally regarded with exceeding respect and awe. It is not surprising that after the Great Flood, they became for some cultures, The Creator himself—God or Jehovah!

I have gone into a lot of detail in this chapter, so that readers can get a clear picture of the post-diluvial circumstances forcing the Kuberas and Krishtayanis to India. Edward Pococke, in *India in Greece,* said that the Mt. Meru dispersal caused the banishment of the Aryan Krishtayas (Christians) from India. He should have referred to the banishment of Abraham and Sarah, which occurred one or two thousand years later. The ones who were banished from Mt. Meru were India's incorrigibles. During the Abrahamic dispersal from India, the Krishtayas or Kristihans fled to Europe.

In other chapters, I will emphasize more that blood relationship between the Turks and Hindus in *Tala* and the Meso-Americans (Mexicans) in *Atala,* for they are connected by an invisible but powerful psychic and physical umbilical cord. The Mexicans and Central Americans in *Atala*, and their Turkic-Hindu brothers in *Tala* have a major part to play in the "Spiritual Cure" of the problems now plaguing the earth. Will they take what I have said seriously? Or will I be laughed off the stage? Who knows?

11

Who Was the King of the Five Krishtaya Races?

When I wrote my prior books about the evils of "belief," I thought they would be sufficient to show people that only Zion (Science), not Babel (Belief), could lead people out of darkness. Furthermore, I wanted people to realize that The Cross, The Holy Trinity, Jacob's Ladder, and The Holy Directions were actual verifiable sciences and could be depended on to help mankind remove the cobwebs from his eyes. However, I was mistaken. It was then that I decided to write this book, showing how cabalists use both the *Torah* and the holy books of the Hindus, to get some sense out of humanity and the reasons for our being here. I will use Murad Adji's description of the ancient Turkish Tengri religion, making my own comments where appropriate:

> Tengri sent his favorite son, Gheser, to the Ancient Altai to teach the tribes to lead a righteous life. Gheser was the first ever Prophet on Earth. The messenger of the God of Heaven, he illuminated people on Tengri.
>
> Central Asian peoples have composed many legends about Gheser and his holy deeds. True, Gheser's name has been modified over the centuries, by accident or intent, to Keder or even Khyzer, which is now his most common name among the Turkic people. And he is now best remembered in association with Tengri, the God of Heaven.
>
> Gheser is a wise guardian of life on Earth. An immortal hero, who to some people is a bearded old man leaning on his staff, and a strong young man brimming with health and vigour to others.

To make some sense out of these two names, *Ghezer* and *Keder*, we must separate them from the suffix *er*, leaving *Ked* and *Ghez*. I'll now use linguistic analysis to show how the people of different language backgrounds would have pronounced them. In each of the blanks, we can substitute A, E, I, O, or U: K__d, K__s, K__sh; K__t, K__th; K__z; H__d, H__s, H__sh; H__t, H__th, H__z. Next: Gh__d, Gh__s, Gh__sh; Gh__t, Gh__th; Gh__z. Additionally, in some cultures, the hard G would pronounce as a soft G or J__d; J__s; J__sh; J__t; J__z. Y and Z are often used in place of a J.

From the syllables Ked and Ghez, we can derive not only the name of the perpetual and divinely appointed kings of all the nations on earth a.ka. the *Nuphylum,* who are the five Aryan Krishtayas (Christian) races of man (Yadu, Druhyus, Turvasa, Anu, and Puru), but the titles of virtually all the ruling classes on earth!

The *er* suffix is like the *er* or *or* we place at the end of a noun to identify members of a particular nationality or group: Britisher; Hollander; Sailor; Banker; Kaiser, Caesar, Soldier; Grantor. We may also place an *ite* suffix to get Hittite, Kassite, Kuthite; Midianite, etc. The Nahuatl or Toltec speaking tribes of Meso-America used such endings as *tl, tle, stle, ztle, etc.* Example: Nahua-tl (Nahua-speaker); Toltecatl (Toltec gentility or governing class).

In the case of words beginning with a J sound, we can get Jesse, Joshua, Jesus, etc. Without the *er* ending, we even get the words *Hodai, Khodai,* and *God.* Yes, Jesus Christ is none other than the son of Tengri, Keder or Ghezer! It seems that from the beginning of Man's appearance on earth, Jesus has been the king, and *Tengri* or *God* has been his father. Notice that Mr. Adji said that Tengri sent his favorite son to rule the five races of *Nuphylum.* Our own New Testament says no less:

> And the Word was made flesh, and dwelt among us, (and we beheld his glory, the glory as of the only begotten of the Father), full of grace and truth. *(John 1:14.)*
> For God so loved the world, that he gave his only begotten Son, that whosoever believe in him should not perish, but have everlasting life. *(John, 3:16.)*

I can continue with many more biblical statements that God gave only one son to the world from the beginning of time, and no other. This, in my opinion, confirms what Murad Adji said about Tengri, which is that other name of Jesus' Celestial Father: God or *Gospodi,* for this name in Sanskrit is *Dyupiter* (Jupiter).

Some readers may want to ask why the Turks insist on claiming Jesus as their own while the Jews do not. This answer is clear. Jesus himself was a Turk. The Turkish Karaite Jews themselves claim to be the original Jews. It has never been hidden from us that one of Jesus' other names was *David Koresh.* The Aryans or Kurus (*Kurush*) were the ruling caste of the world from the very beginning. Even the Bible mentions the Nephilim or Nuphylum. The Bible tells us that when Abraham went to Jerusalem, the Hittites (Turks) were already in control of the city. But we don't need the Bible to tell us that. This is a historical fact that can't be denied. Christ also spoke Aramaic which is a Turkish dialect.

In some way, the Turks found out that their new Divine King was to be born in Israel. The names of the Three Wise Men prove they were Turks.

> *Caspar* was from the Kuru (Turkic) *Krishtaya* populated Caucasus, the Caspian, or Kashmir. He derived his name from the Kashmiri *Kasheph* or the Sanskrit *Kasyapa, the son of God Brahma.* His real title was *Kashephpar* or *Kashayappar.* The Kashmiri *Par* or the Sanskrit *Para* means "highest; greatest; pre-eminent; supreme; he who is supreme; the Supreme Deity. *Caspar* means "King of the Caspians, Caucasus, or Kashmir."
>
> *Baltazar* was a king of the Afghan or Pakistani province of *Balti.* *Sha* means "king; prince; monarch." *Ari* means "faithful; pious; devoted." At the end of a word, just the *Ar* suffix is added. Thus, *Baltishar* means "The Pious King of Balti."
>
> *Melchior* could have been the leader of the North Indian province of *Kuruksetra* or *Kurustan.* *Melik* is the Turkic and Kashmiri term for "King." *Kur, Kuru,* or *Kyur* means what it says. Malik-Kuru means *King of the Kuru (Turkic)* peoples. Even in modern Turkic, the word *Kral* or *Kural* means "a chief ruler; a sovereign; one invested with supreme authority; a head of a country tribe; a prince." We've been taught that *Caesar* was the Latin word for "emperor." *Kurios* was also a Latin word for the Roman emperor, sovereign, prince, and chief. It was also a word for God and the Messiah. For the Greeks, the root meaning for Lord, *Kurios,* was "Power; Force." From that word, they derived *Kristos.* Another Greek word for Lord or "The Highest One" was *Kurion.* The word "crown" was derived from *Kurion. Kristis* was the Greek term describing how the spirit, after the body dies, contemplates the good and bad deeds it did in its past life and realizes what opportunities it missed. We must bear in mind that at one time, the Turks, Greeks and Armenians were the same people. We should not doubt the origins of the Three Wise Men. (*Christianity-Mankind's First Worldwide Religion!* By Gene D. Matlock; p. 34.)

Murad Adji continues, as follows:

> Curiously, the figure of Khyzer (Keder or even Kederles) is common among many nations of the world, those that had links with the ancient culture of the Turkis and their god, Tengri. A keen person will hardly need any persuading to get the message.

If any of my readers have not yet "gotten the message," I have more information to support Murad Adji's claims. His comments about Keder or Gheser explain how these names spread to India, and afterwards throughout the world,

enabling us to find out the true source of mankind's institutions and governments. All I had to do after that was to open up my Online Sanskrit Lexicon to
find out about the world's governing caste.

> Sanskrit *Kashi* = "The Sun; Descendants of Prince Kashi; the family of
> Bharata (India's true name). *Shikha* = "chief; head; sheik; best of a kind."
> *Kashikha* = "Chiefs or Sheiks of Kashi (the Sun) or Bharata." The words *Hat-
> tiya* and *Kashitriya* are even today the caste names of India's ruling and warrior
> caste.

Up to this point, it seems that Keder and Gheser became the names of the ruling castes of India. Let us put these two names to the test, to see if we can come to
a more rigorous proof that Mr. Adji is correct in saying that these two words
reveal the true source of all mankind's institutions and governments throughout
the world.

The following is a list of many Amerindian leadership castes which I compiled
from studying the traditions of most American Indian tribes:

> *Keshua* (Inca leadership caste); *Kashitl; Kashikeh* (Aztec, Toltec, and
> Nahuatl chiefs); *Kashikel; Kisheh* (Mayan leaders); *Kashekwa; Kashikah* (Carib-
> bean and Florida Taino and Arawak chieftains); *Kushuu* (Mexican Mixtec and
> Zapotec rulers); *Kashonsee* (Mexican Tarascan leaders); *Kais* (Arizona
> O'odham word for "rich, wealthy people"); *Katsina* (Hopi and other Puebloan
> protective deities); *Koshair* (Southwestern Puebloan sun priests); *Koshikwe*
> (Zuñi leadership clan); *Gasha* (Seneca Indian chiefs); *Kaddi* (leaders of the
> Caddoan tribe); etc., etc.

Notice the similarity of the Amerindian names for "leadership caste" with
their Old World equivalents:

> *Kush* (ancient rulers of Egypt, Ethiopia, and other parts of Africa); *Kais*
> (hereditary leaders of Afghanistan); *Kish* (hereditary leaders of Persia); *Kassi*
> (Kassites; ancient rulers of Assyria and Mesopotamia); *Kashu* (Babylonian
> leaders); *Kastra* (Roman hereditary leaders); *Kish* (Hereditary leaders of Kish-
> tawar, Kashmir); *Kathay* (China's ancient leadership caste); *Kshatriya; Hattiya*
> (India's ruling caste); *Kossoei* (Persian or Iranian aristocracy); *Kshatrap* (early
> Greek leaders); *Hessian* (German warrior caste) *Katholic* (universal religion of
> mankind); *Kashteel* (a name of Spain's first leadership caste); *Kastro* (another
> name of Spain's leadership caste); *Kaesar/Caesar* (mispronounced as "Seezar";
> title of Roman kings); *Kushang* (a fierce warrior tribe that once left Eastern
> Siberia, moved across Mongolia, swept across China, and kept on going to

India); *Kaiser* (title of German kings); *Kzar* (title of Russian rulers); *Jutes, Goths, Guti, Gades, Cadis, etc.,* (ancient Rajput or Yadava warriors that once overran Europe); *Kossaks; Kazaks* (hereditary warrior class of Russia); *Castle* (home of hereditary leaders).

I know that many, many readers are wanting to find out why Keder a.k.a. Ghezer is no longer ruling mankind but instead the villainous politicians and usurpers of his holy name? Has no one guessed by now? The Noah's Ark and Tower of Babylon tragedies did nothing to change mankind. At various times in history, evil men crucify the reincarnation of Keder/Ghezer (originally Krishtis), and then hide behind the name of Caesar.

12

How and Why the Hebrews (Phoenicians and Jews) Brought Our Amerindians to the Americas.

What do the Turkish-Ramanaka origins of the American Indians have to do with the mysteries linking the Turkish people, the Hindus, the Cross, Jesus Christ, the Holy Trinity, and Mexico? Actually, everything-and more. However, that is something I cannot explain effectively at this moment but in a later chapter. Describing the origins of all our American tribes would fill an encyclopedic volume or two. So, I will try to accomplish this objective by going into detail about the origins of the *Purépecha*-speaking tribe of Mexico's Michoacán and the Toltec Nahuatl-speaking tribes, including the Aztecs, Zapotecs, and Mayans. In my preceding book, *Christianity-Mankind's Oldest Religion*, I gave a reasonable description of the origins of the Mayans and Hopis, with just a vignette of some other tribes. Even so, I left out more vital imformation about the Hopis and Mayans, which I'll include in this book. Hopefully, what I say about these tribes may help me accomplish my objectives adequately. I must keep this book as short as possible.

One Mexican Tribe with Three Turkish Identities: *Michoacán, Tarasco, Purépecha.*

The Old Testament or Torah gave the Nahuas, Nahoas, Aztecs, Toltecs, Mexicans, and the above tribe having three identities a passionate scathing, even mentioning their collective names. The Christian New Testament also alludes to them, saying that if they can be persuaded-or forced-to become ecumenical, mankind will enjoy a thousand years of peace. They are the Meshechs.

The Bible says the following about them. First, it identifies them accurately, just as the Turks and Hindus have done in their legends and mythology:

> The descendants of Japheth: Gomer, Magog, Madai, Javan, Tubal, Mesech, and Tiras. The descendants of Gomer: Ashkenaz, Riphath, and Togamah. The descendants of Javan: Elisha and Tarshish, the Kittim and Dodanim. From these the maritime nations branched out-each with its own language-their clans and their nations. (*Genesis* 10:2-5.)

With regard to the Mexican (*Meshika, Mehsech*) tribe with three Turkish names, the Bible mentions them as Meshech and Tiras. The Hindu holy books not only mention them accurately, but include one that the Bible, for some reason, has left out: Puru. However, the name Puru just represents collectively all of them. It is the collective name of the Krishtaya Aryan Turkish-related tribes in Central Asia and India.

The origin legends, cultural, and linguistic evidence of the Mayas, Hopis, Toltecs, Nahuas, Nahoas, Aztecs, Huicholes, O'odham, Cherokees, Caddo, Zuñis, Incas, Caribs, Zapotecs-plus many others-are, perhaps, more accurate than the accounts that the most erudite of European historians can "dream up." However, those of the Mexican tribe having three Turkish names easily top all of them. They tell us everything, to the dotting of the I's and crossing of the "Ts." They even know where they came from: the Himalayan state of Himachal Pradesh, India. To me, it is a mystery that no one has ever noticed this until now!

If I revealed no other information than their names, I might stand vindicated:

Michoacán, a Turkish compound word meaning "Kingdom of the Meshechs." The Phoenicians, who generally spoke Aramaic in the Middle East and Turkey, first regarded them and all the other Meshechs they distributed all over both Americas with reverence They called them *Meshika,* the Aramaic word for "Messiah." The suffix *Can* derives from the Turkish *Khan,* meaning "king; kingdom."

Tarasco. This name derives from the Sanskrit *Turushka,* meaning Turks; a Turkish prince; Turkestan.

Purépecha, derived from the Turkish and Sanskrit words Puru (all the Turkish-speaking tribes in Central Asia and India, plus *Cha* or *Shah,* meaning "king; emperor."

The Turks also called themselves *Kuru, Koresh, Kuresh, Quresh* (Arab hereditary theocratic leadership caste. Mohammed was a Quresh). Even our Jesus Christ was Turkish, for he was also known as David Koresh. Saul of Tarshish, later to become Paul, was a Turk. The word "Tarshish" proves it. Mary, mother of Jesus, went to live in Turkey (Anatolia) after Jesus' martyrdom. Both St. John and Paul are buried in Turkey. Thousands of Christians and Moslems yearly visit their graves as well as the home of Mary.

The Michoacán tribe's God of Gods exiled them to Mexico. He was ancient Bulgarian king Kubera, the Hindu god of all metals, both base and precious, fine gems, artisans, farmers, merchants, and good fortune. Kubera was supposed to be an ugly, dwarfish hunchback. The Michoacán idol of their God of Gods, *Kuri-Kuvera*, wouldn't have won a beauty contest either. But at least he was made of gold. Even today, the people of Michoacán are enamoured of gold and the ways it can be earned. They pride themselves with the gold ornaments they wear. The Michoacanos living in this country have more rich entrepreneurs among them than the rest of their Mexican immigrant co-nationals.

Naturally, I should not omit Kuri-Kuvera's consort: *Kuvera-pperi*. The term means "Goddess of Nature and Fairy Goddess." In Sanskrit, *Para*="The Supreme Spirit; The Absolute."

The cultural hero of the Michoacanos, who led them to Mexico and helped establish their kingdom was *Tariák-Kuri*. Evidently, Tariak had been a bad boy back in India. There, he was known as *Tarak-Yuddhi* (The Turkish Conqueror). The Hindu holy books called him a demon (*Asura*). The Hindu books say that a son of Shiva killed him, but he turned up very much alive in ancient Mexico. Michoacano history does not treat him so shabbily as he was regarded back in India.

The Tarascans also worshiped a god called *Taras,* which appears to be linguistically related to the biblical *Tiras* mentioned in Genesis. (Reference: *The Conquest of Michoacán,* by Benedict Warren, p. 6.)

The Michoacano words for "water, places of water," etc., are *Dara* and *Doro.*

Here's another valid proof that they came from Northern India. In Sanskrit, *Jhara*='river;' *Dhara* (stream, jet, gush, flood); *Adhara* (canal); Farsi, a Persian dialect spoken in Afghanistan and Pakistan: *Darya* (river); *Dar'ya'cheh* (lake); Pashto, another Persian dialect: *Deria* (sea); Kashmiri: *Dara* (small water channel for irrigation; current or flow of water in a river); *Jori* (running; flowing).

I shall never forget when I became aware of the similarity of the Michoacano's definitions of water with those of Northern India. My wife and I had been staying at the home of a Mexican friend in the beautiful little city of Huandacareo. Before dawn one morning, we left Micaela's house to visit my wife's hometown in Manalisco, Jalisco. We boarded a rickety old bus, the kind the Mexicans call "chicken buses."

Just as dawn broke, we entered a town called Puruándaro. The bus stopped there to take on more passengers. I almost screamed in astonishment: "Look," I said to my wife, "That's one of the names of India's God Shiva!" I asked a woman who boarded the bus whether she knew what that word meant in Purépecha. She said, "It means 'sacred health waters.' This town is famous for its health-bestowing waters." After that, I started doing research on Michoacán fanatically.

Here are just a tiny few of scores of Tarascan towns and villages named after "water:" *Ahijadero, Córondoro; Corongoros; Copandaro; Guándaro; Zirimondiro; Urundareo; Uringuítaro; Puruándaro, etc, ad infinitim.*

I know without asking that my Hindu readers automatically know what some of those prefixes mean. For example, Coróndoro and Corongoros may derive from *Khairon,* the name of an extremely ancient Kashmiri tribe. Cóndoro and Guándaro also appear to have been derived from the Kandahar and/or the Ghandahar regions of Afghanistan. The word Corongoros seems to derive also from *Kurungurus* (Turkish Wise Men).

An ancient Sumerian and North Indian word meaning "city; place" was *Ur* or *Uru.* That word abounds in Michoacán, for it, too, means "city; place:" *Uru; Uru; Uranden; Ururuta; Uren; Urapa;Uruápan Uringuítaro;Urapicho; Uripitio; Uripito,* again, *etc.*

The ancient Scythians (*Saka*) were an extremely warlike but civilized Central Asian tribe. They lived throughout Central Asia, from Siberia down to Northern India. They still live in Siberia. One of their brethren was the immortal deified saint, *Sakyamuni Buddha.* These same Scythians populated large parts of Mexico.

Among the dozens of Michoacán towns named after the Saka, we have *Sacapu* (Saka-Bhu, meaning Scythians who came from *Bhu,* the sacred land around Mt. Meru); *Sacapuri* (Scythian City); *Zakan* (Scythia).

Some other Michoacan towns of Turkish-Hindu origin should not be left out of this discussion: *Ichan* (Ishan or God Shiva); *Ixtapa* (Shiva Our Lord and Protector); *Arapari* (Fairy Lights); *Iztaro/Ixtala* (Ishtar, the Phoenician Moon Goddess); *Angao* (the North Indian Anga tribe. It seems that not all of them were sent to India. The English and Angles are descended from the *Angas.* The Michoacano town of *Kuchis* derived its name from the ancient Afghan tribe of Kuchis, who still live there. The name of one Michoacano town fascinated me and tells us a lot: *Puruátiro,* meaning "The-Purus-Who-Crossed-Over-The Ocean."

Naturally, many Michoacano towns were named after their God of Gods, Kubera, and his faithful Juddhi (Jewish) warrior caste: *Yurécuaro* (Kubera's Juddhi/Yuddhi (Jewish) warriors; *Yuri* (Yuddhi); *Yuríria* (The Aryan Juddhis); *Yoricostio* (Yuddhi-Kashatriya, meaning Yuddhi-Hindu Leadership Caste); *Yurécuaro* (Kubera's Warriors); *Itzicuaro* (Shiva-Kubera. Shiva and Kubera were allies and close friends. Some authorities think they could have been the same person.) The name of the beautiful colonial city of *Pátzcuaro* fascinates me. It means, "Lord Buddha Kubera." Pátzcuaro was the most sacred religious center of the Michoacanos.

The Indic-Phoenicians were also called *Pani,* meaning "merchant and trading caste." A number of cities and towns in Michoacán have names ending in *Pan,* and they are still well-known as centers of trading. The grand old city of *Uruápan* is famous for its textiles, ceramics, clothing manufacture, and Mexican curios of all kinds. In order to make their lacquer ware, they were employing the Chinese tung nut centuries before the Spaniards arrived. Its Mexican name is still "tung."

The Michoacano temple pyramids were called *Yácata.* The Sanskrit word for "Guardian Angel" is *Yah, Yakhu, Yahhu, Yaksha, etc.* The Sanskrit suffix *Ata* indicates the animate-inanimate, spiritual-physical nature of a being is indistinguishable. The Michoacano ruling oligarchy was called *Kashonsee,* which means "Hindu Ruling Class). Naturally, I wouldn't want to leave out the ancient Tarascan nobility who prided themselves on being called *Inti* and *Henditre* (Hindu).

Like the Hindus, Tarascan society was sharply divided in castes. Special priests presided over all the labor guilds. The word *Esha* (God Shiva) was added after each priest's labor classification.

Punga-Barato was the name of the Pacific coastal port where their forefathers first landed, obviously derived from the Sanskrit *Panka-Bharata* (Phoenician India).

They claimed that their land of origin was *Naran-Shan. Shan* was a Northern Indian, Chinese, and Tibetan name of "region." In the Himalayan state of Himachal-Pradesh, there is a region called *Naran.* It is beautiful, heavily wooded, and mountainous, just as Michoacán is. The architecture of Naran and the physiognomy of the humans living there are nearly identical to those of the Tarascans.

As I have stated, the Tarascan words *Yuri/Yori* meant "warrior; conqueror." The Michoacanos told the Spaniards that they were once masters of a vast empire extending all the way north, including what are now Arizona and New Mexico. They must have been telling the truth, for the legends of the Yaquis mention that valiant legions of warriors called *Yoris/Yuris* (pronounced like Jodees or Joodees), once marched northward through the Yaqui nation. The Utes of Utah (pronounced as Yute and Yutah) were also a large warrior class. The Hopi legends say that the Utes accompanied them on their strange and ancient Odyssey.

The anthropologist José Corona Núñez cites the Codex Plancarte to support his contention that at one time the Tarascan kingdom included a large part of Northwestern New Mexico and even extended as far as Zuñi in New

Mexico. He bases his argument on the place name *Zibulan,* which appears in the codex, another name for Zuñi. It is interesting to note that there appears to be some linguistic connection between the Tarascan and the Zuñian. (*The Conquest of Michoacán,* by Benedict Warren; (p. 4.)

The legends of the Purépechas imply that the Phoenicians arrived there regularly, near what is now the city of Lázaro Cardenas, anchoring their barks in the breathtakingly beautiful fiords of the Balsas River.

Rodrigo de Albornoz, in a letter that he wrote to the king of Spain in 1525…said that the Indians of Zacatula, at the mouth of the Río Balsas, said that their fathers and grandfathers had told them that from time to time, Indians had come to that coast from certain southern islands in large dugout canoes, bringing excellent things to trade and to take other things from the land…those who came…stayed for five or six months. (*The Conquest of Michoacán;* p. 8.)

The legends of the Yaquis and other northern Mexican Indian tribes mention a strange horde of short, pigmy-like people called *Surén* who, with their queen, passed through their nations on their way northward. They worshiped the sun (*Surya?*). The *Suren* were a Turkish Tribe. Archeologists studying the ancient puebloan remains in Arizona and New Mexico, have intuited that the early puebloans must have been of extremely short stature because of the low doorways and childlike handprints found on the mud-plastered walls.

The Michoacanos even told the Spaniards that they were closely related to the Incas of Peru.

…I was surprised to find an analogy between ancient Perú and Michoacán. The two people had the same institutions, the same religious practices, similar legends, and both adored the sun. In Perú, in Venezuela, and in other regions of South America, we find many Tarsascan names. on whose nearly identical similarities I have to insist in this work. (*Michoacán,* by Eduardo Ruíz. p. 25.)

Who says that Turkish, Hindu and American Indian legends are not to be trusted? On the contrary, the highly literate and "scientific" Europoid historians are the ones who don't know what they're talking about. Although the Mayans and Aztecs were literate, the Hopis and Michoacanos, who were illiterate, had an accurate, valid, detailed history of their struggles to reach the Americas. Through their oral myths and legends, our American Indians have proved themselves better historians than those who have several degrees backing them up!

The Nahuatl-speaking Tribes: Nahua, Nahoa, Toltecs, Aztecs, and Others.

When I went to college in Mexico, during the late 1940s, it didn't take me long to notice that this country had to have some kind of connection with India and/or the Bible. The first enigma was their name: Mexican, which in Nahuatl is *Meshika.* I had noticed in my studies that there were a lot of Mesech-like names in both Americas. And then, there were the words, *Nahua* and *Nahoa.* The Nahoa were a tribe in what is now Mexico's states of Nayarit and Sinaloa. They were reputed to be the primogenitors of the Nahuas of Central Mexico. That word appeared similar to "Noah" which it, indeed, was. The Nahuatl-speaking tribes couldn't pronounce the "V" sound. In Sanskrit, *Nava* means "ship." The Aztec legend about their "exodus" from Aztlán, Nayarit, Mexico to what is now Mexico City, was unbelievably similar to the story of Moses and the exodus of the Hebrews from Egypt. In the Hebrew version of the same story, Moses (Moshe) and his people were enslaved for a number of years. They had to build pyramids, make adobe bricks, and perform other menial chores for the Egyptians. Finally, the Pharaoh released them.

In the Aztec legend, they left an island just off the Pacific Coast, now called Mexcaltitán (Mesh-Kahl-tee-than). When they reached the Mexican mainland, they were enslaved by the king of Aztlán. For a number of years, they, too, had to build pyramids and make adobe bricks. Finally, they were allowed to leave, being led by their prophet Meshi whose name was similar to Moshe, the real name of Moses.

During the biblical Exodus, the Jews camped for awhile in a place having many poisonous snakes in it, called *Nehusthan.* These Nehusthan snakes appeared to be evil demi-gods. They killed many Israelites. Finally, Moses had a brazen image made of Nehusthan and placed on a pole, telling the Israelites to salute (worship) it. After that, it didn't kill any more Israelites.

In the Aztec version of the same story, the Aztecs camped in an extremely rocky area outside what is now Mexico City, called *El Pedregal* (The Place of Rocks). Poisonous snakes were everywhere. But the Mexican Meshi was some-what more practical and realistic than our Moses. He told his followers to eat them. The Aztecs did such a thorough job of eating all those snakes, that not even today can one find snakes in El Pedregal.

In India, *Aztika* was a Brahman leadership sect. A similar word in Turkish, *Uztika,* means "Upper Class; Nobility." Those names are strangely similar to the word *Azteca.* According to the Spanish historian and priest, *Fray Diego de Durán,*

The Aztecs claimed to have arrived in the Western Hemisphere from a country on the other side of the world. They first inhabited a land located more or less where the Florida Cays are now. A severe earthquake or other cataclysm caused their land to sink under the waters of the Gulf of Mexico. They were rescued by a maritime nation and taken to the upper East Coast of Mexico in ships. From there, they and the Michoacanos, who appear to have been two clans of the same tribal family, walked to Western Mexico in search of a new land. During their journey southward, they separated from the Michoacanos in what is now known as Lake Pátzcuaro.

The Aztec gentility was called *Aztecatl;* The common people were *Azteca.* The leadership of the Phoenicians was known as *Khatti,* Their commoners were just called *Kah.* These two class distinctions are too similar to be a coincidence. The Phoenician *Meshikas* were a special caste of Phoenicians who specialized in obtaining and overseeing slaves, as well as being artisans for the Phoenicians. *Meshika* meant "Messiah" in Aramaic, a Turkic language once spoken throughout Central Asia, but not exclusively. The Aztecs were known for their fine gold work and their enslavement of the other tribes in Meso-America. Their harshness led the surrounding tribes to ally themselves with the Spaniards against the Aztecs. It has been said that the Spaniards never really conquered Mexico. They just oversaw and supported the other Amerindian tribes in such a mission.

Emperor Montezuma told the Spaniards that his family clan came from a far-away land called *Teocolhuacán.* The Aztecs couldn't pronounce "R" or "V." Therefore, this Teocolhuacán had to have been the Turkish *Teo-Kaurava-Khan,* meaning "The Deified Kaurava (Turkic) Kingdom."

The Aztecs were descendants of the Toltecs. This Teocolhuacán from which the Aztecs descended was located in a far away nation on the other side of the world, called *Tula, Tolan,* or *Tullan.* Keeping in mind that they couldn't pronounce "R," they were really the Turs, Turan, or Turan, a name of the Turks. Many Turkish Huna tribes couldn't pronounce "R" either. They called themselves Tulas, Tulas, or Tulan. In Southern Russia, there was, and is today, a Tula. The Aztecs called the Spaniards *Tules.* Even today, we find this word Tul or Tol scattered all over both Americas. *Toltec* derived from Skt. *Toltuk* (Son of the Tola People). In Turkish, *Tulteki=*"The Unrivalled Tula."

The Toltec or Aztec word for "warrior," *Yaotl,* is similar to its Sanskrit equivalent: *Yaudi* or *Yuddhi.*

Tepe is the Turkish word for "hill." *Tepes are* scattered all over Mexico. My estimate is that there are more than two hundred. The most famous *Tepe* is *Tepeyác,* "Hill of the Guardian Angel" in Sanskrit. Before the Virgin of Guadalupe was substituted in her place, Tepeyác was the abode of Mexico's Mother Goddess: *Nan; Inana; Nantzin* (Honored or Revered Mother. *Tzin* is an honorific)*; Ton-nantzin (Resplendent Mother); No-Nantzin (Our Mother); Citl-ali* (Star Goddess)*; Malin-Ali* (Flower Goddess).

The Mother Goddess Innana was especially revered in Sumeria and all over Central Asia. The ancient Turks were the progenitors of Sumeria. In Sumeria and Central Asia, she was called *Nana; Innana; Nan-sin* (Honored or Revered Mother)*; Ishtar* (Star Goddess)*; Str-ila* (Star Goddess)*; Malin-ila* (Flower Goddess).

It does not seem possible to me that these identical names for Mother Goddess are coincidences.

The Sumerian word for a pyramidical temple mount is *Ziggurat*. In Sanskrit, such a temple is a *Sakharu* or *Sakhari*. In Nahuatl it is *Zacualli*. The linguistic differences in these words are trivial.

The names of the popular Aztec Gods, *Quetzalcoatl* and *Tezcatlipoca*, derive from India and Central Asia. Both these names were probably derived from both Turkish and Sanskrit. In Turkish, we have *Kutsal* (Sacred; Holy) *Kuru* (Turk), which the Toltecs would have pronounced as *Kutsalkutl*. The word could have also derived from *Kutsalkrl*. In Mexico, it would have been *Kutsalkatal* (Holy Turkish King). This word also has a Sanskrit equivalent: *Ket* (chief; leader) plus *Shul* (Scepter or Shiva's Trident) plus *Kubera* (partnership of the Phoenicians and Jews or Khyber, another name of Kubera). This could have only been pronounced in Nahuatl as *Ketsalkuwatl*. Although both of these names certainly derived from Turkish and Sanskrit, I am of the opinion that Quetzalcoatl was probably a holy man from today's state of Bihar. In ancient times, Bihar was known for its monasteries called Bihars. But then it was called *Pala*. Quetzalcoatl's native land was *Tlapallan*. In India, it would have been pronounced as *Tala-Palan*, meaning, "The Upper World *Palan*." It was named thusly because Meso-America, which was settled by Kubera and his *Nagastas* (Nagas of the West or Setting Sun), had brought people from *Pala* with him. In the Bible, the Pelegs or Phalegs were great builders, especially of canals and waterways. They surely built the old Mayan city of *Palenque,* meaning *Pala-Lanka*. Even today, in Central America, a large container for water is called *Palangana* (Tribe of Peleg).

Paulisti is Assyrian Palastu or Pilastu, Egyptian Pulesati, Biblical Philistine, Greek Pelasgos, Puranic Pulasta, possibly also Pulama (predatory Poligars of Deccan)…(*Racial History of India,* by Chandra Chakraberty; p. 84.)

In Sanskrit, *Palaka*="World Protector." (See the Sanskrit Lexicon.) Kubera (Heber) and Peleg/Phaleg transported the Meshechs and others to the Americas in order to protect the Middle East, Central Asia, and India, just as the Bible says.

While we are on the subject of biblical names in Mexico, I want to mention the coastal city of *Papaloapan,* in Veracruz. The Nahuatl-speaking people could not pronounce "B." *Pan* derived from what they saw the Phoenicians (Pani) doing; crossing waters. In Mexico, it came to mean any crossing, such as a bridge, and also a Cross, such as the main subject of this book. Therefore, *Papaloapan* meant "Babylonian Crossing."

Have you ever wondered what the word *Panama* means? It derives from the Sanskrit *Pani-maha* (The Great Phoenician Crossing). In ancient times, small ships could regularly sail through the swampy Isthmus of Panama.

I must now return to my discussion about Quetzalcoatl and Tezcatlipoca. The Nahua people couldn't pronounce D, B, or G. Therefore, Tezcatlipoca, who is usually regarded as Kubera, had a Turkish name: *Desh-Keder-Bhoga* (The Sacred God Kheder). In other words, "The Begotten Son of the Unbegotten Father). All these names are too similar, both in pronunciation and function, to be "mere coincidences."

Sanskrit, Turkish, and Tamil place names abound in Meso-America. Nayarit was named after the Central Indian province of *Nayariti*; Chihuahua (*Shivava,* Residence of God Shiva); Jalisco (pronounced Hah-LEES-koh), named after a Greek Sun God. Halys was also the name of the capital city of the Turkic Hittites. Sonora, a burning desert, derived from the Sanskrit name of a terrible devil called *Sunita.* Sinaloa's Old World counterpart derived from the ancient Ceylonese people was called *Sinhala.* Zacatecas derives from the Turkish *Sakatika* (Unique Scythian People). The list goes on and on.

Just as the Michoacanos have a Turkish name for their type of Tamal, *Corunda,* the Nahuatl people had their *Tamal,* derived from the Tamil *Tamal,* which was wrapped in bamboo shucks instead of corn shucks.

The Mayans

The Mayans pinpointed their Old World origins accurately. They claimed that their forefathers came from a western land lying 150 days' sailing time from Meso-America. They gave several names for this land:

Shilanka (Xilanca)—an ancient name of Ceylon (*Zeilan-Ka*).
Shikalanka (Xicalanca)—Ceylon. In Tamil, *Shikalam.*

Itzamna was one of their culture heroes. He claimed to have come from a western country. *Isham,* meaning 'Tiger, "Land of Gold," was a Dravidian name of Ceylon. The *Na* in Isham-na is an honorific.

Ishbalanka (Xbalanca), another culture hero. In Tamil, it means "Shiva of Lanka." India's God Shiva was supposed to have made the footprint on top of Adam's Peak in today's Sri Lanka.

Shibalba The Mayan underworld. This word stems From the Sanskrit *Shivulba,* meaning "from the fountainhead of God Shiva-Mt. Meru, in India."

Palenke (Palenque). This name derives from the Tamil *Pal-Lanka,* meaning "Protectorate of Lanka." Ancient Lanka was India's "Atlantis."

Ceren, a name of Ceylon. Some Mayan ruins in El Salvador are called *Ceren.*

Lacandon, a tribe of Yucatan. India's god Kubera banished the Laks, a Tartarian Huna or Rakshasha tribe from Northern India to Ceylon, giving the country one of its many names and becoming the Lakan or Lakam people. The *Don* in *Lacan-don* derives from *Dan.* (See the online Cologne Sanskrit and Tamil dictionaries for comparison of ancient Ceylon names with those of Mayan tribes and places.)

Ancient Ceylon was divided into three provinces: *Maya,* the central division of the island; *Ruhuna,* and *Pihitee,* the northernmost of the three. The Ceylonese *Maya* were known for their impressive architectural marvels, temples, and irrigation ponds. (Reference: *The History of Ceylon,* by William Knighton, first published in Colombo Ceylon, in 1845.)

One of the names of Ceylon's cult religions was *Mayon.* It still exists among a few aboriginals living on the island.

As I have stated previously, about 4,000 BC, perhaps even earlier, Kubera or Khyber *(Kheeber/Heber),* India's God of Good Luck, Gold, Riches, Merchants, Traders, Mariners and Miners, tried to rid Northern India *(Sivapuri; Sivabhu; Shivulva)* of its most barbarous tribes. These were mainly the Tartarian *Hunas,* also called *Rakshasas* (barbarians). They came from *Huna-Bhu,* meaning "Hunas (Tartars) from the Sacred Land around Mt. Meru." Many of these tribes were cannibalistic, given to intertribal fighting, practitioners of human sacrifice in their religious rites, flattened the foreheads of their babies, took scalps in battle, and observed other customs attributed to many Amerindian tribes.

Ramayana tells us that Kubera (really a group) exiled them to Lanka or Ceylon, taking along with him many of his *Yaksha* or *Yakkha* subjects. These would be the *Veddhas,* considered to be Ceylon's first inhabitants. In Ceylon, the Hunas (Huns) refused to settle down and become peaceful. Therefore, Kubera took them to *Patala* (Meso-America), along with his fellow *Yakkhas*. The Mayans remember them as the culture hero, *Hunapu (Huna-Bhu?)*.

Had the natives of Meso-America been able to pronounce the "ST" combination, today's Yucatan would be *Yucasthan*. Even today, the Mexican Indians and peasants cannot pronounce this combination. For example, instead of *Cómo está?* (How are you?), they can only say, "*¿Cómo tá?*"

Guatemala derives from Sanskrit *Guadhaamala*, meaning *Guha* (Cosmic Intelligence) + *Dha* (Serpentine) + *Amala* (Umbilical Cord), the Sacred Umbilical Cord Linking Western Asia and India with Meso-America. Besides the Ceylonese and Tamil tribal names *Yakkha, Maya,* and *Lak* in Maya country, there are also the *Lenca* and *Rama* tribes. I want to add that no less than two-thirds of all the aboriginal regional names of Mexico are either variations of the name of Lanka or Tamil names of West Indian regions.

The architecture of ancient Ceylonese temples and buildings is also nearly exactly like that of the Mayans.

Kubera even gave his name to North America. The Meso-Americans told the Spaniards that North America was *Quivira* (Land of the Khyber People).

Most of us have heard of the Mayan holy book, *Chilam Balam. Chilan* or *Chilam* is a title of Mayan priests. *Balam* is the Mayan name for Jaguar. In Sanskrit, *Cheilan* = Ceylonese and *Vyalam* = tiger; lion; hunting leopard. "Jaguar" probably stems from the Sanskrit *Higkara*, meaning Tiger-like or "sounding like a tiger."

Chak was the Mayan God of thunder, lightning, rain, and crops. His equivalent in other parts of the world was *Zeus, Dyaus, Jupiter, Ca, Jah, Ju, Jahve, Jehova Jeho, Sakh, Sagg, Sa-ga-ga, Sakko, Zagg, Zax. a.k.a. Zeus,* is often depicted holding a serpentine thunderbolt and a grail, or someone is handing it to him. The Mayan *Chak* is equally depicted. He, too, is God Shiva!

They claim to have been brought to Meso-America by a person or group called *Votan*. This name means "Boat People" in Sanskrit.

The Mayans called their "Quetzalcoatl" Kukulcan and Gukumats. These names derive directly from the Turkic language. Kuk or Gok derived from the Turkic Gog and Gok, names of Ancient Turkish tribes. *Ulu* means "high placed." *Mats* derives from *Masi,* the Turkic word for "Messiah." *Khan* is a Turkic word for "King." Therefore, Kukulcan=Gogulkhan (The Revered King of Gog.) Gukumats = Gokumasi (The Revered Gok Messiah).

The word Huna occurs a number of times in Mayan mythology. I have said that the second island of Ceylon was named Ruhuna. In Turkic, that means "Soul of the Huna." Mayan mythology speaks of a God of Wind: Huracán, from which we derived our word Hurricane. Kubera and his people went to Southern

Mexico either in sailing ships, airships, or both, being taken there by the wind. Hurácan may derive from Kuru-Khan, meaning "The Turkish King." I have much more to say about the Mayans, but I must stop here.

The Zapotecs

This name derives from the Sanskrit *Sapota* (Owners of Boats). The Zapotecs lived and still live in Oaxaca (pronounced in Spanish as wah-HAH-kah). It was pronounced in olden times as *Vashaka,* "Saka Boat People."

M. Oldfield Howey said the following about the natives of Oaxaca in his book, *The Encircled Serpent:*

> …Saint Patrice writes: '…The high priest of the Mixtecs bore the title of *Tay Sacca,* the man of *Sakya,* Tay meaning 'men,' *sacca* having no meaning in their language, but merely to designate a monk. Some other significant terms are *Zaca-than,* 'the place of Sakya,' *Zaka-tepec,* 'the mountain of Sakya.' In China, Buddhists were often spoken of as 'Sons of Sakya,' Sakamuni being the name that was bestowed upon Buddha in his lifetime, his original name being Guatama.' Nor is this all. Saint-Patrice further quotes Vining as saying, 'The country known as Guatemala, in Central America, is named after Buddha, being a corruption of Guatama-than, the Land of Guatama.' (p. 296.)

Note: I have shown that Guatemala was really called "Guhadhaamala," meaning "The Transcendental Intelligence Flowing in The Serpentine Umbilical Cord." There is no doubt that such peoples as the Aztecs, Mayans, and Incas knew about the Turks and Hindus.

I have given my readers just a crumb of all my collected research about the Indians of both Americas. But I don't want this book to be too meaty. I want to put the Turks and the Hindus back on the map in both spiritual and physical ways. I hope that my description of these great tribes have proven my point.

13

What Is the Right Religion?
(Cross Science 101.)

Some readers who have read my last two books, *The Ego-Mankind's Inner Terrorist and Christianity-Mankind's First Worldwide Religion*, cannot understand why I simultaneously warn people about the evil of proselytizing for any religion, Christian or not. What people should not do is belong to the wrong religion. So what is the right Religion?

In truth, all but one of the major religions on earth are the "right ones." No matter what name they go by, they are just overlays hiding the original religion from which they originated; Krishti or Krishtaya. Even that "wrong one" could be made "right" if its theocratic leaders wanted it to become so. Most people know what that "wrong" one is without me having to point it out to them. If they don't, they surely will when they finish this book.

Essentially, *The Right Religion* is all the religions of the world that accept Duality, the Cross, and The Holy Trinity as the foundation stones (Krishti) of all human existence. Here's an example: Let's suppose I want to persuade someone to leave the Baptist Church and join the Jehovah's Witnesses. That would be a lot like carrying coals to Newcastle. The goal of the Baptists is to teach people the mysteries of the Cross and the Holy Trinity. Therefore, they and the Jehovah's Witnesses belong to the same family. Why turn brother against brother? If I did this, I'd be a common criminal and spiritual murderer. Of course, someone (Guess who?) might knock on your front door frequently, wanting to teach you how to read the scriptures correctly. There is no correct way to read any kind of scriptures, for all are Babel.

Let's suppose that I become a missionary for the Methodist Church. I go to India and try to persuade the Hindus to become Methodists. That, too, would be a mortal crime. The Hindus also accept the Cross, Duality and The Holy Trinity as the foundation stones of all human existence.

The word "Catholic" derives from the Turkic-Armenian *Ketylika,* meaning "Alliance" and the Sanskrit *Ketu-Loka* (Phoenician Universal Religion). It derived from the ancient five Central Asian tribes of *Panchala Kristaya* (Phoenician Christian) or *Panchala Kristihan* (Phoenician Christian Soldiers or Conquerors). They were the Yadu (Yayati, Yahuda, Japheth, or Dyu-Piter); Turvasa (Turk); Druhyus (Druze of the Middle East); Anu (Mongoloids, Japanese, Sumerians, etc.); Puru (the Collective Phoenician Christian Tribes of Central Asia and Northern India)

Tengiri or *Tangiri,* the "Adam" of all the religions on Earth, which apparently took the place of Krishti or Krishtaya, originated in what is now the Turkish Republic of Altai, now a part of Russia. Tangiri's Sanskrit meaning may derive from *Danu* (Conqueror or The Tribe of Dan) + *Giri* (Mountain). Tengiri/Tangiri is just another way of saying "Mt. Meru," the navel of the world, or *Siyoni* (Zion), meaning "Born from the Vulva of Mt. Meru" or "The Source." According to the Torah or Five Books of Moses, as well as the Hindu Holy Books, the primogenitor races of mankind left Tangiri, Mt. Meru, or Zion and populated the entire earth.

The Tengiri religion changed Krishtaya from the way of life of original mankind to a religion with a specific name, separating it from all others that might have been in existence in those ancient times. It preached The Holy Trinity (Father, Son, and Holy Ghost), the archetypical and spiritual significance of the Cross, and the Doctrine of Duality (Male and Female Polarities in the World).

According to the Five Krishtayas, the knowledge and skill in applying correctly the spiritual technology of The Holy Trinity, Duality, and the symbolism of their *Kurus* or *Krus,* from which we derived our word "Cross," enabled them to live at least a thousand years, enter and leave their bodies at will, travel to any place in the universe at the speed of light, heal themselves instantly of any affliction, enjoy peace and happiness, know all skills and arts without studying, and instantly attain a peak of civilization which, if it still existed, would, in comparison, make us so-called "modern humans" seem Neanderthal. They lived in a state of bliss.

Overly confident that their lofty status as Spiritual Humans was their inalienable right, they became egotistical, conceited, and uncaring about the collective welfare of their brothers. Gradually forgetting the spiritual technologies I have described, they became more and more atheistic and forgetful of the art of living in Eternal Heaven. Finally, Nature could tolerate no more their fanatical efforts to turn Heaven into Hell. The earth tilted off its normal orbit, turning their frigid Arctic Circle paradise into a frozen wasteland. Therefore, they fled southward, eventually settling in North India.

Who Were the Nephilim?

These original five races, who presumably came from Outer Space to populate the earth, were what the Torah calls "the maritime nations:" the Phoenicians. The Greeks called them *Nuphylum,* meaning "The Five Leadership Clans of Noah." The Bible calls them *Nephilim.*

The Sanskrit Lexicon throws further light on this word *Nuphylum. Nu/ Na=*"ship; boat; knowledge; certainty; the descendancy from Noah or Lord Krishna; God Shiva; Buddha; Noah." *Nu* additionally means "a ship or vessel leading to Heaven." *Navak=*"prayer as a spiritual vessel leading to Heaven."

Unlike Greek, the Sanskrit word for "offspring" or "progeny" is *Vela. Nuphylum=Nephilim=Nuvelan.*

More About the Etymology of *Torah.*

As I have said, the Turkic word for "story" is *Tarih;* In the Hebrew Bible, *Torah* is The Five Books of Moses. In Kashmiri, a North Indian language, *Tarikh=*"Book." In a few other languages, *Torah* goes to the soul of what the Five Books of Moses want us to know: The Holy Trinity Itself. In Sanskrit, it is mentioned as *Traya,* "the triple sacred science; Triad of Buddha; *Dharma,* the real name of Hinduism, meaning "The Science of Life." *Trayavida =*"Knowing the Sacred Science." *Tarana* is a large equilateral triangle supporting a large balance. It symbolizes God Shiva as Atlas, holding up the world.

The Japanese call their symbol of "The Holy Trinity" *Torii.* It is seen everywhere in Japan, especially just outside shrines. During the Korean War, I truly enjoyed worshiping in their very beautiful brand of Christianity. I would drink sweet water from a tank. Then, I would go to the shrine itself, bow, and clap my hands three times; There was also a bell hanging in front of the shrine. After bowing and clapping three times, the Japanese Shintoist (Christian) rings a bell three times, which hangs in front of the altar. All this symbolism means exactly what it does to Catholics-no more-no less: The Holy Trinity, the Father, Son, and Holy Ghost.

We also see Torii and Tarana in various parts of the world. We call them *Dolmen.* Some authorities insist that the ancient Japanese put them there. While it is true that the Japanese are as Turkic Ramanaka as the rest of us humans, they were not the original Krishtayas. We must always give credit to the Kurus-Ramanaka, the progenitors of all mankind.

Do Symbols mean anything?

When Westerners come face to face with Hindu religious philosophy, they tend to become frustrated with and confused about mountains of symbolism, depictions of natural phenomena as animals, parts of animals, different geographical configurations, geometrical symbols such as energy swirls, circles, concentric circles, swastikas, crosses, and other designs, outlandish descriptions of the lives of the "gods," using "gods" to represent aspects of Nature, and other anomalies. They see Hindu religious Babel as the ravings of lunatics. For example, the renowned Hindu geographer, Dr. Shyam Narain Pande, said the following to describe the tribe of Persian people called Pahlava: "The people of this country sprang from the tail of Vashistha's cow…" (*Ancient Geography of Ayhodhya,* p. 41.) Or, how about the statement in the Ramayana, saying that Kubera stuck his head under the water for 10,000 years? The Hindus, through thousands of years of study and experience, know that Nature or God does not speak human words. It can communicate with mankind only through sending him visions of women holding babies in their laps, gods standing on one foot for a thousand years, sticking one's head under water for 10,000 years, a goddess as the symbol of learning, white doves descending from the vagina of a woman or from the sun, the sun, the moon, humans with animal heads, snakes wrapped around God Shiva's neck, geometric forms of all kinds, etc. These seemingly impenetrable jungles of anomalies are called "natural archetypes" or God's way of explaining all the different phenomena in the only way Creation can explain them at a time when mankind could not understand the universe in any other way. Through millenniums of experience, the Hindus have come to understand and apply these strange symbols and anomalies as we understand physics and other sciences with words, mathematical statements, chemical formulas, etc. You might call them "vital memory associations." This may be a reason why Hindus generally excel in scientific and technological scholarship, for they have been able to align archetypical, natural thinking with man-created mathematical and other scientific models. Here in California, Hindus and other Asian students are known for their high scholastic standards and accomplishments. Even the Sanskrit language itself is regarded as an ideal computer language.

Naturally, some readers may want to inquire about India's poverty, caste distinctions, high crime rate, worship of gurus, fights between religious factions, and other problems with which Hindus have to cope. There is a reason for this also, which many educated Hindus have explained to me. Most Hindus themselves can't understand Nature's archetypical language. The archetypical language of

Nature is a science that only the finest and most highly developed of minds can comprehend and unravel. In itself it engenders an intellectual aristocratic minority, caste distinctions, and the like. It is a fact that our western, manmade approach to learning brings the wonders of the human mind, material comforts, and the secrets of Nature to the majority. Having battled for millenniums with Nature's archetypical messages, the Hindus find our western methods of learning childishly simple.

How The Word "Cross" Got Its Name.

Because the Turks were and are collectively called *Kurus,* and because the "Cross" was their collective and religious emblem, "Cross" is named after them. However, they call it *Aji,* meaning "sign." The Hindus call it *Svastika (Swastika).* It is one of their most powerfully effective religious symbols. It is a combination of *Sva* (soul; one's self; ego; wealth; riches; power, etc.) plus a contraction with *Astika* (one's eternal existence in this world and any other). As Hitler and his Nazis found out, the wrong use of this symbol can destroy anyone who uses it to hurt others. The Aztecs named it after the Phoenicians (Pani) who brought them the Cross: *Pan; Pana.*

Another name for this chapter is Cross Science 101. A Cross may not seem like much to rational thinkers, but it has a power over the human spirit and mind that no amount of rational reasoning can grasp. You may not understand the technology behind it, but that isn't necessary. Just apply it. Symbolism does mean something. Take it seriously.

The Cross Symbolizes The World Tree.

Isn't it strange that even little children are attracted to the Cross, although they have never been taught its significance? Notice their doodlings when they are scribbling on paper. You'll see that they never fail to draw a Cross or two.

There are two basic symbols of the original five *Panchala Krishtaya.* The first is the unseen spiritual Father of The Original Races. As part of the Cross, he is represented as a vertical beam, signifying a phallus. It symbolizes the eternal movement of the sun's light-giving energy around the world. In Sanskrit, it is called *Lingam, Sivalinga,* or *Shivling.* This lingam is either a vertical post or a standing stone. Through its reproductive powers, it sends the "Son" or *Phyla* to The Material Dimension of Life. For us, the "Father" is called *Krsti* or *Kristi.* The horizontal beam symbolize a tree with its branches, the leaves, along with its fruits or nuts. It is the son or *Krstis/Kristis.* The nails on his hands symbolizes that they are frozen to the North and South Poles. The "Holy Ghost," meaning "Life Emanating From the Sun," is represented by the apex of the *Krus* or a dove perched on top of the vertical beam or fastened to the apex. A circle around the apex symbolizes the sun also. This is called the Celtic Cross. This Cross may be enclosed within a larger circle, symbolizing The Circle of Life. Sometimes we see a snake wound around the Cross. I'll explain why later. The Lingam, all varieties of Crosses, and World Tree symbols are major religious symbols in every crook and cranny of the world.

How do we know that the Jews are also *Krishtaya?* Their Mogen David is their most sacred symbol. They also recognize the *Tau.* Besides, they are descendants of Yadu. Kubera's (Heber) favorite religious symbol was also a Mogen David. When I was living in Mexico City during the late 1950s, a brilliant Hebrew scholar-cabalist, a close friend of mine, told me about its significance. He said that anyone who meditated and reflected at all times on the significance of the Mogen David would ultimately acquire all power and all knowledge. He told me that once, when King David and his men were going to fight against an overwhelming force, he had the warriors carry shields in the form of the Mogen David. They defeated their enemy easily. The upright triangle symbolizes the archetypical Father, called the Ayeen, sending his son, The Yesh, down to the material dimension. The upside down triangle symbolizes the Son, or Yesh, who will someday have to return to the Ayeen. Sometimes there is a circle around the Mogen David, symbolizing light, the Holy Ghost, and the Circle of Life.

The Hindus also worship the Holy Trinity as a small tree standing in a pot or box filled with earth. It is called *Deepstumba.* The earth in the planter symbolizes "The Earth Mother," She receives the rays of the sun as a woman receives a phallus. The Sun plants within her womb the archetypical human spirit. It mixes with the water, minerals and earth, becoming a living physical being. Then, this new physical being rises up from the earth as a linga or phallus and keeps on perpetuating the Circle of Life. When this happens, the earth also becomes The Male Principal.

Murad Adji says the following about the World Tree:

> ...Turkic settlements were established and new cities built in the part of the Caucasus under their control. One of them was Hamrin. The city was famous for its sacred tree, the Tengri Khan tree, which was mentioned in almost every history of the Caucasus at the time.
>
> It was certainly not a sacred tree of a kind typically adulated by pagans. No, the Turkis kept alive a legend of a world tree embodying everything created by Great Tengri. (Incidentally, this is an occasion when Tengri was to be addressed as Hodai [our Christian God], the Creator.)

The world tree concept is a full-scale science that gives ultimate knowledge to a man who, by learning it, begins to see the essence of the world and to comprehend the way it works. Europeans call this science philosophy.

The world tree has branches reaching up to the sky and belonging to God and birds. The roots of the tree go deep down into the underworld, into the Serpent's kingdom. The tree trunk extends through the mid-world inhabited by humans and animals.

My comment: The Serpent's Kingdom Nagasta, or Guhadhaamala, lies on the other end of the umbilical cord linking Turkey, India, The Holy Trinity, and Mexico. You'll get undeniable proof in this book.

This tree of life is as eternal as God himself, and you cannot see as you will never be able to see God.

According to legend, the tree of life is a channel for spirits and thoughts to flow from one world to the other. The world tree gives humans the knowledge they need. Could it be that Hamrin was a city of wise men and philosophers? Was it possible that here, in the shade of the world tree, the Kipchaks sought counsel from Tengri? Surrounded as they were by enemies?

Churches were shortly built in Hamrin, followed many decades later by mosques. Whatever went on around, the tree remained the city's main sanctuary. Today it is the site of a village called Kayakent. It has a regular urban plan, and the sacred Tengri Khan tree still grows on its fringe as a reminder of the place's glorious past. The Kumyks living here and beyond do not remember or know much about the tree, but they have a very deep respect for that tree growing in Kayakent.

Another representation of The Holy Trinity is a mountain, especially if it has two smaller mountains beside it. These sacred mountains are generally called *Meru, Peru, Beru*, but not always. A single mountain becomes a *Shivalinga*. The Egyptian word for mountain is *M'ru*. There are two smaller pyramids beside it. Here in Southwestern United states, the O'odham Indians have their own Meru, with two nearby peaks. However, in this case, they call it *Babo-Quivari* (Grandfather on our Mother's Side-Khyber/Hibori). In Turkish and Sanskrit, the equivalent of that name is *Baba-Khyber/Hibori,* meaning the Pope or Supreme Priest of All Mankind, the Phoenicians and Jews, a.k.a. The Turks and Hindus. Baboquivari is, indeed, an American representation of Mt. Meru.

In India, Kubera and God Shiva supposedly live inside Mt. Meru. However, the O'odhams depict Kubera as being the mountain itself. I'itoi, or Sewa as he is also called, lives within Baboquivari. Meru, Peru, and Beru also mean "Golden Mountain." Baboquivari has so much gold in it that nearly all the gold panned in

Southern Arizona leaks out of the Baboquivari mountain range. The O'odhams told me that anyone who tries to take gold out of the mountain itself, instead of contenting himself with what leaks out of it, will be either killed outright or doomed to a life of tragedy and shame.

I have to admit that I am drawn to Baboquivari as if it were a magnet. It fills my heart with awe. I visit it whenever I get the opportunity. Even the Whites living in Southern Arizona regard it in awe and reverence.

About Duality.

God or Creation requires that we mentally and physically emulate Nature's cycles from activity to repose, at every single moment of our lives. In my daily walks in the desert every day, when the sun starts rising, I observe the Joshua trees. I envision them as the Lingam or "Father." Its "semen" forms the branches, leaves and the beautiful white flowers that soon dry up and fall to the ground as seed, perpetuating constantly the regenerative process. I even do this when I observe the telephone posts transferring energy to the rest of the posts down the line. When I finished this paragraph, I decided to go to the kitchen for a drink of water. I turned on the kitchen lights, making the light become The Male Principle. The kitchen then became bathed in light, becoming The Female Principle.

A friend recently asked me: "If the *Kristi* is "The Heavenly Father" and the *Kristis* is "The Earthly Son," what place do we women have in this scheme of things?"

I told her that depending on whether we are giving and receiving, we are both male and female. If someone extends me some courtesy on the freeway, he becomes The Male Principle and I The Female Principle. If I am swimming and start drowning, and a woman life guard dives in to save me, she becomes the Male and I the Female. Let's suppose a man and his wife are both teaching a class of students. Both of them become The Single Male Principle and the students become The Single Female Principle. We may be physically male and female, but in regard to spirituality, we are all androgynous.

> Simon Peter said to them, "Let Mary leave us, for women are not worthy of life."
> Jesus said, "I myself shall lead her in order to make her male, so that she too may become a living spirit resembling you males. For every woman who will make herself male will enter the kingdom of heaven." (Thomas Saying 114.)

In the Thomas Gospel, the human body is regarded as an animated corpse. It is just dirt and water. The spirit is the only reality. At all times, people are in motion and repose, or giving and receiving. Spiritually, there is no difference between men and women.

Karma.

Since we all live eternally, we must at all times remember that we reap what we sow. The harvest is called Karma. What I do to others I also do to myself. If I commit an evil or violent act, I become The Evil Male Principle. Because as a physical human being I am the Son of the Father, the Father naturally takes measures to punish anyone who does evil and unseemly things to any of his Sons. Somewhere along the line, I must become the Evil Female Principle and let an Evil Male Principle ravish and harm me-or, I must suffer in some other horrible way. It is the Law of the Universe. It is the *Tao*. This is why humans should always be kind and good to all beings on this earth and to Mother Earth herself. If I take trash out in the desert and deposit it there, I am actually raping Mother Earth without her permission. Someday and somewhere, I'll have to pay the price.

When I was in Nichiren Shoshu Buddhism, we were taught that when someone treats us favorably, we always must reciprocate in some way, in order to keep a favorable balance between us. It is a fundamental tenet of Buddhism that when someone does me some good act or service, I must reciprocate as soon as possible. If not, I'll always have a karmic debt with him.

Sometimes, we help people out of some difficulty when they cannot promptly return such a favor. The person receiving help can repay his karmic debt by helping someone else.

The day before I worked on this part of the chapter, a Mexican friend who can't speak English asked me to go to the City Building and arrange for the building inspector to go to his home and inspect his newly built patio. When I returned, his wife insisted on serving me a delicious plate of beans, chicken, rice, and tortillas. I gladly accepted. Not only did I enjoy a tasty repast, but I also let them pay their karmic debt. Naturally, when I received the meal, I became the Female Principle. That meant that I then had to pay back the debt either to them or to someone else. We are never free of our mutual debts to one another. It is like a gigantic wheel. Round and round it goes, and where it stops nobody knows.

Jesus said that he came to this world to divide people; not to unite them. This is as it should be, for if God favors any one religious organization over another to force people to conduct themselves correctly, the Laws of Karma could not possibly exist. If the clerics of a certain religious sect in Afghanistan decide to execute a man for having converted to Christianity, they are inventing their own conterfeit Laws of Karma. They, not the man they intended to kill, would fall within the judgement of the Laws of Karma. The Laws of Karma were not created by mortals. Therefore, God does not recognize theocracies. Naturally, such Divine Ecumenicalism would divide sectarian people who can not see that God is for everybody.

How does the principle of Duality work when a beggar wants a handout? That depends. All of us have received the gift of life. Life demands that we emulate God which is Creation. If I am young and capable of creating (working) and giving (becoming the husband or phallus), but I just want to receive, like a female prostitute, I upset Natural Balance and must suffer the consequences. As for the person who gives alms to a hale and hearty beggar, he angers the Father. The Father wants his Son to grow up to self-sufficiency. He will turn on the person who seeks to spoil and ruin his Son.

Naturally, the Father smiles upon anyone who will befriend, feed, and help a son who is truly in need, such as elderly and handicapped people.

People are surprised to find out that Hindu Shiva-ism condones capital punishment. The Father frowns on people who want to be merciful and kind to those who have murdered and raped his Sons. The Father sees them as working in collusion with such evil people. He says, "Such people themselves are not worthy of kindness. Man lives forever anyway. Why won't they make it possible for him to leave this Hell he has made for himself and begin life all over again? If they will not do this, I will visit upon them the same karma as the evil people they want to protect."

What about such practices as abortion? The Buddhists say that a spirit seeking rebirth looks for a suitable couple who are copulating. If it desires the male in the act of copulation, it will be born as a male. If it desires the female, it will be born as a woman. I will leave it up to your conscience to decide whether a fetus is human.

How about homosexuality? I prefer to let the homosexuals define themselves; not me.

If any of my readers understand that both men and women must always practice the Male Principle at all of times, which consists of always protecting and nurturing the Son of the Father, what will this constant practice do for them? The answer should be obvious. They will start climbing Jacob's Ladder again.

An Easy Way to Understand Exactly What Karma Is.

The word "androgynous" means "both male and female." Physically, people don't always appear androgynous. But if you examine people closely, you'll see that they are physically androgynous to a degree. A male usually doesn't have protruding breasts. A woman has protruding breasts, but inside her vagina, one sees a tiny penis called "clitoris." Where the Holy Spirit is concerned, both males and females are entirely androgynous. And this is where Karma manifests itself. If a person demonstrates the Good Male Principle, he must become later on the Good Female Principle. If he demonstrates the Bad Male Principle, he becomes later on The Bad Female Principle. If he is inconsistent and irregular in the polarities of Male and Female Principles, he becomes later on, in both bad and good ways, variations of the opposite. "Pay Back Time" is not always immediately reflexive. Sometimes it can be accumulative and retroactive.

How long will it take the practitioner of the Dual Principle to return to the lofty status of Spiritual Man or Woman? That, also, depends on how faithfully and constantly one practices. A person who sinks his whole being into the practice may attain Divine Status in a few years. Those who are careless and insincere in the practice, occasionally or frequently falling by the wayside, may need hundreds of lifetimes and blood-dripping Karma before freeing themselves of the Hell in which most humans now find themselves. The practice is like anything else. You get as much back as you put into it. Practice this until it becomes a conditioned reflex.

We read a lot about the ineffectiveness of psychologists and psychiatrists. People having mental afflictions should know that by constantly practicing Tao or Duality in their daily lives, they can ultimately become mentally stable again.

Why Does Conscious and Constant Practice in Searching For the Male and Female Principles in Everything We Do and Say Strengthen and Expand Us Mentally and Spiritually?

The human mind works simultaneously at a conscious and subconscious level. When we were learning how to read, write, and calculate, we repeated the required disciplines over and over until we could perform these operations automatically without thinking about them. For example, people regard me as a good typist. I can type as fast as I want without having to look at the keyboard. When a thought occurs to me while I'm keyboarding, my mind doesn't have to wonder where the tips of my fingers are going to land. In time, after you have practiced diligently for a year or two, you will begin to do it inwardly as well. When that happens, you will be well on your way to imitating the Tao in your daily life and working your way up Jacob's ladder.

The famous mathematician-philosopher, Alfred North Whitehead, wrote, "Civilization advances by extending the number of operations which we can perform without thinking about them."

Aryan Krishtaya spiritual development science doesn't demand that we have gurus, read murky scriptures, or study intricate yogic and other such disciplines. All one needs for spiritual advancement to the highest degree is to practice constantly the science of the Holy Trinity, the Cross, and develop within one's self the ability to recognize duality in all things and within one's own being. This is really not hard to do. I hope you will agree.

To keep ourselves aware at all times of the Triple Alliance and Duality, we not only observe closely all that goes on around us, determining whether it is the Father or the Son, Male or Female, we can wear the symbols, in order to keep ourselves reminded of all times that we have a sacred duty to perform in this world. In the Catholic Church, members remind themselves of this during mass and in their daily lives by making the sign of the Cross with their hands. All this may seem irrational to the uninitiated, but Nature is getting the message, and she strengthens us to grow spiritually.

Many people criticize the fact that Catholics wear crucifixes with the effigy of Jesus Christ affixed to them. Is this paganism? It is not in any way paganism. Such a crucifix is a powerful reminder that there is no way on earth for any of us to escape from the Cross.

According to the ancient Krishtaya, the sacred word *Akristi* was more powerful than the Hindu sacred syllable *AUM.* Those who chanted this sacred word while thinking of or looking at a Cross were said to be able to attain anything they wanted.

The Circumstances Making the Ancient World Aware of The Power of The Cross.

Murad Adj tells how the Turks taught Europe about the power of The Cross. Mr. Adj's free online book is of such importance to the world, I had to fight the temptation to quote most of it. Therefore, if he mentions certain individuals or nations with which you are unacquainted, I advise you to do some independent investigation.

A Christian soothsayer, Gregory, had a vision of a fiery column, with a cross on top of it, rising to the sky. The cross radiated bright light, exactly like a lightning.

At the time, the Armenians held little faith in the salvational power of the cross-they were still pagans. They did remember well, however, the cross-spangled banners the Kipchaks had fought under and were struck by coincidence-Saint Gregory saw a similar cross in the sky. Was it a sign of God?

"The Turkis must be helped by their God of Heaven," the Armenians decided.

Rumour about the Turkis' all-powerful God swept across Europe like wild fire. News of it was carried far and wide by Christians. They spread Jesus Christ's prophetic words of horsemen who would liberate the world from Rome's rule. You can read this prophesy in the Apocalypse, one of Christians' most revered books. It was looked to with hope. People would read every line time and again, relating the prophetic words to what was happening around them. There was a complete match. Everything was turning out exactly as the man called Christ had said.

"The prophecy has been fulfilled. Now wait," St. Gregory addressed his followers, after he had seen the shining cross of Tengri in the sky. Weren't those words why Armenians called the Saint Gregory the Illuminator?

Victory was round the corner. Bide your time and wait, was the message.

The Turkis, of course, did not know, or even guess, what was happening in Europe at the time, until a young Armenian priest who came to them told them all. The Armenian's name was Gregoris, he was a grandson of St. Gregory the Illuminator, and he was only sixteen years old. Gregoris made a low bow and asked, in broken Turkic, for a meeting with the Kipchak king.

Doesn't the Holy Book tell us, "What Tengri says will be"?

Why did the young Bishop Gregoris come to see the khan and what did he ask for? No, it was not military assistance.

This time, the Armenians were asking to be taught how to win. They (both pagans and Christians) wanted to adopt faith in the God of Heaven who had made the Turkis invincible. Christian Bishop Gregoris was the first European to come to the Turkis to learn about the faith in Tengri so he could then teach it to his people. In fact, he wanted to follow the example of Gheser and Khan Erke, this time in Europe...

The Kipchaks' arrival at the boundaries of the Roman Empire and their brilliant victory over Iran impressed all, Christians above all. The Kipchaks were on everybody's lips-they were too outlandish to go unnoticed. Their iron armour and weapons made them look out of a different world in the Europeans' eyes. And they really were-from the bright world under the high sky of Tengri.

Heathen Europe looked at them bottom-up, like a foot soldier does at a horseman. Europe lost to the Turkis on all counts, the principal of which was faith in God-really an asset it lacked conspicuously, in God who gave the Turkic people plenty of iron and an ability to make the most of it.

A simple example will emphasize the importance of iron. A well-landed blow with an iron sword could cut a bronze one in two. In other words, Roman troops had no arms to resist the Kipchaks. Like prehistoric men with nothing else but wooden clubs.

You can say whatever and however you like about the collapse of the Roman Empire, put forward any hypotheses and make any guesses. All discussion would be a waste of time unless you consider this simple fact.

Turkic Tengri stood for iron and Rome's Jupiter symbolized bronze. The Kipchaks were to win inevitably, just as iron was superior to bronze. The Roman Empire was doomed, fully at the mercy of the Kipchaks, if and when they cared to finish it off.

The Armenians would not send Bishop Gregoris for nothing. They were probably the only Europeans who made the correct guess about the course of future events, and did whatever they could to distance themselves from Rome on its deathbed, even if not dead yet.

These were the reasons that brought the teenage bishop to Derbent. He was baptised there (ary-sili or ary-alkyn in Turkic) by immersion in water blessed by a priest holding a silver cross over it three times.

My Comment: Notice that word Ary. It means Aryan or the "Aryan Baptism."

Baptism with water is a key rite of the Tengri worship. In fact, initiation into the faith or, in other words, into the Turkic world. Baptism originated in the Ancient Altai where newborn babies were dipped in ice-cold water before they entered into the realm of the Eternal Blue Sky. (The baptismal bath made a child tiurk, which the Chinese translated as "strong" or "robust".)

Another ancient Turkic word, aryg, meant "pure" in spirit. It was applied to a person that had gone through a cleansing ceremony.

The use of water for baptism goes back to the Ancient Altai, among people who cared for their bodily and spiritual purity. Today, introduction of baptism is ascribed to Christians or to some other creed. It is completely wrong. Early Christians could not use baptism for the simple reason that Europe first learned about the ritual with the arrival of Kipchaks. This is an indisputable fact that is not covered up by Christian historians themselves. Baptisteries, or basins to have Christians baptised, were first built in the 4th century.

As added evidence, Tibetans, who adhere to traditions of faith in Tengri, still perform ary-alkyn and ary-sili rites.

The Armenian bishop was, therefore, the first European to be admitted to the faith in Tengri. That was the Turkis' own way, full of spiritual symbolism, to express their relation to alliance with the West. Gregoris was baptised in a lake, Aji or Lake Cross, near the village of Kayakent.

Turkic priests took the spiritually pure Gregoris to Hamrin where he was initiated into the mystery of the World Tree. He was shown the Turkis' sacred texts, in particular, Tengri's covenants, which have, as far as can be judged by fragments, been incorporated in the Koran. And then, following an admission ceremony, he was allowed to join together the thumb and fourth finger of his right hand, a godly sign of reconciliation.

In Oriental symbolism, the two joined fingers signified allegiance to Heaven. They were then lifted to the forehead, lowered to the chest, raised again to the left shoulder and then the right shoulder. The Turkis used this gesture to ask the God of Heaven for protection and patronage. (Bishop Gregoris was thus the first Christian who made the sign of the cross.)

Early Christians did not cross themselves, being unaware of the force of the cross, and they adopted this practice from the Kipchaks.

Gregoris told his hosts of Christ, whom he worshipped, about Europe and persecution of Christians. The Turkis believed him, accepting Christ for the Son of the God of Heaven, because they knew of other sons of Tengri, in particular, Gheser, the Turkic people's Prophet. Gheser is extolled in a prayer, which is very brief and emotional.

"We gave you Gheser, so say your prayers to God...." This is a phrase from Tengri's Testament. (Today, it makes up Sura 108 of the Koran.) The East still remembers these words, even though the meaning of Gheser (Kawsar or Kewser) is not clear to all.

Gregoris spent a long time learning the mysteries of divine service. Turkis helped him to set up a Christian church in Derbent. (Many years later, it was renamed Albanian Church, after a new country in the Caucasus, Albania, Gheser being probably one of its cities.)

Armenia was the first country in Europe to have a new Christian church in 301. The Armenian church accepted Tengri and adopted His cross. And more, Armenians borrowed the principles of divine service from the Turkis. (Previously, Christians had no rite of their own and followed Judaic practices in synagogues.)

Armenians also were the first defectors from the old practices, causing ire and indignation in Rome. In response, Emperor Diocletian unleashed his notorious persecutions of new Christians.

No Christian was, however, frightened by executions and banishment. The new faith acquired growing numbers of followers instead. The seeds of Turkic culture sprouted into plentiful shoots on the barren soil of heathen Rome. Indeed, no one can defy the omnipotence of the God of Heaven.

Now, the various peoples comprising the Roman Empire talked without fear about the helplessness of the old gods. They openly rejected Jupiter, crushed Mercury's statues and smashed idols. "What Tengri says will be."

In the end, Rome saw light as well. At one time, Emperor Diocletian wanted to convert to new Christianity, but took fright at the last minute. In desperation he abdicated and left the imperial palace. A wise politician, he realised that he had lost to the Turkis.

He was defeated without ever engaging the Turkis on the battlefield.

On his departure exactly, the Roman Empire gave way, without war or catastrophe. It ceased to be so self-assured and believe in itself, the greatest of earthly sins.

The Turkis conferred a high, indeed very high, honour upon the head of the Armenian Church, giving him the title of katylic, which is "ally" or "initiated" in Turkic. This title, modified to Catholicos over centuries (with the Greek ending "-os" added on later), has been retained to our day.

Why did the Turkish Tengri Cross and Religion Disappear?

An aggressive religion conquered the Turkish nations a few hundred years after the crucifixion of Christ. It did not permit people to honor and revere sacred icons representing divine natural archetypes. For them, Cross symbolism was idolatry; the Holy Trinity became anathema. When the new religion swept over Central Asia, the Tengri religion, the original Krishtaya, died painfully in a holocaust of fire and bloody sword play. However, I have read that some Turks still keep the religion alive in secret. Don't let that word Tengri dismay you. It does not represent a pagan idol. It is just another word for *Hodai/Khodai,* from which we derived the word "God." The other Turkic word, "Bogh," is commonly used in Central Asian countries and in Northern India. Murad Adji is not lying to us. We know that non-Italians were dominant in the Roman army before it fell to the so-called "barbarians." We call them Goths, Ostrogoths, Visgoths, Alans, Vandals, Celts, and other names. The Turks referred to themselves collectively as Kipchaks, Kurus, or Aryans. After Christ's crucifixion, the Greek and Turkic Apolloites, convinced that our Jesus Christ was an incarnation of Apollo by all of his names, such as Keder or Keser, converted almost overnight. When that happened, the infant Christianity became divided into two main groups: The type of Christianity forming the present Roman and Orthodox Catholicism, and the type that the Goths, Ostrogoths, Visigoths, Celts, etc., understood to be the Aryan Son of God, Apollo, Keder, or Keser. Check your religious history books to confirm what I have just stated. That branch of Christianity was known as Arianism, or Aryanism, as it should've been spelled in the first place. English is a strange language. Just a different letter, though it stands for the same sound, can lead people astray. In Spanish, one gets a better idea of what "Y" is: *I-Griega* (Greek I).

I hope that pious Christians will be broad-minded enough to accept what Murad Adji has to say about the combining of Judeo-Christian and Tengri religious practices. He has history on his side. We should pay attention to him. The world is having a difficult time right now. The truth will make us all free.

Will some power come along someday and yank the Cross away from us as it was torn out of the hands of our Turkish brethren? Not if there is there any truth to that popular song of Christians everywhere! Here are a few excerpts:

Onward, Christian soldiers, marching as to war,
with the cross of Jesus going on before.
Christ, the royal Master, leads against the foe;
forward into battle see his banners go!
Crowns and thrones may perish, kingdoms rise and
wane, but the church of Jesus constant will remain.
Gates of hell can never against that church prevail;
we have Christ's own promise, and that cannot fail.
Onward then, ye people, join our happy throng,
blend with ours your voices in the triumph song.
Glory, laud, and honor unto Christ the King,
this through countless ages men and angels sing.

Not Even The Most Educated of Clerics Understand The Significance of The Holy Trinity!

The analytical psychologist Carl Jung's father was a Protestant minister. Yet, his father knew absolutely nothing about the mystery he was supposed to teach to his congregation. Jung wrote in his *Memories, Dreams, Reflections:*

> One day I was leafing through the catechism...I came upon the paragraph on the Trinity. Here was something that challenged my interest: a oneness that was simultaneously a threeness. This was a problem that fascinated me because of its inner contradiction. I waited longingly for the moment when we would reach this question. But when we got that far, my father said, "We now come to the Trinity, but we'll skip that, for I really understand nothing of it myself." (pp. 52-63.)

A Popular Salvadoran Folk Tale About The Holy Trinity.

My next-door Salvadoran neighbor and friend, Mauricio Velásquez, said that his grandmother told him a popular folk tale in his country.

One day, a certain priest was walking along the shore of a Salvadoran beach called *El Obispo* (The Bishop). He was trying to make himself understand the full significance of The Holy Trinity.

Suddenly, he came upon a little boy who was poking a hole in the sand. He said, "My son, why are you doing that?"

The child answered, "I'm punching this hole because I want to drain the entire ocean into it."

The priest responded, "But my son, that is impossible."

The child said, "You're correct. And likewise it is impossible for mere mankind to know the full meaning of The Holy Trinity." After saying that, the little boy disappeared instantly, before the priest's eyes.

What would atheists say about all that Mr. Murad Adji and I have said thus far? Do they think that The Holy Trinity is just a silly superstition? Will it someday disappear as that little boy did? Do they think that if they shut their eyes and stop up their ears, Christ will go away soon? I think not. He has been with us since the beginning of the world! He will be here until the end as well.

14

The Brain and Spinal Cord Are Receptors and Processors of Solar Energy.
(Cross Science 102)

The problem about Life Energy emanating from the sun and Outer Space in general is that people can't usually see or feel it. Therefore, they think it is non-existent. However, if they could be made to see and feel the mind-boggling amounts of radiation and solar energy battering all of us night and day, many people might die of fright. For example, if mankind could find a way to capture just enough solar energy in a coffee cup, he could make all the oceans of the world boil over! There are elements of solar energy that mankind has not even discovered yet. By using light correctly, we could heal all diseases, rejuvenate old bodies, make plants grow without water, energize the minds of all humans sufficiently to turn idiots into geniuses, run automobiles and airplanes without fuel, turn ordinary dirt into metals many times stronger than steel, and help us live for hundreds of years as Noah and the patriarchs of old did. I am not stating an opinion, but an actual fact.

Here's something that I'll bet you haven't yet been told in Sunday School and biology class. Nighttime is not just for snoozing and early evening love-making. It is the time when we humans must recharge the batteries storing our life energy, just as we recharge cell phones, fuel cells, and other kinds of equipment requiring electrical power. We're not supposed to be out dancing and carousing around, drinking booze and watching sports events on TV, or working all night in some factory. Nighttime is for getting recharged!

If I were to explain this concept to you as the Hindus understand it, leaving it at that, you would probably want to put me in a strait-jacket and lock me up for my own safety. I'll just quote a few passages from Dr. Pande's "geography book," to give you an idea of what I'm referring to.

> The Sun-dynasty is such a riddle that the meaning which is conceived is that the Ikshwakus and their capital city of Ayodhya is shining like the almighty sun at the top. This symbolizes the ever-shining city of Ayodhya. The sun does not see tomorrow. It has been said in the Rigveda. Due to the creation of the earth, the sun's light makes a horizon which is always moving toward the west. The union with the light and darkness has been curiously conceived as a fight going on between these two. In a symbolic way, the king of Ayodhya rules on the earth like that of the sun in the heaven. The geographical accounts are connected with the astronomical riddle all over the world e.g. the word 'Ra' in Egypt means sun. Raja title for the king in India is the same as Rex in Italy. All these titles are related with the sun. Sun's rays are mostly associated with the north and south Tropics of Cancer and Capricorn, in Sanskrit, Uttarayana and Dakshinayana.
>
> Ayodhya, connected with the Ramayana makes unity in between north and south in the manner as we see one thing by two eyes with the help of spinal cord (the Merudana in Sanskrit) in the bodies of living beings like that of the Meru Mountain on the earth....
>
> God Rama is also known as Ramachandra.

My comment: The Epic, Ramayana, is actually a history book, hidden in strange mythological terms, telling how mankind, with the help of Heber and Phaleg, left Mt. Meru and settled the world. Rama represents Mt. Meru. Chandra (the moon and stars) represents Mt. Kumeru, in the Western Hemisphere. Kumeru can be no other mountain except Mt. Orizaba in Mexico's state of Veracruz. The word Veracruz is supposedly a Spanish term, meaning "Where the Cross was seen." Rama, or Mt. Meru, is where the movement from the Eastern Hemisphere passes eternally over Mt. Orizaba (Kumeru or Citlaltepec) in Southern Mexico because Chandra (Moon) symbolizes the place where the Turks (Nagas) and Hindus first landed in the New World.

Dr. Pande confirms my comments:

> It is only to associate sun with the moon. Likewise, the 'Singh' title for the king in India, introduced later on, has not come out from the forest, as it was the strongest animal, but it is associated with the sky as the group of stars 'Singh Rashi,' the lion. Still better example we see...where the stars are appointed as soldiers. Similarly the riddle of the sun assumed as sitting on the 7 horses should be compared with the Rigveda symbol 'Ashva' meaning ('A'-No and 'Shva'=tomorrow) no tomorrow. The sun is always shining. Therefore, it may be realized that the yesterday, today and tomorrow are meaningless words on the surface of the sun. Nowadays, the television sets are

propagating this view. Even a child at night beholds the match going on in the day light somewhere else on this very earth at the same time. The seven colours from the rays of the sun have been scientifically proved, which are shown also by the flowers which have been the cause for beauty and bliss. It seems that people have stolen smile from the flowers. Thus, peace and unity may well be associated with the almighty sun or God Rama or nature. Now we shall see how this smiling nature comes to help the humanity for peaceful life through the democracy. In politics of the day whatever be the cause for increasing percentage in the demoralized activities all over the world, it will be reduced if the source study based on the geographical astronomical and spiritual aspects is grasped by every person. (pp. 68-69 *in passim.*)

…the spinal cord is symbolized as the Meru mountain in the Vedic hymn 'Devanam pu' which also points out that the human body becomes the main source of expansion of culture. The body is representing the sun, Ayodhya and the Meru mountain. Man's movement causes an ever-changing horizon in every direction. Sun's horizon is moving toward the west. Meru mountain's horizon is static. But, as soon as the body moves, it combines the three strands-geographical, astronomical and spiritual-in a beautiful manner.

Ayodhya was safe as its position was on the 'roof of the world' identified as Meru Mountain on the earth and in the body on the uppermost portions. Like 'Atharvaveda' in the Manusmrita, Vishnu and Shiva have been shown in residing in the human body. These two examples are the roots of the democratic form of government in the world. Everyone's life, thus, becomes the epic Ramayana….

We have seen that the Atharvaveda and the Science of String, 'Tantra Shastra' have rightly explained the history of cultural and democratic expansion of the ancient city of Ayodhya. The point of confusion was only the separation of Meru from Ayodhya and understanding the symbolic as well as condensed form of Kailash mountain and the Earth for Meru mountain as conceived by the Science of String or the Tantra Shastra.

In order to understand the culture and democracy we have to analyse that the geographical static Meru mountain has been equated with the static and ever-shining almighty sun or the Vedic 'Ashva' meaning 'no tomorrow.' Thus the real realizations of the all pervading God of all the religions can well be visualized by eyes, hearts and minds. This point will harmonise the differences of views becoming mythical 'Ashwa' meaning horse with apparent movement, equated with the dynamic human spinal cord. We should not be dissatisfied with such mythical expressions but keep in mind that the truth is emphasized by nature, teaching a lesson to the humanity to establish a strong centre which may equal the capital cities politically…

My comment: Pay particular attention to what he said about "mythical expressions." Nature or God speaks no words. Just Man. God broadcasts these strange images to our minds. Soon or later, certain individuals learn that these archetypes are a type of foreign language. Additionally, these archetypes are the same in all religions and cultures except one. The "exception" regards these archetypes as "idolatrous." I've heard Christians say the same thing. If people could understand that mythological expressions are the Original Words of God, mankind could progress more than he has, especially in the social sciences. The author mentioned Science of String. Science of String was derived from Hindu mythological sources.

> ...it is our pious duty to protect ourselves while going towards the horizon, periphery, south or depth because due to the vast and uncontrollable expansion these areas are not so protective as the centre...(pp. 70-71 *in passim.*)

The following is an illustration provided by Dr. Pande, showing how the energy of the sun enters the brain and moves down the spinal cord when we have our heads and spinal cords properly aligned while we're sleeping.

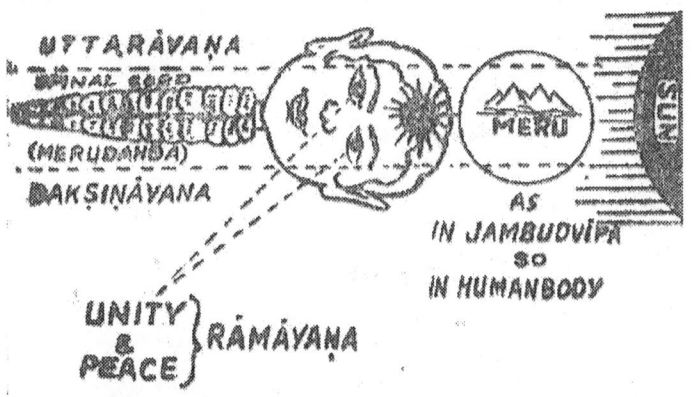

Fig. 2. Dr. Pande's illustration shows how all life energy from the sun enters the brain, moves down through the spina lcord and continues westward, entering the brain and spine of anyone lying correctly in the Sacred Directions. As it moves along, it throws its rays toward the North and South. The western coordinate of the movement of this energy is Mt. Orizaba, in Mexico!

Dr. Pande is trying to show us that a powerful energy constantly moves around the world from East to West, by day and by night, millennium after millennium-forever. This energy extends thousands of miles in both Outer and Inner Space; East and West; up and down; round and round. If people align themselves with it when they are sleeping or just lying in bed, it will eventually unite in peace and harmony as many people on earth who will obey Natural Law as God or Nature intended. The greater number of humans who obey and live by this Natural Law (Tao), the more united in peace and harmony they become. They will be attuning themselves to the Source of All Life. Finally, fewer wars. Less violence. Less crime. Less hunger and suffering. Less unhappiness. And if all humans aligned themselves correctly while sleeping? We'd probably return to Eden.

I find it strange that most humans think nothing of picking up a cell phone and calling friends and relatives, some of whom are on the other side of the world. Yet, they poke fun at the idea that the life energy of the sun is sweeping around the world 24 hours a day, and that it, too, communicates with mankind in its own way. How can they be so conceited as to think that God can't communicate with them in the same way, and even on a much superior and more powerful level?

They cannot ackowledge the reality of this Divine Energy because it doesn't speak to them in words. Dr. Pande said that this is the very energy that caused world civilization to develop from East to West. We will now put his statement to the test, to see if what he says are just the ravings of a congenital crackpot or is advice that we should all take seriously. See the following map:

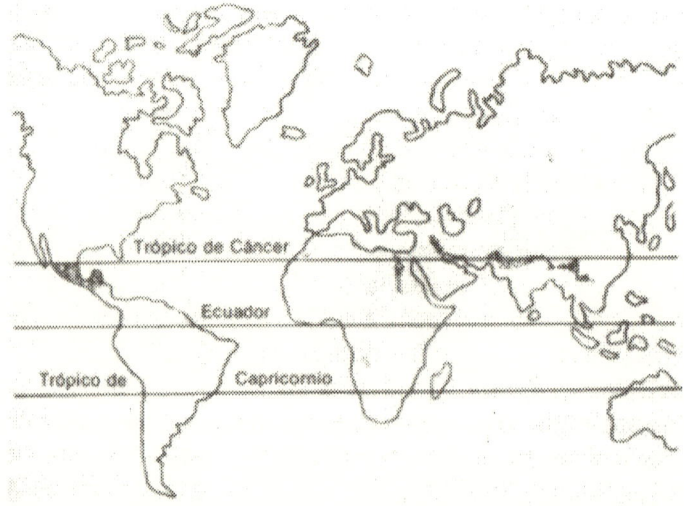

Fig. 3. Civilization always follows the sun and the trade winds. Wherever it takes root, it then fans out from north to south, just as the sun's rays do.

As Dr. Pande said, "Sun's rays are mostly associated with the north and south Tropics of Cancer and Capricorn, in Sanskrit, Uttarayana and Dakshinayana."

Notice that Mexico and Guatemala are marked in black on the map,. This is what Dr. Pande was calling *Chandra* (Moon) or Mt. Orizaba, Mexico. It is here that the Turkish and Hindu Nagas (Snakes) first delivered civilization to the Americas. Some skeptics or critics may say that it is just a coincidence that civilization moved from East to West. It is no coincidence. It cannot move in any other way.

I make some fantastic claims in this book, that we rarely get in Sunday School class or in Bible-thumping sermons accompanied by throaty shouts of "Hallelujah." Some people may want to say, "Figure Three just shows where the most favorable trade winds are. The spread of civilization has nothing to do with the movement of solar energy from East to West." Therefore, I will put the ancient Ramayana Path of Unity theory to another test. See the following map:

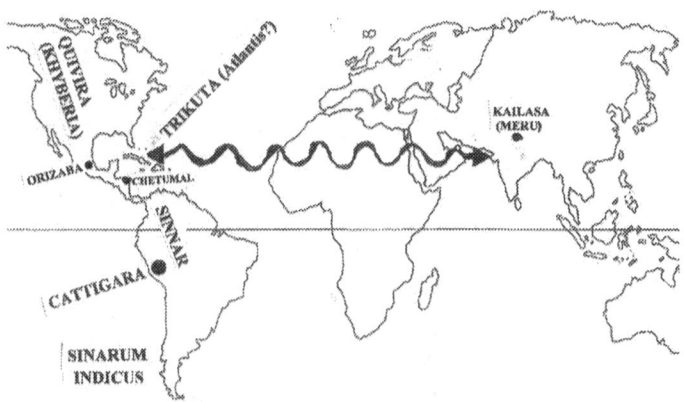

Fig. 4. The greatest concentration of solar energy, symbolically shown as a serpent with a head on each end, passing through Mt. Meru in Western Tibet, and Mt. Orizaba (Citlaltepec), in Veracruz, Mexico.

I have already discussed how Hindu teachers prove to their students that such holy books as the Ramayana are reliable and valid in spite of the cumbersome myths and metaphysical expressions contained in them. They can stand up to scrutiny. The teachers get a world map, folding it at 0° Longitude. Then, they stick a pin through mouth of the Indus or Sarasvati rivers. The pinpoint emerges in the Western Hemisphere in what we now call the Antilles or West Indies, in the Caribbean area.

On the above map, I have illustrated the eternal flow of solar and life energy between those two parts of the world as an undulating line, representing serpent energy. The arrow on each side of the line represents the head of a snake or Naga. This is also how this energy was portrayed by the ancient Aztecs and Mayans. (See the picture of Quetzalcoatl in Chapter Sixteen.) Kailasa (Meru) in Western Tibet is located at 81'10º L. East. Mt. Orizaba (Citlaltepetl) lies at 97'26º L. West. Although Meru and Citlaltepec are not exactly lined up together, they are close enough to show that any disalignment is trivial. But this in itself is not enough proof. I must provide more evidence.

According to the Ramayana, Kubera (really our Heber and Phaleg), who was a Naga, banished many tribes of the most barbaric and savage Rakshasas (lowland Huns) and Pisacas (mountain Huns) to Lanka (Ceylon). Athough tropical Lanka contained ideal conditions for life and happiness, they behaved no better there than they did back in Northern India and Central Asia. In desperation, he and his followers, the Yakshas or Yakhus, who gave their name to Yucatan, transported them to Patala (Meso-America), to what is now the southern coast of Veracruz and Belize. There is a safe port in Belize, next to Mexico's state of Quintana Roo, called *Chetumal.* The Hindu representation of Mt. Meru looks like a flower with four petals representing the four directions, north, south, east, and west. The center of the flower represents Mt. Meru. It is the world's first map of this globe. The left petal points west toward a western coastal area called *Chetumala* or *Ketumala,* which was also supposed to be an ancient port. See the Meso-American Chetumal on the map. In order to keep the Rakshasas and Pisacas from returning to India, and possibly to keep competitors from going to Meso-America, Kubera built his palace on a huge island off the coast of Veracruz, the vestiges of which we now call Greater Antilles or West Indies. This island was called *Trikuta.* The island, plus the surrounding areas, then as now, was called *Antipodes,* derived from the Sanskrit *Anta* (Outer Boundary) + *Pa* (Guard; Protector) + *Deza* (Territory).

According to Hindu mythology, Lanka was an immense territory, stretching nearly all around the world. About 2,000 B.C., when Abraham and Sarah fled to the Middle East, nearly all of Lanka sank under the sea. In the Americas, the only part of Trikuta that we can still see, are the islands we today called Antilles or West Indies. Archeologists will someday discover many ruins at the bottom of the Gulf of Mexico and the Caribbean Sea. (See my *The Last Atlantis Book.*)

The Amerindians told the Spaniards that North America was named *Quivira (Khyberia).* The upper western coast of South America was called *Sinnar,* a term connoting "property of India." The Indians told the Spaniards that the people living in Sinnar were called *Sinu.* Even today, there are tribes in the area called *Sinu, Zeno,* and *Zinyu.* These were the Chimu, Incas, and other highly developed tribes. The ancient maps copied from Ptolemy's world map called what is now the Pacific Ocean, *Oceanus Indicus* and *Mar Sinarum.* The Ptolemy map called the ancient Peruvian ruins of Chan-Chan, *Cattigara.* This word derives from the Sanskrit *Khatti-Gatta,* meaning "Phoenician Quay."

I have much more evidence on hand to buttress my claims that the invisible coils of solar energy flowing between Mt. Meru and Citlaltepetl form "The Ramayana Path of Unity," but I feel what I have stated thus far should be convincing enough.

Although Mt. Kailasa is the world's most sacred mountain, it is in such a cold and inhospitable part of Western Tibet, that only a few people visit it. On the other hand, Citlalteptl (Orizaba) lies in a tropical area, surrounded by ancient Olmec and Mayan ruins, plus many other tourist attractions. I predict that eventually, when the Hindus and Buddhists find out that Citlaltepetl is in fact the fabled mountain *Chandra* (Moon Mountain), that part of Mexico will become one of the most popular places to visit on earth. Because solar energy is more powerful in that area, I predict that many health resorts will be built there.

Everything I have said thus far can have true meaning for all humanity, only if we are willing to accept the fact that *Bel,* or Confusion, is the god of those foolish enough to think that mere words can convey truth. The truth lies only in the archetypes and symbols of solar energy. When we see that this energy, not the names mankind gives to it, is the real god of the world, we humans will someday reduce wars and misunderstandings to non-lethal levels.

How did Dr. Pande come up with his drawing of a human lying with the back of his head facing the East, symbolized by Mt. Meru? He "translated" his drawing into human language as he received it in mythological language from God, which we call archetypes.

By now, you may want to ask: "Is there any other way for mankind to understand that message from God, other than the one Dr. Pande provided? If I start understanding this type of message, I might be classified either as an Anti-Christ or a witch."

Yes, there is another archetypical symbol for recognizing this energy, Remember, I am describing the movement of Universal Life Energy around the world eternally, from East to West. Man's life is fastened to this energy. He is nailed to it, just as Jesus was nailed to the Cross. This energy is the same, for all peoples, of all religions, but not all the names are the same. Don't forget: God just gives the "games." Only humans give the names. If you can accept that fact, then you may be able to accept in your mind what you are about to see next.

Every major religion on earth, and in every known nation and tribe, from the beginning of time, has provided this example for mankind to see and understand. We inherited it from the Turkish Krishtaya Aryan Nephilim when they first arrived on and populated the world. The following is what the followers of the Hindu worshippers of God Krishna often receive:

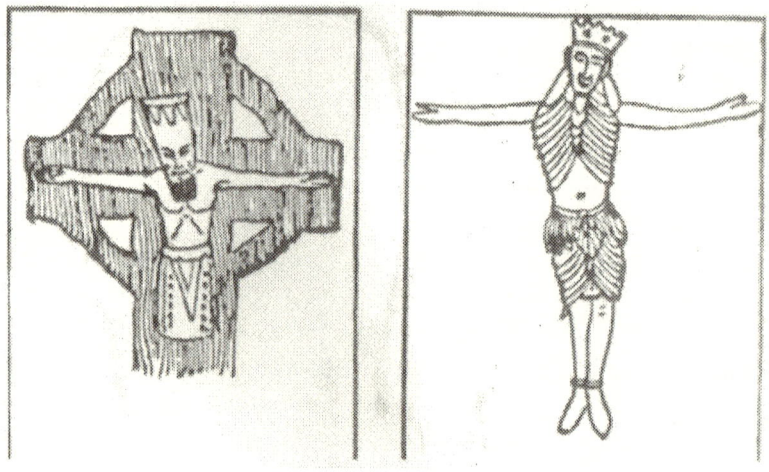

Fig. 5. The Hindu God Krishna.

Have you noticed that the figure at the left is nailed to an Aryan (Turkish) or Celtic Cross? Did you know that these figures existed a thousand or more years before our Jesus Christ was born?

The famous American atheist, Kersey Graves, discussed in detail sixteen crucified saviors in his book, *The World's Sixteen Crucified Saviors*. He listed many more. I will not list them in this book for various reasons. However, as I said at the beginning of this book, I want interested readers to study Graves' book carefully, as well as to discuss these things with educated atheists. It is of utmost importance that they do this, for sooner or later, if we humans are going to progress to our full potential, we'll have to redefine "atheism" to reflect the Sanatana Dharmaist (Hindu) and Buddhist definition of the term.

Fig.6. This plate I copied from Moore's "Hindu Pantheon," called "Krishna's Crucifixion in Space. The editors of Moore's first edition removed this picture from their first edition because they thought it would be too controversial. This one is reproduced from Godfrey Higgins, "Anacalypsis," Vol. II. (1836.) Notice the rays of the sun above Lord Krishna's head. This figure symbolizes the East-West Holy Directions, carrying the energy of Kristi, the Archetypical Father, from Mt. Meru down to where you see the nail holes on his feet, which is Citlaltepetl or Mt. Orizaba, Veracruz, Mexico. According to the ancient Hindu scriptures, the most powerful currents of life energy whirl around the world unceasingly, just like the body of a snake, between the Tropics of Cancer and Capricorn.

I now ask these questions of my atheistic, skeptic, "scientific," and fundamentalist Christian readers: A lot of people go around these days, accusing others of being "Anti-Christs." Who are the real Anti-Christs in this world? Those who say that our Jesus Christ came into this world only once-and no more? And only to the existing 24,000 existing Christian sects on earth? Or those who say he has always been with us, among all peoples and all religions, often with different names, since the beginning of time? Forget about all the idols or "natural archetypes" that Hindus or Sanatana Dharmaists worship. To know whether the Hindus are our brothers in Christ, consider the following: They adore a Cross which they call Swastika. The pith of their teachings is the Holy Trinity. They know that mankind aligns himself with the Infinite through training his mind to live Duality (real spirituality). They know that all life energy emanates from the sun. Are they our brothers in Christ, or are they not? Is the Cross for all religions and peoples, or is it not? Must they be converted to the Jehovah's Witnesses or the Mormons? After all, their sons and daughters may be doing better in school and in life than yours and mine. You decide.

Bulgarian King Kubera (Heber) and his Yakshas or Yakhus (Phaleg) brought settlers to Mexico and Meso-America, wanting them to civilize themselves and support *Talan,* The Eastern Hemisphere, on their backs as "Guardians and Protectors of the Upper World:" *Patala* (The Western Hemisphere, Land of Buddha, or The Underworld). Therefore, The Western Hemisphere is also known as *Atala(n).* To help my readers understand this concept more easily, I would like to discuss the legend of Atlantis, but I have found out, through experience, that such a discussion always produces losers; not winners. However, I do want to describe what the word "Atlas" really means. It is a compound word derived from both Turkic and Nahuatl. In ancient times, people thought of the continents as floating on water. The Nahuatl word for water is *Atl;* its Turkic equivalent is *Su.* The ancient Turks and Mexicans felt that both their "waters" were holding up the world. Therefore, they combined them as "partners." *Atlasu,* meaning "water on water," eventually became the Greek god Atlas. What I have just stated should give my readers an idea of the tight unity that once linked Turkey, India, and Meso-America.

My discussion thus far gives me the opportunity to prove to the world that the Roman Catholic Church is not so "unscientific" as its enemies and detractors claim. On the contrary, just the opposite. In the past few years, we have noticed that the Vatican is more and more emphasizing the importance of Mexico. The "rationalist" haters of Rome claim confidently that the Church is becoming steadily weakened, wanting to protect its vested interests in Mexico in order to survive. But the Church doesn't need to grasp for a lifeline. It is destined to survive for tens of thousands of years more, just as it has existed since the arrival of the Five Krishtaya tribes with the Nephilim.

The enemies of Catholicism like to poke fun at and criticize the Catholic Crucifix with the body of Christ nailed to it.

Many people cannot accept the idea that all our religious knowledge has come from the Turks and the Hindus. Even the deities have similar names. In order to make the science of the Cross more understandable to those who practice our brand of Christianity, I have used only icons and archetypes that Europoid Christians can understand easily. I said to myself: How would I see this situation if I were a Hindu? I came up with this; I know it to be accurate in every way. I hope this does not make fundamentalists think I'm an Anti-Christ. When our forefathers were chased out of North India, each tribe carried with them a piece of truth. Those who stayed behind also remained with a piece of truth. If we can get all those pieces back (The Hopi Indians insist that there are five pieces needed to solve the riddle), we humans will be much the better for having done so. The spiritual or dual solution does not consist of "killing infidels" or forcing everyone to kiss each other when they'd be happier bloodying their respective adversaries' noses. Just because we call it "spiritual" doesn't mean it isn't "scientific."

Go With the Flow!

In figures 7 and 8 at the left, I am showing Christ hanging on a Cross. But in this case, his back is wrapped around what is called the "World Egg." A snake wrapped around the World Egg could also represent the spinal cord. In this case, I am showing the eternal circumbalatory movement of life energy as a human fastened to a vertical beam (of light) and its arms (light beams) extending North and South as the horizontal beam (of light) Christ's outstretched arms are nailed to the North and South Poles.

Christ's head is placed in the Eastern Hemisphere or Upper World, representing Mt. Meru, the origin of all mankind, and the source of all knowledge and phenomena. The vertical beam represents the spinal cord and the constant flow of universal energy through it.

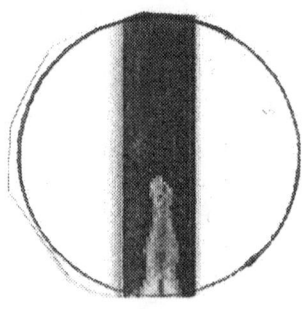

On the backside of the World Egg, we see Christ's feet nailed approximately opposite to the head of Christ on the other side. So where would Christ's feet be nailed symbolically in Mexico? And how do I know his feet are symbolically nailed there? Once again, God's language comes to the rescue. We must remember what Dr. Pande said about the word Ramachandra, meaning Sun-Moon. Mt. Orizaba was also once one of the holiest places in ancient Mexico. The father of God Quetzalcoatl was buried there. Anyone who is conversant with the mythologies of the ancient world can readily identify Quetzalcoatl with the Hindu *Dyaus Nahusha* (Dionysius), God Vishnu, and God Krishna, for the three are the same spiritual being. The Hindu myths say that *Dyaus Nahusha* was turned into a Naga. To where did the mother of the Nagas, Kadru, send her sons? Was it not Mexico?

Did you see the movie, *The Passion of Christ?* When Christ and his disciples were in the Garden of Gethsemane, he crushed a serpent's head beneath his feet. I don't remember reading anything about that in the Bible. Why did the producers show him doing that? They knew that the Buddhist, Turkish and Hindu viewers would understand, sending them a powerful message that was sure to result in long lines of Buddhists, Turks and Hindus wanting to see that movie. You may not want to accept what I say, but that serpent represented the Nagas living in Southeastern Mexico!

Most modern Mexicans may not know that Christ's feet are symbolically nailed on Vera Cruz's Mt. Orizaba, the third largest mountain in North America. It, Mt. Ararat, Mt. Meru, and Adam's Peak, in Sri Lanka, possibly others in the world, are the world's most sacred mountain peaks. The Aztecs and Nahuatl-speaking people called Mt. Orizaba *Citlaltepetl,* meaning "Mountain of the Stars." This would conform to Dr. Pande's description of the connection between Rama (the sun) and Chandra (the moon). I have already stated in my discussion of the Toltecs and Aztecs that the Virgin of Guadalupe is also the ancient Innan of the Sumerians. The Sumerians were Turks. The Virgin of Guadalupe even wears the same colors of vestments that the Aztec Mother Goddess did. Remember, like you, I am not insane enough to think that Jesus Christ himself as a physical person is wrapped around the center of the world, between the Tropics of Cancer and Capricorn. If I truly thought that, I myself would seek refuge in a padded cell in the nearest insane asylum and have "Anti-Christ" tattooed on my forehead. All I am doing is visualizing "Christ" as the maximum force of life energy circulating around the spine of the world-the space between the Tropics of Cancer and Capricorn.

Here is another way to visualize this so-called Sanatana-Dharmaist archetype. Picture in your mind a real human brain connected to the spinal column. Now, visualize tha veins and nerves extending outward throughout the body. These veins and nerves are "the rays of the sun" spreading North and South. Now, let us suppose you are religious. You pray gratefully, "God, thank you for giving me the life energy from the sun, enabling me to experience life."

What can possibly be "pagan" and "Anti-Christian" about reverentially worshiping the earth, the sun, the stars, the moon, the deserts, mountains, and all other blessings of existence and the Creations of God. Is not Creation (God) the

Father and Mother of us all? Can we not honor our real Father and Mother? If we cannot reverentially honor our "Father and Mother," protecting them from harm, we have only ourselves to blame for all the troubles on this earth, the damage done to it, and the real possibilities of a future destructive Great Flood or other catastrophe that may destroy all that we have accomplished and send us back to primitivity. Always honor your father and mother-both temporal and eternal.

If what I have said is not yet sufficient to convince you that Christ's feet are nailed symbolically, not physically, to Orizaba, I still have more to say in this chapter and in my special message to the Mexican people.

In Sanskrit, Mt. Orizaba would also be called Kumeru or Meriku, which was their name for Orizaba or Citlaltepetl. It is from this name we derived America.

Naturally, I am not talking about a physical Christ nailed to a wooden Cross. In this case, I am talking about pure solar life energy moving around the world night and day: *Guhadhamaala*. Even the most skeptical of scientists will admit that all life emanates from the sun. Without light, there can be no life.

The vertical beam itself symbolizes a snake, the energy of the sun, or the Primordial Father coiled around the World Egg. When our bodies are aligned correctly at night, the energy of the sun, even at night, recharges our respective spirits through the brain and spinal cord. The disks on the spinal cord are called *Chakras* in Sanskrit. When we are mentally attuned to the *Tao*, behaving and thinking as I described in preceding chapters, our spirits gradually accumulate enough Divine Power to climb back up Jacob's Ladder. As we make the return climb, we acquire new insights and Divine Knowledge which will help us evolve as God intended.

Is The Idea of An Unseen Umbilical Cord a Laughable Superstition?

Mt. Meru, the Tree of Hamrin, or any other similar symbol is another natural archetype. The umbilical cord extends downward into the earth as far as the center of the Earth. The center of the earth is like another sun-a molten mass of extremely high temperatures. This center is the earth's heart, just as the blood red, flaming Sacred Heart of Jesus is his heart. Your own heart is a microscopic version of the heart of the earth and of the heart of our galaxy, which is the sun. Anything that has a heart is also a living being. The invisible umbilical cord (*Guatemala*) passes through the earth's core until it reaches the Navel of The Underworld, which is Mt. Orizaba (*Citlalteptl*), to which Jesus, Surya, Krishna, Indra, Agni (God of Fire), Vishnu or Rama's feet are symbolically nailed.

The "arms" or "rays" of the earth's heart spread out from North to South, symbolized also by a Cross. Just picture a Cross jutting out in four directions from the earth's molten core. The solar power roaring around the surface of the earth constantly also roars through and around its interior as well, making the earth's molten core a kind of axis of a giant wheel of energy. Often, this energy is symbolized as an energy swirl or spiral rising out of the earth's molten core.

If Mother Earth has a "flaming heart of Jesus," we can be sure that she, too, is a living being just like us. What do we do with our Mother Earth? Do we not litter her and damage her any way we can? Do we not fight over pieces of her flesh? Can we be sure that she will not retailiate someday? Or am I just being "superstitious?"

A Message to Those Who Reject What I Have Just Said.

By now, many readers who do not know anything about God's Archetypical Language, and who see the Devil's work in such matters, may be wishing to throttle those of us who know that archetypes are the language of God and say, "How dare you teach a philosophy that was also a mainstay of Mithraism, Apolloism, Krishnaism, and all the other two or three dozen ancient crucified sun-gods. You heretics are Anti-Christs."

The Bible tells us exactly how to recognize the Anti-Christ:

> This is Antichrist, who denies the Father and the Son…Every Spirit that dissolves Jesus is Antichrist…(John 1:2:22 and 4:3.)

This is my answer to those who think I'm some kind of "Anti-Christ:"

Have I denied or affirmed the Father and the Son in this book? Have I tried to dissolve Jesus or make him more visible? All I have done is declare that Christ is as much a Christian as he is a Jew, Buddhist or Hindu. Look around you; see how today's world is floundering in wars, tears, and tragedy. Are you willing to allow religious provincialism, ignorance and stubbornness to blow it out of the solar system? If you are, look to yourself as the Anti-Christ; not to those of us who insist that all the sun gods of mankind, by whatever name, are Jesus Christ. What can possibly be wrong with a universal spiritual or dual solution to the problems of the world? This is the only solution capable of working. Don't let the words Mithra, Kukulkan, Surya, Rama, Shiva, Vishnu, etc., blind you to reality. That energy concentrated between the Tropics of Cancer and Capricorn is none other than the archetype of the original Krishtis-our own Jesus Christ.

You may want to ask me: "If what you say is true, why do the same horrible conditions under which mankind lived in the past still exist?"

There is no question easier to answer than that. What I have told you did not help ancient mankind because he was just as rebellious and irascible then as now. The Great Flood and the dispersal at Mt. Meru weren't enough inducement for him to love God sufficiently to improve himself, just as they are not now. Hardly anyone in those days was "going by the rules." The solution which I recommend, and which God guarantees "or your money back," will work when, and only when, men humbly surrender to the Will of God.

That the Panchala Krishtayas brought the ancient Mexicans the Religion of the Turkish God Tengri, there is no doubt. Murad Adji said that the Turk's World Tree extended downward symbolically to the world of the Snakes. The world of the Snakes or Nagas is Mexico. The Hindu holy books are emphatic about this. The American Indians themselves told the Spaniards that all of North America was named Quivira (Kheever, Khyber, Heber, etc.) (See *El Orígen de los Indios*, by Father Gregorio Garcia). We must not forget that the dispersal of nations took place in the time of Heber and his son Phaleg. The Bible does not lie to us.

So far, I have discussed the mythology concerning Mt. Meru. So how does this tell us anything about a spiritual or dual solution to many of the problems now plaguing mankind?

As I have stated, these unseen dimensions, beings, and powerful energies roar around the earth constantly, from East to West. These dimensions, beings, and energies are hundreds of thousands of miles high, perhaps reaching the sun itself. They pass through the human body and spirit just as water leaks through a sieve. During our working days, we move around in these energies, but we get the greatest benefit from them at night. I should also emphasize that these dimensions, beings and energies are omnidirectional, even inwardly.

Those who have read my books know that I am as much resentful of gurus and political activists as I am of those who want people to convert to other religions. Neither of the two groups know anything yet as they should know. As I have said, I once thought that by just exposing the specter of Bel (the Phoenician God of the Underworld), people would get the hint. I was mistaken. So, I decided to reveal what I know about Christ as a a truly educated Hindu would understand him. The omni-directional Christ nailed to a Cross says it all. Any Christian who can understand that I'm not being blasphemous or "sacreligious," will surely see that I'm talking about an energy that can someday be measured with scientific instrumentation.

I know without investigating that many people reading this book will some-day be able to travel within that domain (bilocation, etc.), just as easily as they travel in airplanes, ships, buses, trains, and automobiles. Once that happens, they may need another type of symbol to be their guiding light, which will be either a Mogen David or a Swastika. We should not be prejudiced against the Swastika because of what Hitler did with it. The wrong use of the Mogen David and Swastika will always destroy "the bad guys." I guarantee it.

Why Is It Absolutely Necessary For People to Sleep With Their Heads Facing East, and Their Feet Pointing Toward The West.

Although I have already explained why the Sacred Directions are important for having peace in the world, I must emphasize this fact. All humans are different, each from the other. Furthermore, because the Ego makes us all different, it is impossible for us to to see life collectively in the same way. As Christ said, "There will always be wars and rumors of wars." But Nature assures us that we can keep war at a bare minimum if we'll all sleep in the Sacred Directions. In this way, Life Solar Energy can penetrate every human equally, synchronizing and harmonizing all individuals within the five races, so that contention will be minimal. In time, and if enough people sleep with their bodies aligned in the sacred directions, mankind will begin to regenerate himself and do better in life. All prison, hospital, military, private, and any other kinds of beds must face East and West. This includes all churches and temples. Again, I say: Our heads must point toward East and our feet toward the West. Don't forget: Christ's head symbolically, but not physically, represents Mt. Meru. His feet are nailed symbolically, not physically, to Mt. Orizaba. His hands are frozen or "nailed" to the North and South Poles. Symbolically and not physically, of course. I am talking about an incredibly powerful energy that is personalized.

Why Is The Spiritual and Energetic Umbilical Cord Connecting Central Asia and India With Mexico So Important For Health, Wealth, and Happiness Among All Mankind?

The story about the Eastern and Western Nagas is much more than a story. It is a symbolical reality of realities. The Nagas represent the very real spiritual and energetic umbilical cord connecting Central Asia and India with Mexico. This "umbilical cord" or the vertical beam of Christ's Cross, which is the space between the Tropics of Cancer and Capricorn, contains the most powerful elements of Solar and Life Energy. Therefore, it throws out the most powerful rays in all directions. If the inhabitants of Central Asia, India, and Mexico unite spiritually, totally, in every way, their "rays" will regenerate the North and South as well. For this reason, all mankind must encourage the Central Asians, Indians, and Mexicans to get their act together.

What I Have Just Written Is Symbolic Reality; Not Mystical Guesswork!

I did a lot of careful research and study before writing this book. Even in the Turkish republics, people are getting increasingly restless. They're thinking more and more about their ancient religion of Tengri, and his Only Begotten Son Keder/Keser. Once the Mexicans (really all Meso-Americans), Turks and Hindu Sanatanists remember how tied together they are genetically, mythologically, and historically, a quick change will take place on earth. Even if these peoples don't orient themselves in the Sacred Directions simultaneously, the Cross-hating religion will begin to weaken and crumble, for any religion rejecting the Cross and the Holy Trinity is destined to fall. I predict that if my message gets to the Mexicans and Turks, the Cross-hating religion will weaken beyond redemptionin during the lifetimes of many people reading this book! At the same time, the problem of millions of Meso-Americans seeking to flee to the USA will dramatically decrease.

What Is The Difference Between Europoid Christian Atheists and Sanatana Dharma (Hindu) and Buddhist Atheists?

I will use the natural archetypes of Jesus and Krishna hanging on a cross as an example. The Hindu and Buddhist atheists do not need natural archetypes or any other kinds of archetypes to know that the greatest amount of life and solar energies whirl eternally around the world, between the Tropics of Cancer and Capricorn. They know that the energy exists, but they will not, or cannot, visual it as an archetype. And they will worship this energy that they cannot see, feel, and identify. So, according to Europoid Christian criteria, they are not atheists but religious Sanatana Dharmaists which they, indeed, are. On the other hand, the Europoid Christian atheist might insist that there is no divine, solar, or any other kind of energy circling the globe constantly and maximally between the Tropics of Cancer and Capricorn. Therefore, Europoid Christian atheist scientists may not even bother to find out. And if they do take the Sanatanist and Buddhist ideas seriously about these things, their Europoid Christian fundamentalist brothers might label them as devilish "Anti-Christs." So where do I stand on these matters? I myself am certain that these energies exist in the world. But I must honestly confess that I can't visualize them as men hanging on crosses or as serpents wound around the World Egg. And for certain, I am in no way a Europoid Christian atheist.

What Is The *Aryuveda?*

The *Aryuveda,* meaning "Truth of the Aryans," is, perhaps, the world's most ancient book on the art of healing. It even predates the Chinese *Nei-Ching* and the science of Tao. When the Aryan Kurus entered India, they brought the Aryuveda with them, containing the science of healing they used back in Hyperborea, in pre-Noachide times. The Aryuveda insists that anyone wanting a true healing of his body, mind, and spirit must always sleep in the East-West direction I have described, if he wants to heal himself effectively. It is the starting point for any kind of healing to take place.

A world-famous Hindu medical researcher, Dr. Asoke K. Bagchi, said the following about the Ramayana Path of Unity in his essay, *Concept of Neurophysiology in Ancient India:*

> To the medical historians the Aryan civilization is of prime importance. Various historical facts derived from the treatises on the same are still of profound scientific value...their metaphysical ideas were so potent and rational that we cannot still refute some of their primitive concepts.

Is It Possible For Sectarian Fundamentalists, Wishing to Remain Aloof From Other "Non-Christian" Religions to Achieve Salvation?

If a sectarian religionist refuses to accept the the eternal universality of Christ in all religions, but prefers to practice his religion as if Jesus Christ was born 2,000 years ago, and at no other time, he has absolutely nothing to worry about. God is merciful. *He/She/It/They* seeks to place Christ, the true medicine of the body, mind, and spirit in the innermost pith of each human, according to his respective level of spiritual and intellectual development. Regardless of what his conscious mind, the Ego, tells him, The Doctrine of the Cross helps keep his mind and soul attuned to the Infinite. He may think consciously that he worships the Jesus Christ who once lived in Israel. But inwardly, he worships the Eternal Energy of Life, just as many so-called "pagans" do outwardly in their own respective religious persuasions. However, he should never try to convert anyone to his particular brand of religious sectarianism or condemn others to Hell. Only

God can do that. Let each person reach Christ-Conscious in his own way and in his own religion.

Some of the religions we mistakenly call "pagan" are culturally correct for the societies in which they are practiced. Since their outward appearances appear strange, with a plethora of idols, strange rituals, etc., we think of them negatively. But as I said, if they are practicing Cross Science, as outlined in this book, regardless of the excess baggage bending their backs, they stand on equal ground with the Christianity to which we are accustomed. It's their business, not ours, whether they want to mash themselves to the ground with non-essentials. We, too, appear suspiciously strange to them. Additionally, we should not forget that we don't need any of the trivial, useless lead we throw on our own backs. All of us, Christian, Jewish, Hindu, Buddhist, or whatever, would do well to just stick to the basics and not burden ourselves unnecessarily. True religious practice should be kept simple and easy. I hope I have made it appear so in this book.

Mankind has become so smug and conceited that he can't accept the archetypical symbolism of Mounts Meru and Orizaba seriously. A friend of mine, who has read my books, told me that some of his friends were shocked and dismayed to find out that I, an educated man, would take Cross Symbolism, Christ as representing solar energy, and the extra-cerebral flow of the mind seriously. I have no apologies to make about that. I'm glad I found out this information. I have no doubt that the Catholic Church already knows this as well. There's an old Spanish saying: *Dime con quién andas, y te diré quién eres. (Tell me with whom you associate, and I'll tell you who you are.)* If such a saying has any truth to it, I'm running around with the right people. Also, as I've told you previously, I'm giving the "spiritual or dual cure" for Man's predicament. It's not like the so-called "scientific solutions" given by Europoid Christian mathematicians, physicists, biologists, social scientists, and politicians. Spiritual technology abides by its own laws. We should not be afraid to try it on for size.

The life-giving, recharging action of the sun is especially powerful from sunup until around ten o'clock in the morning. Take advantage of this extra charge of energy. Get up early in the morning; take a walk; get a little exercise; greet the rising sun.

A few hundred years after Christ's crucifixion, the new religion to which I've been alluding came along, insisting that the sacred directions were really North and South. Any adoration of or trust in the Cross was considered idolatry. At sword point, many millions of people, especially in the Turkish nations, were forced to join this religion and point their bodies North and South while sleeping. It could also be true, as it is with so-called Christians, Jews, Buddhists, and

Hindus, that they slept in whatever direction they wanted. But when people were forced to align their bodies North and South, the archetypical Son's (Jesus) body became a huge impermeable dam, preventing free flow of the sun's energy. His arms pointed helplessly toward the East and West. This time, Christ was crucified again, and without the protection of the Heavenly Father. No rising on "the third day" this time. The result was devastating for mankind. No longer able to pass through mankind's head and spinal column, the energy roared and tumbled over his body just like a nightmarish tsunami, destroying mankind's body, peace, and happiness. This is a fundamental reason for much of mankind's suffering. This is an entirely scientific spiritual or dual solution. What are we going to do about it? If we must, let's use "rational, scientifically acceptable" Europoid Christian atheist terminology for Divine Energy and get on with our lives. After all, we invented the words. God gave us the archetypical symbolic language.

Developing The Faith That Can Move Mountains. How All Humans Can Become Super-Beings!

What I am about to tell you is, perhaps, the most important metaphysical secret any human being can ever learn. It is certainly the most amazing fact taught in this book. It is the best kept secret in Hinduism, Buddhism, and Christianity. True spiritual leaders fear that if this information becomes generally known and made easy to understand, the wrong people can acquire it and destroy the world. I say that "the bad guys" are already in at least partial control, using this same secret. Perhaps this is the reason why they are the masters of this earth!

It is now time for the "good guys" to get this information. My greatest regret is that I did not find this out when I was a child. If people can accept and practice what you are about to learn, we humans could rise to the status of "super-beings" in just three or four generations!

"Faith" and "belief" are really opposites. "Belief" is something we erroneously think can happen if we will it to happen. It is a way of making lying seem real. "Faith" is something that really happens if we will it to happen. It is based on truth; not brainwashing. Faith=Zion or Science. Belief=Bel; the Underworld; the Devil.

You have learned that just the amount of solar energy in a cup can make the oceans of the world boil over. I have also described how solar energy, the energy of all life, a.k.a. The Breath of God, swirls around the world from East to West eternally, by day and by night. The greatest concentrations of this energy pass between the Tropics of Cancer and Capricorn, the symbolical spinal cord of Jesus Christ, with the nerves and veins (the sun's rays) spreading toward the North and

South. All that I have said will be proven scientifically someday, if not already. It does not demand blind belief on our part.

We symbolize this symbolical head, body, and feet as Jesus Christ, with his head being the sun, the swirl of energy being his spine, the veins and nerves being the rays, and his feet being the moon and stars. The polar regions symbolize Christ's hands nailed to the Cross. Anyone wanting to unify his mind with that unlimited energy must, from now on, condition it to become confident that the sun, along with its movements across the sky, is symbolically the head of Jesus Christ. The suns rays are his halo, as depicted in pictures of Jesus. What we don't see is his body and spinal cord, but it's there nonetheless in the unseen form of infinite energy. At night, the moon symbolizes his feet. Even during cloudy days and at night, this energy moves around and through the earth perpetually.

You may be wondering how Christ can help us if his back is facing the earth and not his face. But Christ is omnidirectional. His face is as much looking directly at us as his back. The Hindus teach this truth to their people by depicting their principal Gods as having faces pointing in all directions. No matter what we do or where we go, Christ is looking directly at us, both from the sky and in our hearts.

If a person will constantly remind himself that the Christ is moving with the sun around the world, he will ultimately become the instrument of his own personal evolution. Like my recommended exercises in reacting subconsciously to duality, so also must our awareness of Christ's head being the sun, his body the flow of energy, and his feet being the moon and stars, as a subconscious reflex. In time, what is locality (the individual mind) will fuse with infinity (non-locality), welding each individual and Jesus Christ as one and the same mind. Even the Bible assures us that this will happen:

> Let this mind be in you, which was also in Christ Jesus; who, being in the form of God, thought it not robbery to be equal with God…*(Philippians 2:5-6.)*

The children of parents who teach them what I have described in this book, will cause their grandchildren and beyond to evolve toward becoming super-minds and super-beings in every sense of the word.

Those who discount the importance of what I have just said should study the history of mankind. All ancient ruling houses, of every nation on earth, claimed to be the flesh-and-blood manifestations of the sun (*Kashi*): the Hindus, Sumerians, Greeks, Egyptians, French, Germans, Romans, Japanese, Aztecs, Mayans,

Incas, *ad infinitum, without exception.* They kept the common people in control by convincing them that they, the ruling houses, were the official intermediaries of the sun. When the now deceased Chinese dictator, Mao Tsung, was totally in control of Communist China, banners and posters of his face staring out from the middle of the sun were displayed all over China. In this way, he was able to get the Chinese people to follow him blindly. In doing so, however, he nearly destroyed China, for the honor of being The Only Begotten Son belongs to Jesus Christ, not to any mortal man. Even now, this secret metaphysical knowledge has been kept exclusive so that the ruling oligarchies in religion, government, and business can continue being the "alpha wolves" on earth. Don't accept naively what I have stated in this paragraph. Investigate for yourself.

The secret of the sun (Kashi) and solar energy, not communism and other "isms," promises salvation to all mankind. Jesus Christ was the first person on earth to reveal this secret to the common man. It is now time for all the "betas" on earth to become "alphas." There is a lot more I would like to say about this, but I don't want it to dominate this book which gives the general natural laws of the dual universe. I will deal with this subject in greater length in my next book.

Psychologist Carl Jung wrote in his work *Mysterium Coniunctionis:*

> The arcane substance [of alchemy] corresponds to the Christian dominant, which was originally alive and present in consciousness but then sank into the unconscious and must now be restored in renewed form. (CW 14, par. 466.)

This so-called "Christian dominant" is still known and used by a few famous Hindu metaphysicians. By deliberately making their scriptures appear overly fantastic, incomprehensible, and preposterous, they maintain a monopoly on this knowledge. I have taken this knowledge and made it understandable to the masses, thus restoring it in renewed form. I have also clothed this Christ archetype in acceptable cultural and theological garb familiar to Christians so that it will not threaten their sectarian sensibilities and provincialism. If those Hindus who monopolize this knowledge are worried that the masses in general will grasp the synthesis of what I say in this book, they need not worry.

When I tell you that the head of Jesus Christ lies symbolically at Mt. Meru, and his feet at Mt. Orizaba, while the Hindus say that the honor belongs to God Rama, there is no contradiction because we are dealing with natural archetypes and not with man-created names. Mt. Orizaba should become as sacred for the Turks, Buddhists, and Hindus, as it should be for the Christians. Regardless of the various names of this deified archetype, it is the same for all humans. If you can accept this, then no more tensions and misunderstandings about religions being "different" will ever again keep humanity divided-that is, every religion except the one which is still too stubborn to present that "fifth stone tablet" to the patient Hopi Indians. Hopefully, sooner or later, the Hopis will receive that tablet.

Carl Jung wrote:

> ...the conception of the unitarian and trinitarian ideas...were in existence many centuries before the birth of Christianity. Whether these ideas were handed down to posterity as a result of migration and tradition or whether they arose spontaneously in such case is a question of little importance. The important thing is that they occurred because one, having sprung forth from the unconscious of the human race (and not just in Asia Minor!), they should re-arise anywhere at any time. It is, for instance, more than doubtful whether the Church Fathers...were even remotely acquainted with the ancient Egyptian theology of kingship. Nevertheless, they neither paused in their labours nor rested until they had finally reconstructed the ancient Egyptian archetype. (*Psychology and Religion: West and East*, CW 11, pars. 194-206, *in passim*.)

Again, my readers may inquire, "If what you say is true, why hasn't the world improved over the millenniums? Why do most people still value evil, stupidity and ignorance over enlightenment?" As usual, I say that this is the easiest of all riddles to clear up. Only a few people in the past took this "sun secret" seriously, just as many people who read what I have just said will laugh their heads off, wondering how an educated man like me can be so "superstitious" or "anti-Christlike." Instead of getting on the sun's (Christ's) bandwagon themselves, they go back to their movie, artistic, and music idols, politicians, social activists, ignorant clerics, or whatever and whomever else specializing in keeping the masses' heads buried in the sand. However, I do know that some people will act on what I have just written, and they will reap extraordinary benefits for having done so. Jesus Christ will not disappoint them. This is his objective: Let each man and woman become his and her own king and queen.

The Mexicans and people of Meso-America are directly in the path of this radiant energy. They, including their Turkish and Hindu brothers who also live within the spine of Keder, Keyser, Shiva, Mithra, Horus, Indra, Agni, Quetzalcoatl, Kukulkan, Bochica, Surya, Rama, Krishna, Vishnu or Jesus Christ will be the first to benefit if they take seriously what I say in this book. God's plan for the world is kindergarten simple. It is not exclusively for the members of a particular ruling oligarchy, religion or sect. If this were so, Karma would be just a superstition, which it isn't. Even a child can visualize and apply "The Spiritual Solution." It is entirely scientific. Don't wait until the scientists discover it in order to get benefits. Start now.

How I Discovered The Power of The Sun.

Since I retired from the teaching profession in late 1988, I have been taking daily walks in order to stay in satisfactory physical condition. Unfortunately, the California High Desert is not the most pleasant place on earth in which to live. It is consistently windy. The summers often get intolerably hot. The winters tend to be mild, but we get our share of cold days also. For these reasons, I can't walk every day. I also start my walks just before dawn breaks, even in cold weather.

Soon after my retirement, I started suffering from a king-sized case of acid reflux (heart burn). I found out through experience that I could control this ailment and eventually rid myself of pain by walking as regularly as possible. I also felt unusually energized after these walks. However, on the days I couldn't walk, I'd suffer a relapse and would have to start all over again.

For years, I attributed my success in controlling my condition to the daily exercise. However, I discovered accidently that some other factors, not the walking, were freeing me of pain and giving me extra energy. It took me more than a decade to discover that if I stopped walking and faced the east at the break of dawn, the pain would disappear in seconds. I also noticed the extra burst of energy. Whereas before I'd greet the rising sun only during my walks, I now drive to the desert and face my car toward the east during windy and cold weather. I can free myself of pain immediately, without getting out of my car. I have not yet freed myself of acid reflux, but as long as I face the sun at dawn every morning, I feel completely normal and free of pain. I can also eat spicy foods. As the Bible says, "…bodily exercise profits little…" *(Timothy 1:4:8.)*

It is not necessary to see the orb in order to get immediate relief. As soon as the eastern sky lights up, good things start happening to me. And when the orb does finally appear, it is a welcome sight indeed! I have noticed that the effects are always greatest at the break of dawn, continuing to be strong until the sun has risen about 45 degrees. After that, the healing power of the sun begins to weaken dramatically, but not completely. Additionally, I have found out why the different religions of the world have holidays dedicated to the sun on almost identical dates. The power of the sun on such days becomes dramatically intensified.

At first, I felt like a "Columbus" who discovered something that nobody else had ever found out before. But research on the Internet showed me that many thousands of people have also discovered the power of the sun. One man, an ex-

Protestant preacher, wrote that when he discovered the power of the sun, concluding that it is truly the energy emanating from Jesus Christ, and the fact that it unifies all religious teachings, he left his pastorate. He knew that if he declared that God, Jesus, Vishnu, Shiva, Mithra, Apollo, Indra, Agni, or whatever else we call the Divine Sun is no respecter of particular religions and man-created names, his congregation would think that he had become an Anti-Christ and kick him out of the church. He might have said to himself: "They can't fire me. I quit."

In his book *Spontaneous Healing*, the world-famous medical doctor and researcher, Andrew Weil, told how a non-Christian Japanese man suffering from terminal cancer became healed by the rising sun:

> Shin…went to the eighth-floor rooftop of his apartment house, where he could look over the skyline of Tokyo. He recited Buddhist mantras and poems, put his hands together to pray, and awaited the sun. When it rose, he felt a ray enter his chest, sending energy through his body. "I felt something wonderful was going to happen, and I started to cry," he says. "I was just so happy to be alive. I saw the sun as God. When I came back down to my apartment, I saw auras around all my family members. I thought everyone was God." (p. 128-129).

Andrew Weil said that Shin's recovery was not immediate. He had to get up on that rooftop for several weeks more and watch his diet carefully. But he eventually made a complete recovery. Not bad for a terminally ill cancer patient.

> About twenty-five years ago I had an experience with the Sun of God. For about a week I got up every morning to watch the Sun come up. On that last day I felt a liquid electricity from the Sun enter the top of my head. It was in earth-time about 30 seconds of ecstasy. I have not had that particular experience again, but I feel some of its light has stayed with me. (*Outer and Inner Sun Worship*, by Wendell E. Wilkinson.

Shin and Wendell Wilkinson's experiences are not uncommon among people who have discovered the power of the sun. I hold the view that some particles of sunlight, bombarding the earth, are supercharged, renewing and invigorating the mind and body of anyone lucky enough to be in their path.

Suntan salon companies are well aware of the divine nature of the sun and its healing powers. They insist that artificial but full spectrum lighting can do all the sun can do. Don't listen to them. All you'll get from them is a magnificent suntan. The sun emits much more than "full spectrum lighting." Only the sun itself can bless us physically and spiritually. If you are interested in learning more about the healing power of the sun, I recommend *The Healing Sun,* by Richard Hobday, published by Findhorn Press.

If you want maximum benefit, both spiritual and physical, from the light emanating from the sun, you must go outside and wait for the sun to rise before dawn breaks. As dawn begins to break, face the east and absorb the incoming energy. The moment the sun rises, look at it directly; contemplate its beauty and visualize mentally the energy penetrating every cell of your body. Extend your arms outward, with the palms of your hand facing the sun. Most people feel a curious tingling on the palms. Think of something you want for yourself or others. Ask for a miracle. I know many people who got their miracles in the form of spontaneous healing, greater energy, and other benefits. As you acquire more skill and experience in benefiting from Christ's light shining at you from the sun, you'll find out that you'll get maximum benefits about 15 minutes before down up to an hour after the sun rises.

This is what I do: I face the sun for a few minutes and then walk, letting the energy circulate throughout my body. Then, I stop, face the sun again, and continue walking. Before I found out about the power of the sun, I customarily walked from five to seven miles a day. I now walk just one or two miles. Do not stare at the sun for more than a few minutes after dawn breaks. Keep a pair of dark sun glasses on hand.

I want to emphasize that beyond the archetypical Keder, Keyser, Indra, Mitra, Apollo, Shiva, Rama, Krishna, Vishnu or Jesus encasing us with and in its eternally revolving energy, there is even another energy manifestation. The Hindus call it *Brahma.* However, it is beyond our comprehension. The reader will note also that I have not discussed the feminine aspect of this solar energy. That becomes easy to understand if you can visualize that the receptors of the energy are the feminine aspect, whether physically male or female.

Readers familiar with Sanatana Dharma religious practices, which emphasize natural archetypes, such as the constellations, to help people recognize the Divine within themselves, have probably noticed that I studiously omitted a recounting of that first, foremost, and most long-lived war in human history: India's immortal *War of the Mahabharata,* the war that sent Abraham and Sarah to the Middle East. It was and is known as the war between the Sun and Moon dynasties. Until people get accustomed to understanding the place that natural and cosmic archetypes have in human religions and psychology, I have deliberately avoided mention of those whose spiritual emblems were and are moon and star symbols from which they derive their power. In that first of human world wars, which is still being fought, the Krishtayas or Krishtihans, the original tribes to teach about the sun, were driven out of India, to the Middle East, Europe, and other parts of the world. Christ told us over and over, and as the doctrine of The Holy Trinity demonstrates, that he belonged to the Sun Dynasty and wanted to re-establish its authority in the world.

I hope by now that I have shown all my readers, even the so-called atheists, skeptics, and "scientists," that real religious practice is not a speculative and purely subjective practice, although its enemies and ignorant clerics have made it appear to be so. In reality, it is the most exciting and nearly exact science to learn of all Man's other sciences-and the easiest to learn. I feel that I have said nothing in this book that "rationalists" and their comrades-in-arms, the religious provincialists of all the world's different religions, can effectively reject and mock.

I want to emphasize that our bodies and our homes are temples to the Holy Spirit. Remember: There are non-human phylum on earth. Each type of being emanates a unique type of energy. Don't put yourself in danger of absorbing it, for, like it or not, all beings are in competition for supremacy over all the others. We don't want their energies to accompany us on our interminable circumambulations around the Wheel of Life. Mankind must not sleep near non-human phylum or allow them to inhabit his private domiciles. In time, these non-nephilim phylum will mix their energies with their human masters, destroying them in the end. Like most people, I, too, love pets like dogs, cats, fish, canaries, etc. Just keep them out of your home. And if you must have a pet in your home, keep only one or two.

Why do we humans congregate in churches when we're worshipping collectively? We are just combining our Nephilim, Panchala Krishtaya energies in order to strengthen ourselves both individually and collectively, giving thanks to God for appointing us as Alpha-Phylum on Earth.

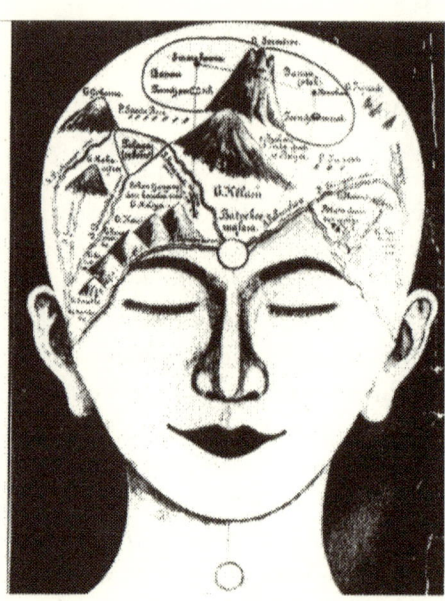

Fig. 9. Balinese drawing of the Ramayana Path of Unity, showing that
cerebral images are the microcosmic mirror reflections of the macrocosm
itself. It shows that each individual is at one and the same time existing in
locality and non-locality. Whatever happens in the universe also happens
simultaneously in his brain. "Happening" likewise includes the flow of
Universal Energy. When a person lies down to sleep at night, aligning
himself properly in the Sacred Directions, he and all others who are doing it
simultaneously synchronize and harmonize themselves with one another
and the Universal Life Energy. (Picture donated by T. L. Subash, Chandra
Bose.)

Throughout this book, I have "lawyered" in defense of the Cross, the Holy
Trinity, and the importance of regarding the sun as the actual archetype of Jesus
Christ's blindingly bright face as he stares at us lovingly from Outer Space. I have
described the infinite solar energy sweeping around the earth by day and night as
moving endlessly between the Tropics of Cancer and Capricorn, the spinal cord
of our Lord Jesus. The rays shining from his face move out towards the north and
the south, illuminating the minds, bodies, and souls of anyone knowing this
truth of truths. The frozen North and South poles represent the nails holding fast
his arms. The moon and stars reflect the light from Christ, lighting up the darkness of men's souls and minds. They represent his feet that are nailed to the
Cross. When men adhere strictly to this archetype, they automatically begin to
blend their conscious awareness with that of the Cosmos, becoming one with

Christ himself! Some people have used this knowledge and bent it to their own selfish agendas, to achieve domination in all areas of human existence.

Regardless of my Herculean attempts to reveal simply and effectively the eternal truths of the spiritual science handed down to us by the original five races of mankind, the Aryans or Turkic Krishtayas, many readers will continue to laugh at what I call "spiritual science," wondering how such an "educated" man can be such an ignoramus. Some may say, "The ancient Krishtayas or Krishtihans never existed. Several thousand years ago, someone just dreamed them up." Perhaps they agree with those Hindu activists who want people to think that the Turkish Aryans or Krishtayas were an invention of the whites to keep the darker races in subjection. Yet, the Hindu myths plainly state that the Aryans, a term meaning "Noble Ones," were all the races of mankind.

Some agnostics, atheists, and skeptics have also told me that the sun is is not God. They say, "Gene, can't you see that the sun is just a natural creation?"

I must admit that I agree totally with the above argument. I always tell them: "Yes, you are absolutely correct. Nothing can be more natural than Jesus Christ. Jesus as the Divine Archetype of all humanity is the Only Begotten Son of the Unbegotten. There is even a power above him. His Father. You win. You've converted me."

The Hindu equivalent of "The Only Begotten Son" is their God Shiva. He was born of the sun. He also crucified himself voluntarily the minute he became the Only Begotten Son. The images of Shiva show his throat as dark blue from the stain of the deadly poison he swallowed voluntarily. Had he not done that, neither the gods nor mortal men would ever have any hope for immortality. Shiva poisoned himself so that all humans could live forever, both in and out of the physical body.

It is an interesting anomaly that Jesus and Shiva had and have the same names. (See my book, *The Ego-Mankind's Inner Terrorist!*)

Most humans, who truly want to progress and move upward in the world, must crucify themselves for the greater good. Soldiers will fight to the death in order to protect their respective countries. A man who loves his family will work and sacrifice to provide for his wife and children. A student will suffer all kinds of difficulties in order to educate himself for a better life. I can go on and on with proofs that when men want to achieve transcendence, they must make sacrifices for the greater good. Nothing worthwhile is ever free of charge. Those who don't want transcendence will spin their entire lives wallowing in the mud. That, too, is a kind of sacrifice when you consider that they are wallowing in the mud so that those of us who do want better lives will have the least competition.

I stated in Chapter One that some inner force started eating at my soul, forcing me to write this book about spiritual science. I wanted to write it, not only for all mankind, but to encourage my deceased Mexican wife Consuelo's people that spiritual science, not slavery in the United States and starvation in their own country, is the road to both spiritual and material liberation. This book was not at all difficult to write, for I had already accumulated enough knowledge to put it together. Also, this "inner force," that ordered me to write the book, directed me to the right references I needed to complete it.

Almost immediately, some disconcerting pressures from without strove to weaken my will and convince me to doubt myself. But I endured those pressures and prevailed, coming out the better man for having done it.

Manusa

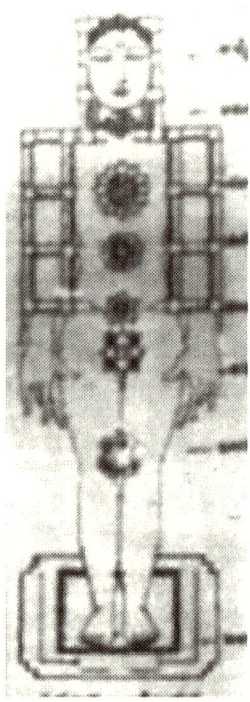

Fig. 10. Manusa, the archetypical representation of mankind. Notice that Manusa is locked in place by a crate or brace. He can only move around in the small space allotted to him under his feet. He cannot merge into the infinite until he reaches a certain spiritual level. (Picture donated by Mr. Subash Bose.)

Some Western Christians, who don't want to know that the Hindus are also full-fledged Christians as well, often send missionaries to India to convince the Hindus that only Western Christians are right and that Hindus or Sanatana Dharmaists are entirely wrong. Fortunately, my Sanatana Dharmaist friend, the Tamil Nadu holy man, Mr. Subash Bose, felt no need to convert me to his religious persuasion. When he found out what I was doing, and some of the pressures endeavoring to weaken my will, which he had predicted before Consuelo died in August, 2004, he put his shoulder to the wheel with me. All humans, of whatever religion, must keep the Cross and the Holy Trinity alive. The word religion is just a word or Bel. It's practice that counts.

The original five races of mankind, the Krishtayas, also had another name: They were called *Man.* Its Sanskrit equivalent is *Manu.* The Cologne Sanskrit Dictionary defines it as "the thinking creature, mankind, the man par excellence, the representative man and father of the human race, Noah, the mental powers, father of men, and most importantly, *Born of the Sun.* Krishta, Krishtaya, Buddha, Krishna, Vishnu, Horus, Mithra, Shiva, and Manu are the one and the same being.

I now have this question to pose to the agnostics, atheists, "scientists," and skeptics: Can you deny that mankind never existed? If you are confident and knowledgeable enough to "guarantee" that the Krishtas or Krishtayas existed only in mythology, then you must be honest and declare that mankind has never existed, either. Or what about Manu being "born of the sun?" Who looks down from the sky at you every day? Why did Jesus tell king Salivahana that God is in the center of the sun? Why did Jesus say he was "The Son of Man?"

Manusa or *Manusha is* a term meaning "the races of Man; the condition or manner or action of men." (Refer to the Sanskrit Lexicon.) In this case, *Manusa* has his shoulders, arms, and head enclosed in a type of packing crate. The symbols on his body show mankind's spiritual centers which, if he were not locked in that packing crate, could make him equal with God Himself. When mankind gets the wisdom and love for all Creation to not defy God or destroy the Universe, God will release him from that packing crate.

I ask you: Will mankind ever be able to free himself from that packing crate? Will he look at Shiva or Jesus staring at him from the sun and emulate him on earth by blessing all things and beings? It often appears doubtful, doesn't it? I know without asking that many people are going to look up at the sun and laugh at the thought of it being an archetype of Jesus or Shiva. They will brag that they aren't "superstitious" and "ignorant."

The Dance of Shiva (Nata Raja)

Another name of God Shiva is *Nata Raja,* King of the Dance of Life. In his book, *Facets of Brahman,* Indian author Swami Chidbhavananda states:

> Beings are normally entangled in states of existence called the wakeful, the dreamy and the dreamless sleep. They come by these experiences successively and not simultaneously. While in the state of wakefulness the other two are negated. In this manner all the three experiences undergo extermination one after another. They have made alliances not to co-exist nor to quit the field all at the same time. In this triple alliance any one state at a time happens to reign supreme in the course of a day. And what takes place in a day is invariably repeated all through the life of an individual. In this shift system slight variation is permitted occasionally, but no one in the party ever thinks of taking a holiday. Now herein comes a bold philosophical statement the truth of which not one in a million is able to grasp. 'Whatsoever exists at one time and ceases to exist in another, has no permanent value.' It has neither absolute existence nor absolute value. This maxim leads one to the logical conclusion that all the three states of existence-the wakeful, the dreamy and that of sound slumber are mere passing phases in life, each in turn exposing the unreliability of the other two…. Nataraja's raised foot indicates his exhortation to spiritual aspirants to transcend the phenomenal experience which is constituted of these three passing phases…(pp. 109-110.)

I would like to quote more from this book, but I prefer to discuss it in greater detail in the next book I'm planning.

Did Jesus learn about Nata Raja in India? Or *was he Nata Raja?* In the Apocryphal *Acts of John,* before his crucifixion, Christ told his twelve disciples to hold hands and form a ring, with him in the center. As they moved around in a circle, Christ sang a special song of praise. I quote from some extracts of this song:

> I will save, and I will be saved, Amen.
> I will be loosed, and I will loose, Amen.
> I will be wounded, and I will wound, Amen.
> I will be begotten, and I will beget, Amen.
> I will be eaten, and I will eat, Amen.
>
> I will be thought, being wholly spirit, Amen.
> I will be washed, and I will wash, Amen.
> Grace paces the round. I will blow the pipe. Dance the round all. Amen…
>
> The Eight sings praises with us, Amen.
> The Twelve paces the round aloft, Amen.

To each and all it is given to dance, Amen.
Who joins not the dance mistakes the event, Amen.
I will be united, and I will unite, Amen.

A lamp am I to you who perceive me, Amen.
A mirror am I to you who know me, Amen.
A door am I to you that knock on me, Amen.
A way am I to you the wayfarer.
Now as you respond to my dancing, behold yourself in me who speaks...

As you dance, ponder what I do, for yours is the human suffering which I will to suffer. For you would be powerless to understand your suffering had I not been sent to you as the Logos by the Father...If you had understood suffering, you would have non-suffering. Learn to suffer, and you shall understand how not to suffer. Understand the word of Wisdom in me.

Notice that Jesus stands in the center of the Circle of Twelve as the Sun shines in the center of the astronomical entities in our galaxy. Why? For he *is the sun shining down on us throughout all of our successive lives!*

15

Reincarnation
(Cross Science 103)

The famous atheist, Kersey Graves, hated Catholicism passionately, but he had to admit that it is the world's greatest success story. Edward Pococke, one of the most distinguished orientalists and theologians of the Age of Enlightenment, was a dedicated Christian Protestant. No one could ever accuse him of being an atheist. However, he, too, had to admit that the Roman Church knew how to reach the hearts, minds, and souls of its adherents.

If Catholicism's critics placed the Church's secret of success under a microscope, they'd convince themselves that the Church teaches religion scientifically. As long as it keeps on teaching religion scientifically, not interfering with scientists working in other areas and staying out of politics, it will always be successful. Just recently, I read in the newspaper a story about a certain Los Angeles Catholic prelate who said he would take political action to insure that people fleeing from Mexico and other countries to this one would not be sent back. Had he adhered tightly to his "job description," that of Catholic priest, no one would need to come to this country in order to build a better life for himself. For whom is he working? For Christ, or for the religion insisting that North and South are the Holy Directions? He should not be ashamed of preaching "the spiritual solution." What does it matter if he gets ridiculed for the type of science he practices? After all, it is the only one that will work in the end. How tragic, that I, a layman, should have to remind him that a priest should do God's work; not that of politicians and wicked money-grabbers wanting cheap labor.

The fathers of Catholicism must have paid attention to Genesis when it stated that God invented things, but Man, not God, invented words.

> ...the Lord God formed out of the earth all the wild beasts and all the birds of the sky, and brought them to the man to see what he would call them; and whatever the man called each living creature, that would be its name. And the

man gave names to all the cattle and to the birds of the sky and to all the wild beasts...(*Genesis,* 2:18-20.)

In all my writings in which I need to describe archetypes, I use the best explanation I have ever read: that of J. Iglesias Janeiro, author of the cabalistic text, *La Arcana de los Números:*

> An archetype is the sovereign and eternal model that molds beings and things, giving them understanding of what they really are...it is the mode by which a thing or being comes to exist in the physical world, making it comprehensible on the psychic plane. The Cabala derives archetypes from the primordial causes...(p. 68.)

Paintings and other representations of the Holy Mother Progenitor of mankind often show rays shining out from around her. Upon observing such images and paintings, the human mind unconsciously intuits that all life comes from the sun and from the vulva or vagina of the female because those rays also look suspiciously like pubic hairs. These representations appear idolatrous and pornographic to the uninitiated, but they do serve a deep and noble purpose-that of leading mankind to the certainty that he will always have life everlasting, both in and out of his physical body.

When does the human spirit become masculine and the sun feminine? When the body dies and the spirit returns to its source, which is the sun. It remains masculine until it re-enters a physical womb. Masculine=movement. Feminine=repose.

Everyone wants desperately to live forever. Since few of us can remember our prior earthly lives, we cannot be convinced by words and other people's positive testimonies alone. It really does no good for clerics to assure us whether or not we are going to live again physically. The members of the religions preaching the doctrine of reincarnation, including the clerics preaching them, are just as unsure and fearful as those belonging to religions denying the pre-existence and eternal life of the human soul. As the old saying goes, "Damned if we do; damned if we don't."

God (Creation) has no knowledge of Time and Space. Man created it while he was naming all the animals and noticing that there were varying intervals between where he was at a certain moment and where he was at another. Therefore, he developed the sciences of time and measurement. Although this knowledge was "dangerous" enough to someday aid mankind in increasing his mental stature on earth, perhaps even leading him to challenge God's authority again, as Adam and

Eve did back in their Hyperborean Paradise, God at least let him retain a few measly crumbs from the table of Divinity-and that included the Mystery of The Cross, the Mystery of the Tree of Life, and the Mystery of the Holy Trinity. In reality, these are all three ways of saying the same thing.

> ...Adam separated the Tree of Life [The Cross} from the Yesh [the material, physical world]-the Tree of the Science of Good and Evil-from the tree of the Ayeen [the invisible, non-materialized archetypes of Creation], The Tree of Life [The Cross or The Holy Trinity]. He insisted on using the Yesh [the material, physical world] for his own selfish pleasure, condemning himself to death, that is, to taste the bitterness of death. (*La Cábala,* by Alexandré Safrán.)
>
> When mankind comes to distinguish the Yesh [the material, physical world] from the Ayeen [the invisible, non-materialized archetypes of Creation], but toward that which he can direct himself willingly, he frees himself from the anguish of death. He understands that his entry into the Yesh [the material, physical world] is a proof of the life that God [Creation] has for him. God [Creation] wants the man to live in the Yesh [the material, physical world], but not exist solely in it, so that he may not die but rise up again, of his own free will, toward Him [Eternal and Constant Creation]. *(Ibid.)*

Note: The words within brackets are my own. I repeated the meanings of the words Yesh and Ayeen each time the Rabbi expressed them, so that no one can misunderstand his message to all mankind. Cabala is not like the teaching of dogmas and scriptures.

Since Man was wise enough to perceive that there were varying intervals between Points A and B, God allowed him to notice that when he made circuitous trips from their origins to their destinations, and from their destinations and back to their origins, he would delude himself into thinking that the return trips, even though one was traveling at the same speed, would pass faster time-wise than the first part of such circumambulations. This is a phenomenon that most humans experience when they pass the first half of their respective journeys throughout life. When I turned 50, my dad called me on the phone and said: "Son, welcome to the over-the-hill club." As middle-aged people and beyond continue to age, they sense that time is passing faster and faster. In the case of a man like me, in my late 70s, time zips by almost like lightning.

Jesus' sayings in *The Thomas Gospel* expain clearly that life is cyclical, always beginning and ending in the same place. I especially appreciate Jesus' commentary about the cyclical nature of life because the Hindus say the same about the fetus' nine-months in gestation:

The man old in days will not hesitate to ask a small child seven days old about the place of life, and he will live. For many who are first will become last, and they will become one and the same.

The Hindu scriptures say that a fetus with bad karma will experience its confinement in the womb as a hellish straightjacket, suffering from indescribably agonizing claustrophobia. While imprisoned within the mother's womb, it is tortured day and night by memories of the evils it committed in its prior life. In most cases, it vows that after leaving the womb, it will never again repeat its past mistakes. Just after birth, it still remembers its recent past for awhile, but these memories soon fade into oblivion. As Jesus said, if an old man could communicate with a recently born infant, he would get a clear account of the penalties God imposes on those who will not live righteously. Will what Jesus and the Hindu scriptures said really happen? Or will nothing happen as the skeptics and atheists assure us so confidently?

As I said, time perception is a learned process. It took thousands of years of mental conditioning for mankind to involve himself so completely in an illusion of his own making. In order to create types of measurements capable of explaining time intervals from one point to another, Man had to make a habit of remembering those intervals by certain definitions, such as seconds, minutes, hours, days, weeks, ears, centuries, millennia, etc.

But not all men allowed themselves to be fooled by the specter of linear time. Some began to reason that time was not speeding up. What was happening? The gap between the beginning of their earthly lives and the ending was just narrowing exponentially to a point where it would reach the point called death and immediately enter birth once more. Our perception of the time processes are memories of things we've done before. The wise-men of old had to reach one conclusion: Time appeared to be speeding up because they had circumambulated from birth to death before—hundreds and even thousands of times. Man's eternal lives are, in every case, cyclical, just as day and night, the seasons, the movements of the planets and stars in space, are cyclical. God has at least given us humans enough intelligence to know that we'll die. This archetype of accelerating time is God's merciful message to us: "You shall never die." God told Moses: "I am that I am." In Nature, everything "is." "Not" is the only philosophical and scientific concept on earth that doesn't exist, but some ignorant people will tell you it does.

Even the world's greatest scientists are beginning to see that time is an illusion. No one can say that the magazine *Scientific American* is "unscientific." The world's brightest minds pen their thoughts in that magnificent periodical. I read an article in a special edition of *Scientific American*, that every thinking human being, especially religious leaders, should study carefully: *That Mysterious Flow*, by scientist Paul Davies. The following is what Mr. Davies said in the conclusion of his article:

> …what if science were able to explain away the flow of time? Perhaps we would no longer fret about the future or grieve for the past. Worries about death might become as irrelevant as worries about birth. Expectation and nostalgia might cease to be part of human vocabulary. Above all, the sense of urgency that attaches to so much of human activity might evaporate. No longer would we be slaves to Henry Wadsworth Longfellow's entreaty to 'act, act in the living present,' for the past, present and future would literally be the things of the past. (Edition on display until February 20, 2006; p. 88.)

If modern scientific thinking has at last led mankind to realize that by explaining away the flow of time, we'll never truly die, there is no doubt that religion and science are at last becoming unified. The singularity is near!

The fact that the singularity *is* near is one of many reasons why I wrote this book about all mankind's need to link his mind and spirit to the doctrine of The Holy Cross, a.ka. The Tree of Life and The Holy Trinity. In my last two books, I was able to discuss the flow of time in relation to the individual. But I did not feel capable of being able to help all humans perceive the collective flow of circular time from points A to B, and from B back to A.

When I first started my studies of the origins of religion back in the 1960s, I thought I would find out that essentially, Christianity was a hoax and that Christ had not really died on that Cross. But as I got deeper and deeper into my studies, I realized that just as my own life after age 50 seemed to be accelerating, I was going back to point A again. I am moving eternally, round and round, from Mt. Meru to Mt. Orizaba, and back again. God is real. Everlasting Life is real. However, I did not abandon my contention that the remains of Jesus Christ are lying in the building called *Rauzabal*, in Srinagar, Kashmir, India. His sarcophagus lies in an East-West direction. The sarcophagi of two saints belonging to the religion that forced so many millions of human beings to accept North and South, causing the violent deaths of approximately forty million Hindus, as the holiest of directions, are also in the *Rauzabal*. Until I get verifiable evidence that I am wrong, such as DNA, I will continue to suspect that the remains lying in the first named sarcophagus, are those of our Jesus.

Little by little, as my knowledge deepened during my researches, I became convinced that the progenitors of all mankind were the Hindus. When I got to that point, the Turks kept popping up. I tried to wipe them from my memory. I said to myself: "Oh, no! This can't be happening." However, later on, I learned about the Panchala Krishtaya, the Five Original Races of Mankind, and how they left their Arctic Circle paradise and entered India. It was then that the Aryan Turkish Krishtayas and the Hindu Ramanakas merged and united, becoming the greatest nation ever to exist on earth: The Eastern Hemisphere or *Talantes.*

Even the Turks are becoming aware that they and the Hindus are the progenitors of all mankind. They are realizing that all Life Energy flows eternally from the East to the West, like a perpetually revolving fly wheel. They are writing more and more books and articles about the Doctrine of the Cross and the enlightenment they originally had when Tengri, also Hodai (God), revealed to them the mysteries of life. Yes, it is true that human civilization began at the Arctic Circle and extended down to what is now Sri Lanka. But from there, the Light of the Sun carried the energy of life from East to West, between the Tropics of Cancer and Capricorn. More and more Turks are realizing that they can no longer afford to keep on thinking that North and South are the sacred directions. I feel in my heart that Tengri is at last returning to them. And in returning to them, the Turks also link up with us, for all of us carry their blood in our veins. Our DNA and our Christianity prove it one hundred percent.

At the time of this writing, a Hindu politico-nationalist movement wants the memory of the Turkish Aryan Krishtayas expunged from all the history books and from the memory of mankind. They say that the Aryan story is a concoction of European white racists. Yet, even today, the Turkish people call themselves Ari and Kurus. Here is my warning to the Hindus: If those ill-informed activists get away with this crime, India will be shattered into tiny pieces, for the Kurus form the backbone of their history. Not only that, but they'll become the laughing stock of the world. What intellectual blindness forces them to deny that one hundred fifty million Aryans and Kurus (Turks) live in Central Asia? How can they convince the world that we Europoids invented them? I, too, once fell sway to the anti-Aryanist error, as evidenced by my book, *Jesus and Most Are Buried in India, et al.* I thank God that I freed my mind from that type of reasoning. If that activist organization succeeds, India will become a Humpty Dumpty, never to be put back together again!

16

An Urgent Message to the Mexican People!

Mexico is an extremely rich country. Its people are hard-working and intelligent. Why doesn't it progress as the United States is doing? The answer to that question is simple for those who know something about the Science of the Cross and the Holy Trinity-and who are not afraid to prove its efficacy. The Mexicans are the *Atlantes*, the name the Aztecs gave to idol columns holding up temple roofs. These idols symbolize the Mexican people themselves. Their source is Mt. Meru, or the Upper World. The Turks and the Hindus are their spiritual fathers. They are connected by a spiritual umbilical cord. Whatever happens to one, happens to the other. This causes another anomaly to spring up. Everyone in the world is Turk also, but on a different frequency. Whatever goes wrong for the "Holy Twins" also affects us adversely. Don't ask me why. God's infinite plan is beyond my understanding. Also, most Mexicans do not care in what position they have placed their beds, just so long as they get a good night's sleep.

A millennium and a half ago, that "certain religion" I've been discussing ousted the Turks' beloved Tengri and his Only Begotten Son, Keder/Keser. They forced the Turks to accept North and South as the true Sacred Directions, insisting that these directions were their only hope. Immediately, the Aryans or Panchala Krishtayas (the original Christians) ceased to be a great people. At the same time, the Mexicans blinded themselves to the blessings of their own country, becoming convinced that their only hope was the North. This is brought out in their mythology. The Aztecs taught that their divine destiny was to conquer the North. However, they were kept from doing so by the Michoacanos and their superior bronze and copper weaponry.

Although I have no definite proof to back me up, I feel that the Aztec myth of "Go North young man" arose when the Turks and Northern Hindus were forced to accept the new religion.

Even the Spaniards, when they first invaded the Americas, noticed that something had gone wrong in both Americas. The Amerindians were falling into unspeakable savagery. Even the civilizations of the Aztecs, Mayans, and Incas were falling apart. No one knew at the time that they were declining because the Turkish and Hindu worlds were falling apart. Since they were sharing the same umbilical cord, each was pumping unhealthful life energy into the other.

My Mexican friends tell me that if not for them, no one would do the dirty slave work in this country, so they have volunteered to become slaves. However, if they would just sleep in beds facing East and West, abiding strictly to the Holy Trinity, they would again become the Atlantes holding up Talantes or the Upper World. This, in turn, would strengthen the Turks sufficiently to again embrace the governorship of Tengri and His Only Begotten Son, Keder/Keser. Gradually, Mexico and Central Asia would become The Hope of the World and no longer The Hopeless of the World. They would stop going North to sell themselves into wage slavery. They would progress as never before.

The Dual Solution Will First Unite Mexico Within Itself!

Regardless of outward appearances and the Mexicans' fondness for flagrant and outrageous flag-waving here in the United States, Mexico is a badly divided and territorial country in which the word *mexicano* does not invoke the same emotions in the different regions and social classes. The Spaniards chose to name the whole country after the *Meshika,* who were the most powerful and hated tribe in Meso-America. Even today in Mexico, there are tribes who don't want to be called "Mexican." Mexico's different social classes are also seriously disparate. Upward mobility is more difficult in that country than in the United States. The upper classes, who generally govern the nation, are often raised and educated outside Mexico itself. As a result, they have no true "national awareness" when they are elected to office. Their definition of power is the opportunity to milk Mexico dry, giving nothing back in return.

When the Mexicans start abiding by God's "dual solution," they will almost immediately notice more solidarity and cohesiveness within their country. That alone could save Mexico.

Adam, a Turkish word meaning Man, was the first of the Spiritual Men to be evicted from the Hyperborean paradise in which he lived. The Koran and Jewish legends state that when he was cast out of Hyperborea (Eden), he went directly to Ceylon.

...When the primal pair fell from their estate of bliss in the heavenly paradise, Adam landed on a mountain in Ceylon and Eve fell at Jiddah, in the western coast of Arabia. (*Arabia: The Cradle of Islam*, by Rev. S. M. Zwemer; p. 17.)

"Wasim" is the high mountain called Adam's Peak in today's Sri Lanka, once called Ceylon. There is a foot-like impression on a stone at the top of the peak, which is regarded as that of Adam himself. It is regarded as the one holy spot on earth, uniting all the religions of the world. The Buddhists teach that it is Buddha's footprint. The Catholics and Syrian Chaldean Christians revere it as the footprint of St. Thomas. According to Hindu traditions, God Shiva flew directly from the top of Mt. Meru, following a longitudinal line called *Vedka*, connecting with the top of Adam's Peak. According to Sri Lankan legends, even Alexander the Great visited Adam's Peak.

When Tengri or God forced Adam out of Eden, he allowed him to take along the hallowed Tengri or Celtic Cross, so that he would not get lost in his wanderings. According to the legends about Adam, he went to Ceylon and then followed the sun westward before making a complete circumference of the globe and returning to Eve in Jiddah. This story tells how mankind and the development of civilization spread throughout the world, from East to West.

The Turks also had two other names for Adam, the man: *Olmak(er)* and *Olman(er)*, meaning "becoming; coming to exist; coming into being."

Let us take these Turks at their word, to see if their hoary legend and our own Bible make any sense. We fly around the world, landing in Southern Mexico and Central America. There we find the impressive ruins of Mexico's first human civilization: that of the *Olmeca* and *Olman*. Not only were they the progenitors of the Mayan civilization, but that of the Nahuatl or Toltec peoples, as well as that of the Zapotecs of Oaxaca.

According to the legends handed down to the Mayans, seven families were taken to Meso-America by a great navigator (really sea peoples) called *Votan* or *Potam*. This would indicate to me that they left from Meso*potam*ia where the Sumerians had their seaports.

This word Votan appears to derive from the Sanskrit words for boat: *Pota; Vah; Vadhu; Vadh; Vahittha; Bohitta.*

The legends of Votan or Potam are known throughout the world: Woden, Odin, Faathan by the natives of the South Pacific island of Yap, Bataan by the Filipinos, and similar names throughout the world. According to the Meso-American myths, Votan was a member of the Chan (Shan) tribe. The Chans were Turks from Central Asia and Northern India.

The *Chiapanecan* Indians, from whom Mexico's state of Chiapas got its name, claim that Votan and his people settled there first. The word "Chiapas" derives from the Sanskrit *Shiva-Pas,* meaning "Shiva, Protector of the World."

Foreign tourists visiting Turkey soon hear about an ancient race of "snake people," called Nagas, who once lived there. I have stated that they were led by the Bulgarian Turkish king, Kubera. His Naga subjects were called Yakshas or Yakhus. These would be the people of today's Siberian Turkish Republic of Yakutstan or Sakastan. Kubera, also known as Khyber, Kheever, Heber, etc. was really the ancient commercial and maritime partnership of the Phoenicians and their Juddhi (Jewish) warriors. The Phoenicians had a privileged slave caste called *Meshechs* or *Meshikas* (in Aramaic), *Tubal,* and *Tiras.* The Kuberas (Khyber, Heber, etc.) respected and honored them in spite of their slave status. If we went back into the past, we'd probably want to be Meshikas ourselves, for they lived as well if not better than their masters. They were regarded with awe as a sacred people because they were the sons of Japhet, the favorite son of Noah whom they called *Na, Nu,* or *Nava* (pronounced as Nahua). *Na/Nu* also meant "Lord Krishna; God Shiva; Buddha." *Nava* meant "Divine Ship or Divine Ark." It was the highest and most honored title that a human could hope for. That's how they received the name *Meshika,* meaning "Messiah." The Phoenicians also gave them another honorary title: *Navak* (pronounced as *Nahuac*), a term meaning "prayer as a vessel leading to Heaven."

I know that by now, my Mexican readers may be shocked to find out all this information. If they doubt me, all they have to do is look in the Sanskrit Lexicon.

After the Great Flood, the Meshechs began to degenerate as a people. They said among themselves, "We are the direct descendants of Japhet. We should be masters; not slaves."

The time came when this slave caste got restless and started rebelling against the Kubera hordes, allying themselves with savage Huns moving into North India. They even wanted to abandon the Kristayani religion, the religion of the Nephilim, and force people to follow them. All this happened at Mt. Meru, or the Tower of Babylon, when God decided to disperse them and the other trouble makers to faraway lands.

In order to bring more peace to Central Asia and Northern India, Kubera and his Yakhus rounded them up, exiling them to Ceylon. But they were as bad or worse there as they were back in Central Asia. Therefore, he took them to America, settling them in the Mayan lowlands. Since they had fallen into a state of disgrace, the Phoenicians started calling them *Anahuac,* or "people with no ship to take them to Heaven." *A* is the Sanskrit term for "not; without; no longer." The

Mexican people have long forgotten that *Anahuac* is a term of disgrace, meaning that not even God in Heaven will give them passage on Noah's heaven-bound ship. However, Anahuac is still regarded as a term for "water" and the Mexican people.

Besides the terms Naga (Snake) and Anahuac, meaning "the people whom God rejected," we also have abundant evidence that the Mayan lowlands were named after the Nagas. Let us now put this legend to the test, to see if it has any merit. After all, we must not be satisfied with mere myths and legends. We need concrete evidence. Even today, all of the Mayan lowlands, extending from Southern Mexico and Central America, are called *Nacaste.* This word derives from the Sanskrit *Nagasta,* meaning "Nagas Living Where the Sun Sets." There is a region of Nicaragua and Costa Rica, which the early natives of the region called *Guanacaste*, derived from the Sanskrit *Guhanagasta,* meaning "The Cosmic Intelligence of the Nagas of the Western Hemisphere." Don't forget what I said about the Sanskrit meaning of Guatemala. Everything is exactly as I say it was and still is.

Mexican Indians and country people believe that each person is born with a *Tona,* or animal guardian angel spirit. It is his individual zodiacal sign. Sometimes the *Tona* (zodiac totem) and the human it protects become so close that they merge. When this happens, the human becomes a Nagual or were-animal. Here is a superstition definitely inherited from India, for a *Naga* is supposed to be simultaneously human and serpent.

In India, the parents of a newly born child generally assign it a zodiacal totem sign as soon as it is born, called *Pa-Thona.* It, too, is an animal. *Pa-Thona* (Sanskrit zodiacal sign) = *Tona* (Nahuatl zodiacal sign)?

Mr. Subash Bose gave me his opinion of how the Mexican were-animal came to be called *Nagual:*

> It appears to sound like *Nagula* or *Nagulan.* one of the brothers of Pancha (five) Pandavas in the Mahabarata epic.
>
> Lord Indira (Indra) has 14 names in which appears the word *Naga,* one of which is *Naga-nagrku nathan. Nagr* = town or *loka*; *Naga nagrku* = town or *loka*) of *Nagas*; *Nathan* = God. We have the traditional practice of titling the name of a child as *Naganathan.*

Before going to live in Mexico, the Hindu God *Dyaus-Nahusha* (Dionysius as the Greeks and his Turkish countrymen called him), was banished from India for having raped the wife of a great Hindu philosopher named Agastya. According to the Hindu legend, he was turned into a snake. In reality, he just boarded a Naga ship and went to Mexico. At first, the Meshika welcomed him with opened arms.

He taught them the arts of civilization. However, the welcome soon wore off. One night, in Tula, a city which he had founded, he got drunk on his home brew and raped his own daughter. Some say it was his sister. For that, the Mexicans sent him back to India. Though *Anahuac,* they still knew the difference between right and wrong. Quetzalcoatl left Mexico (Land of the Meshechs) on a Naga ship from a harbor in Southern Veracruz or Northern Yucatan, near Mt. Orizaba where his father was buried. He left on a raft of Snakes. Mt. Orizaba was probably a navigational marker that ancient mariners used to return to India or wherever else they were going. Quetzalcoatl returned to India via the same route that had brought him to the Mountain of the Stars (Citlaltepetl or Mt. Orizaba) from Meru. Even today, Mexico is connected to Turkey and India by that invisible cord of Solar Energy and Divine Knowledge. Nothing in this world is happening by accident. There is some kind of plan of which we are ignorant. That is because we have rejected the idea that there is a spiritual side of ourselves. We are pawns in a Divine Chess Game. Are we spiritually powerful enough to win it? Or is it more "scientifically authoritative" to reject the Cross?

Fig. 11. Quetzalcoatl (Dionysius) returning to Mt. Meru on his raft of snakes.

Notice the strange Snake Cross at the bottom of Quetzalcoatl's raft. The snake has no tail; just two heads. The two snouts point East and West, showing that it is completing a round trip back to where it came from-the sun or Mt. Meru. The frontal drawing of a snake's head symbolizes the total Divine Unity between the Mexicans of the West, *Nagasta,* and the Nagas of Turkey and India. Could the future of the world depend on a correct understanding of that astonishing archetypical Cross symbol? As Murad Adji said, "The roots of the World Tree [in Hamrin) go deep into the underworld in the serpents' kingdom (Mexico)." Will the Mexicans awaken from their slumber on time to save themselves, Turkey, India, Catholicism, and the world as well? Or will they remain blinded and continue worshiping the North as so many millions of their blood brothers are doing right now, back in the Turkish nations?

Because of their passionate adherence to the flow of Life Energy from East to West, each immigrant tribe to America tried to find a cave or a mountain which could line up with their ancient homelands back in Central Asia and India. The Mayans called their cave to the Underworld, *Xibalba* (pronounced as "Shivalva"). It derives from the Sanskrit *Shivulva,* meaning, "The Vulva or Womb of God Shiva." The Aztecs told the Spaniards they came from an ancient land called *Teocolhuacan.* Since they couldn't pronounce "R," the word meant "Teo-Kaurava-Khan," meaning "The Kuru (Turkic)-God-King." The Southwestern Puebloan tribes of New Mexico claimed that their underworld was *Sipapu,* derived from Sanskrit *Siva-Bhu,* "The Sacred Ground of Shiva, around Mt. Meru." The Olmecs and Aztecs revered Mt. Orizaba. The O'odhams of Arizona look to Baboquivari Mountain near Sells, Arizona and a cave in Northern Mexico as their place of emergence.

The Carib (*Kaurav*) a.k.a. Arawak (*Arak* [Erectheus]) or Taino (*Dannu/ Tannu*) Indians, though entirely illiterate, really facilitated the job of finding out the origin of our American Indians. Not only did they give the Spaniards a wealth of details hidden in their mythology, but they *could* pronounce "R" correctly. They told them that their mythical forefathers were the *Kuru-Rumani.* The *Arak* were a tribe of Afghan Turks. The *Tannu* or *Dannu* were the warrior group of *Tannu,* an ancient Turkish nation that is still very much in business. Their place of emergence on the Carib island of Española was from a cave at the bottom of a hill called *Caunana* These were the *Khan-Anu,* one of the five Krishtaya tribes. After the Krishtayas went to India, the Anus could have settled in what is now Himachal Pradesh, India. After that, many of them went to Ceylon with Kubera, eventually settling on the Caribbean Islands. The Caribs said that a personage called *Machekael* (Skt: Mesech Family) guarded these newcomers carefully, to keep them from escaping. In my opinion, as the old saying goes, that's "telling it like it is." (See *El Orígen de los Indios,* by the Catholic Priest, Gregorio García. pp. 318-319.)

There is no end to evidence that the Mexicans and Central Americans are blood brothers of the Turks and Hindus. Actually we all are, but the Meso-Americans are more so.

Here's my message to my *Mesech* (Mexican) friends, among whom I've lived nearly for about 60 years of my life. The feet of Jesus Christ himself are symbolically nailed to your sacred mountain, Orizaba, in Vera Cruz. You are truly a people blessed by God because you have his spiritual feet symbolically lying directly on your soil. Instead of looking North for your salvation, look to your brothers in *Talantes* or The Upper World. Look to the East, to the rising sun, from which all life and human civilization originated. No longer can your *Atlantes,* which are you yourselves, continue to keep holding them up. A certain religion now prevails in the Upper World, which has decreed that the only hope for mankind originated in the North, which is now the Arctic Circle. They say that the mystical teaching of the movement of Life Energy from East to West is idolatry. They say that only they are right and that everyone else is wrong. As blood brothers of the Turks and North Indians, you, too, are being spiritually forced to look northward. If your blood-brothers' obsession with the North, the original abode of *Olmak* or *Olman,* the Turkic name for Adam, continues this way, your present sufferings, compared to those to come, will seem trivial in comparison.

There is a growing movement among some Mexican-American political activists in this country, who call themselves *Hijos de Anahuac* (Sons of Anahuac), which says that the spiritual homeland of the Mexicans is not Turkey and Southeastern Mexico, but Southwestern United States. They want their Mexican brothers to become obsessed with the idea that North is the sacred direction from which humanity's first civilization left to populate the world. I don't know whether they're doing this out of ignorance or because of some evil intentions. They don't want their brothers to know that they and the Turks and the Hindus are connected by spiritual and blood ties. Furthermore, they want to build up enmity between the European-Americans and them, saying that only Mexicans have a right to North America. But we are all Turks. However, the Mexicans are more so. And their salvation lies not in going North, but in re-establishing their relationship with the Turks and Hindus. We are all brothers, but the misguided Mexican-American activists in this country don't want anyone to know it. Do you think I'm lying? What did I tell you about the history and meaning of that word *Anahuac?* Are they not doing right now in this country what their forefathers did thousands of years ago, at the Tower of Babylon or Mt. Meru?

I have given you the spiritual or dual solution. Take it or leave it. My same advice is for the African-Americans, for they are bending under the same leaden weight on their backs. But their problems are even worse. A large portion of them also belong to this Non-Christian religion, both in this country and in Africa. Not only that, but hundreds of thousands, even millions of Africans are themselves Turks, such as the African Turkmen, Kuris, Somalis, Ethiopians, and others. African-Americans are known for their deep religiosity. If they are tired of trailing behind some other cultural groups, all they have to do is learn Cross Science. Then, they will progress steadily and surely.

Fig. 12. Mayan priests worshiping the Cross which is also the World Tree.
Every religion on the face of the earth at one time worshipped the Cross.
There had to be a reason.

Are You Still Unconvinced That Christology Has Always Been The Original Religion of The Entire World?

Quetzalcoatl, Kukulkan, and Gucumatz were the same person. Even he was crucified, died and then rose from the dead before leaving the coast of South Eastern Mexico on his raft of snakes. The coastal area from where he embarked for Mt. Meru was near Mt. Orizaba (Citlaltepetl) where his father was buried. It doesn't matter whether we call the crucified saviors of the world, Jesus, Rama, Shiva, Indra, Agni, Keder, Keyser, Krishna, Mithra, Apollo, Dionysius (really Quetzalcoatl, Kukulkan, and Gucumatz), or whoever. All are names of God's Only Begotten Son. Atheists and skeptics insist that all these saviors were plagiarized from a common source in Turkey or India. This may not true. And even if it were true, the same archetypical representation would and always will appear in some nation of the world. Peace and understanding will come to the world when we realize that the Ramachandra Path of Unity is, and always will be, the same in every crook and cranny of the world. Notice the following illustration of Kukulkan fastened to a Celtic Cross. The mystery of the Holy Trinity and the Cross, and its implications, are mankind's beginning, existence, end, and eternal repetition of the cycle of existence!

Fig. 13. Kukulkan or Gucumatz-The Mayan Jesus Christ! Just because he looks "culturally different," with a different name, and is stuck on a strange-looking cross, doesn't mean he isn't Christ. Remember, we're talking about an archetypical image of Divine Energy and not about a physical person. We all live in the same universe and are subject to the same physical and spiritual laws.

17

Two Non-Christian Southwestern Indian Tribes Who Want You to Become a Christian!

These two non-Christian tribes don't have any missionaries. They don't want you to join them in their religious services. They'd be delighted beyond measure if you stayed away from their villages and religious services. If you do observe any of their religious dances and gatherings, don't take pictures. Don't ask questions. Don't give "Christianly" advice. Just watch. Don't join them in their dances, prayers, and supplications to God. Anyway, I don't think many people would want be converted to their anti-Christian Christian religion because some of their ceremonies require that the faithful handle rattlesnakes.

The members of a certain Christian sect who knock incessantly on our doors, handing out poorly printed leaflets and tiny booklets, giving every conceivable argument to convince us that the rest of us are wrong, and only they are right, would probably be chased out of these two non-Christian Puebloan villages for trying to make them become Christians. They themselves have no desire to become Christians, but they certainly want you to become one.

It is a historical fact that in 1700, one of these tribes annihilated an entire village for having converted to Catholicism. This tribe, more than the other one, is the more fanatical of the two in wanting you to become a Christian. They keep their dances and prayers going on almost around the clock, 365 days a year. Hypocrisy? Not if you look under the surface.

These two tribes are the Hopis and the Zuñis (pronounced as ZOONyees.) The Hopis are the more "fundamentalist" of the two tribes. They were the ones who annihilated an entire village for submitting to Roman Catholicism.

Why don't they tempt you with attractive and irresistible inducements, as some Protestant sects do, such as promising to let you handle and step on hundreds of rattlesnakes if you'll sign on the dotted line and become one of them? Why will they not let you become a full-fledged card-carrying.old-time snake-loving hallelujah-shoutin' Naga?

This is why. Preaching and scriptures are Babel. Each one of us is different. No one understands Babel in the same way. No one attains spirituality by reading scriptures and listening to deafeningly loud preaching. Not even tithing ten percent of our yearly earnings can help. We can attain spirituality only by recognizing and attuning ourselves to Duality, The Holy Trinity, and letting God's message get to us by understanding the full meaning of the three most powerful natural archetypes in the Universe: the Cross, the Swastika, and the Wheel of Life.

These two tribes opine that only some inner voice within us all can wake us up. So, they are praying that we all remove the cobwebs for our eyes, the cotton stuffed in our ears, and the mush from our brains.

How, When, and Why Did These Two Tribes Get to America?

Mr. José Sandos, a Zuñi authority on Puebloan cultures, wrote in *The Pueblo Indians:*

The people came from the north to their present areas of residence from the place of origin, Shibapu, where they emerged from the underworld, by way of a lake. During their journeys they were led by the war chief…With his assistants and war captains…, they constituted a force responsible for clearing up the path upon which the people traveled. And with them came the Great Spirit, and He guided the ancient ones through the many arduous tasks of daily life…Many of them finally settled at the Four Corners area, where they developed their civilization and settled for some hundreds of years before moving to their present homeland. As the ancient ones relate, it was in order to preserve the people from total annihilation that the Great Spirit impelled them to migrate…They were advised to build fortress-like communities for protection and were promised the guardianship of the warrior twin gods Maseway and Sheoyeway." (p. 17.)

The names of those twin gods appear to be derived from variations of the Hindu God Shiva: *Mahashiva* (pronounced in Sanskrit as Mahasheewa) and *Shiyavha* (Pronounced as SheeYAHwah), meaning "Shiva, The Fast and Swift."

The word *Shibapu* tells exactly where they came from: *Shiva-Bhu,* "The Sacred Land of God Shiva: Mt. Meru."

Mr. Sando gives further evidence that his people came from Northern India which was also the southern frontiers of the Turkish nations:

> Since the caciques (chieftains) and the other leaders were responsible for governing the clowns (*Kushare* in the Keresan language; *Kusa* in the Puebloan Tewa language; *Tabosh* in the Tawa language) were that group of society responsible for the entertainment of the people. All these peoples, with their many and varies responsibilities, were under the titular leadership of the cacique and his staff." (p. 20.)

Kushare and *Kusa* derive from the name of India's leadership caste: *Kashi.* *Tabosh* derives from the North Indian *Tavith* or *Tavish,* meaning "people who impersonate the Divine Mother." These can be either male or female. *Berdaches* (gender benders) play an important part in Zuñi religious practices. *Keresa* derives from the Turkish *Kurusha. Tiwa* and *Tewa* are names of the ancient Turkish nation of *Tannu. Tanu* is also another name of the Keresan, Tiwa, and Tewa languages.

The Hopis are not really a tribe, but a group of clans who escaped from Northern India and went to New Mexico to pray for the "poor lost souls" or those who drove them out of Central Asia. According to them, they escaped from their ancestral home of *Sipapu* through a "hole in the sky." *Sipapu* is just a dialectical variation of Siva-Bhu. After their escape, they met *Masawa* (Shiva the Great) who led them to America.

Hopi accounts of their migration to America differ among all the clans, for they originally were not a tribe but a group of affiliated clans of like mind. However, a good conjunct of their ancient history confirms that the following tribes escaped with them: Navajo, Supai, Paiute, Apache, Ute, Heheya, Bahanna (White men), etc. *Heheya* derives from *Haihaya,* another name for "Phoenician." The *Bahana,* also called *Pahana,* derives from the Sanskrit *Vahana,* meaning "Transporter; Shipper." Hopi historian Edmund Nequatewa explains why they left Northern India and Central Asia:

> The Hopis lived in the underworld, which was the original place of all human life. Here, in the beginning, all life and everything was good, in peace, and happy...the people were classed as common, middle, and first class.
> The time came when the common and middle class grew wise to the doings of the priests and the high priests. All the days of their lives these poor people had been cheated of their family rights by the upper classes of the people. At times the wives of the lower class were visited by their men and by the

priests and high priests, while the poor husbands of the women were away. Now all this kept on from bad to worse.' *(Truth of a Hopi;* p.1)

Notice that Mr. Nequatewa said they came from the original place of all human life. We should know by now that they were from Central Asia, the home of the Krishtayas or Turks.

When the Turkish-North Indian *Hopis* could endure no more suffering, they sought the advice of the chief *Yai-owa* (Jehovah). He decided that they should abandon India and migrate to Southwestern United States.

The Hopi migration account must have happened between 700 and 1000 A.D. At that time, India was in hellish turmoil. The religion that converted everyone at sword point, forcing them to accept North and South as sacred directions, and to forget about that idolatrous "Cross," took the lives of an estimated forty million Hindus. The Brahmanists, the top priestly class of the Hindus, were also on the move, trying to force the tribals to give up their lands and accept the caste system.

The Hopi Wind God (Yaponche), a.k.a. the Hya-Phoenicians, blew them here on the ships of the *Vahana.*

The author of *Truth of a Hopi* goes on to say:

> The legend of the bahannas, white brother, or white savior of the Hopi is firmly established in all the villages. He came up with the people from the underworld and was accredited with great wisdom, and to set out on the journey to the rising sun-promising to return with many benefits for the people. Ever since, his coming has been anticipated. It is said that when he returns there will be no more fighting and trouble, and he will bring much knowledge and wisdom with him. The Spanish priests were allowed to establish their mission in the Hopi country because of this legend, for the people thought at last the Bahana had come..." (p. 108.)

Soon after the Spaniards arrived, the Hopis found out that even they, with their deep spiritual insights, were not so clever as they thought they were. In no way were the Spaniards "The Great White Brothers." Time will also tell that the Hopis have erred in another way. The rapid acceleration of scientific development is bringing the world to "singularity," in which the material and the spiritual halves of mankind again unite as one. They should quit dancing, chanting, and praying long enough to enjoy a few material delights, for their prayers will be answered in the coming years-hopefully. It could also happen that God will bring us down to our knees again as He did in Eden and Mt. Meru. Where spiritual science is concerned, even priests are getting "Fs" these days!

Those who are curious about the Hopi non-Christian religion that prays constantly for the rest of us to become Christians should read the work of a leading authority on Hopi religious practices: Gary A. David. The title of his work is *The Orion Zone-Ancient Star Cities of the American Southwest.*

When Mr. David read this chapter before I sent it, this is what he answered me:

> I don't know why you ask the Hopi to quit dancing and doing their ceremonies. If that happens, according to them, the Fourth World will end, probably violently (i.e. WW III).

As you have read in this book, so little is asked of us in order to prevent the total destruction of mankind. Yet, for the so-called scientists and skeptics, it is too radical and irrational to be a solution. If what I have written is so impractical, why have the Hopis danced almost continually for more than a thousand years, pleading with God to enlighten us a little? Could it be possible that they know something that eludes our educated, "know-it-all" scientists and atheists?

Don't ask the Hopis to sell you a copy of their bible. They don't have one. All they have on hand are four stone tablets with some strange markings on them, which only they can understand. They say they are waiting for a fifth one to arrive, when that Cross-hating religion that I've been describing comes to its senses and brings it to them.

While I was preparing this book, I thought hard and long about the different religious groups who preach the sanctity of Duality, the Cross, The Holy Trinity, and the Holy Directions: All forms of Catholicism, Protestantism, Judaism, Buddhism, Jainism, Tengriism, Hinduism, and of course, the Hopis and the Zuñis. The nearly 60 years I've been in Catholicism have convinced me that these are not religions or organizations at all, but some kind of mask hiding a "thing or being." When people tell me they despise Catholicism, they innocently think they're hating some kind of organization. But these described religions are in no way organizations, but a "being" we can't yet comprehend. It's like hating the tumbled-down barn keeping the finest of horses and cows hidden where we can't see them-and then deciding that the horses and cows are inferior because of the barn. No matter how perverted and ignorant the leaders of these religions are, and no matter how slanted their holy books, this being just stays where it is. It's not going anywhere, and it's not going to die out-ever.

The Los Angeles prelate who forces the priests under his command to tell their Mexican flocks that their happiness lies in the North, would not do this if he knew how much damage he is causing, not only to the "sheep in his barn," but to the world at large. But no matter what he does, no matter how many idols the Hindus worship, no matter how "scientific" and "rational" the Protestants pretend to be, Krishtaya will never die, for it came into to the world with the Nephilim. It will stay here, even though the rest of us, though our ignorance and the evil in our hearts, invite the virtual destruction of the world in scourges designed to wipe out an evil humanity who think that the Cross and the Holy Trinity are a joke! But all the while, Krishtaya will remain what it is-and where it is. It will survive whereas those of us who should be living according to the Tao may not.

Before closing this book, I will include one more chapter, just in case no one has "gotten the message" yet. I ask myself, if no one listens this time, what must I do? I've written several books in this vein already, and everyone still prefers to worship that "Second God," Bel. Will God give me more inspiration and wisdom to make the Holy Trinity and Cross teachings more comprehensible? After all, that little boy told the priest in the Salvadorean folk tale, that no matter how hard we try to understand the full meaning of the Holy Trinity and the Cross, we cannot, for it is a secret that only God knows.

18

Give Christianity Back to the Christians and Tengri Back to the Turks!

The Turkic brand of Christianity emphasized the Aryan (Arianism) teaching that the Unbegotten (God the Father) and his Only Begotten Son Jesus, Keder, or Keser, were born before time began. The Unbegotten was Creator of the World. The Father, working through his Begotten Son, created the Holy Spirit in which, and with which, all men are able to enjoy life in the flesh. We, the descendants of the Aryan Krishtaya Nephilim, must be subservient to the Son, just as the Son (Jesus) is subservient to the Father. What I have just stated is corroborated in *I Corinthians 8:5-6:*

> Indeed, even though there may be so-called gods in heaven or on earth-as in fact, there are many gods and many lords. Yet there is one God (Theos) the Father, from whom all things and for whom we exist, and one Lord (Kurios) Jesus Christ, whom are all things and through whom we exist.

These "other gods and lords" are the archetypes that have created all the non-human beings on earth, such as cats, dogs, bears, worms, fish, etc. Additionally, there are other beings and dimensions among us, that we cannot see with the naked eyes.

In 325 A.D., the Aryan concept of Christ being subject to the Father created much infighting among the different Christian sects at the time. Emperor Constantine organized an assembly called the First Council of Nicaea in what is now Iznik, Turkey, condemning Arius (the name of the Aryan leader), demanding the formulation of the Nicene Creed, which is still enforced in Catholic, Orthodox, and some Protestant churches. The central teaching of the Nicene Creed is that the relation of the Father and the Son is the same. They are not two beings, but one. There was also in those days an Asthanasian Creed which was a more aggressive rejection of the Holy Trinity.

Constantine succeeded in getting the Bible of the Aryans burned. For a few years, the dispute calmed down, but opposition to the Nicean creed continued.

Eusebius of Nicomedia was one of the most outspoken Aryanists. Constantine turned against him but later allowed him to resume preaching. In fact, he even had Eusebius baptize him on his deathbed, for in life he was a hypocrite and an evil man, to boot.

After Constantine's death in 337, the dispute rose up again. Constantine's son, Constantius II, who had become emperor of the eastern part of the Roman Empire, supported the Aryans, vowing to reverse the Nicene Creed. None other than Eusibius of Nicomedia advised him to do it. At the time he was both head of the Aryan party and the bishop of Constantinople.

Constantinius had the Nicean Creed bishops exiled. In 365 A.D., Constantinius became the sole emperor of both the Eastern and Eastern parts of the Roman Empire. He succeeded in exiling Pope Liberius Gregory Nazinzus.

Later on, the Nicene proponents succeeded in gaining power again. At the time, the Temple of Serapeum in Alexandria, included a branch of the library at Alexandria. This library contained several thousand Turkish books consisting of works on history, Tengri religion, science, and the like. To wipe the memory of the Turish Aryan Krishtayas (Kipchaks) from the mind of Man, they marched on the Serapeum and destroyed it.

The Turks to this day bitterly resent the fact that Constantine had religious history rewritten in such a way as to downplay the major part that the Aryans (Goths, Ostrogoths, Visigoths, etc.) played in shaping Christianity. I will quote some comments from Murad Adji's book. I recommend that all people read his books. Give him your full support, for the Turks must return to Tengri if they are ever going to become a great power again.

> The Greeks were the first Europeans to remember the old political axiom: "Your god your rule." So they came to the Turkis in an attempt to steal the God of Heaven and impose their power on Europe. Never before had anyone attempted anything like that. People came to learn, not steal from the Turkis.
>
> A Greek by the name of Constantine was among the seven august pretenders or emperors (rather, claimants to the shaky throne of the Roman Empire). Like his rivals, however, Constantine had only his high title to show for his claim, without an army and, therefore, power. The Mediterranean was in the hands of Maxentius, the real emperor. His army was stationed in Rome, and nothing seemed to forebode trouble. One day, however, the Romans saw

horsemen galloping under banners decorated with a cross (those were labarums) no one had ever seen before. The attack was sudden and daring.

Maxentius' army was dealt a devastating defeat at the Milvian Bridge in sight of the walls of invincible Rome in 312. Maxentius was killed in the battle, and Constantine hastened to proclaim himself emperor. Actually, the Kipchaks who had entered into an alliance with him on his insistence cleared the way to the throne for him. The Turkic cavalry won a battle, victory in which was ascribed to the Greeks. Really, the Greeks had not a single soldier under their banners.

The balance of forces in Europe swung heavily in Constantine's favour. The period of anarchy ended.

In the same year 312, by a mere coincidence, the Greeks invited Turkic priests to say prayers before congregation crowds to the Sole God (in Turkic, of course). Prayers were said on central squares of Greek cities on orders of Licinius, Constantine's rival for power in the empire's East.

Europe first heard about God from those preachers. This is a confirmed historical fact.

The public saw the will of God in the Kipchaks' victory over Maxentium. Fighting under a cross-emblazoned banner, a small Kipchak force had no trouble defeating the Roman army. Its victory was received as a sign of the Heavens. Indeed, "your god your rule" was the general opinion.

A very shrewd politician, Constantine grasped at this chance to show himself off, in the wake of that victory, as a believer in the new God and make the new faith and the Turkis serve his objectives. Following Licinius' example, he came out for recognition of the new Christianity that had come from its birthplace in the Caucasus. He expected to benefit from an alliance with the Kipchaks.

As they write history books, some researchers overturn, pass up or conceal facts of history as politicians tell them. They ignore the old maxim that you cannot conceal the truth for long-it will come out eventually, at the least expected time. The Greeks chose to conceal the truth. They accepted the faith in God under Constantine. This is a fact no one is going to deny. Historians pass up for some reason the fact that they accepted it from Turkic priests, however. They seem to forget that there were no other teachers or bearers of faith in the God of Heaven around at that time, only the Kipchaks.

The Turkic religion gave rise to Buddhism in the East and to new Christianity in the West. Tengri opened up differently to different peoples, and His presence in the new places was added evidence of the Great Migration of the Peoples. Europeans did recognize God and, through Him, Turkic spiritual culture. These facts cannot be denied or concealed.

It is impossible to conceal that Constantine never accepted God and remained a heathen all his life. A heathen High Priest. He was least of all interested in true faith and only cared for power. He went to great lengths to deceive the Kipchaks, so they could be next to him and keep him in power.

He paid a high price for victory over the Romans and lavished gifts and promises on the victors. He stinted no efforts or money to keep the Turkic warriors at his side so they could serve him. And stay behind they did. It looked as though the Greeks had overindulged them on drinks. Those traitors were later known as "foederati" (suggesting the treaty they had signed with the Greeks).

Constantine pampered them as best he could. For example, he introduced a new calendar, with a day-off on Sunday, the Turkic way. Townsfolk were now forced to go to church and pray to the new God of Heaven.

Please note a significant fact: until the year 325 the Greeks prayed to Tengri only and relied on Turkic books and prayers in church service.

This fact is completely forgotten or ignored. Really, it helps explain some of the darker aspects of European history. For example, coins minted in the Byzantine Empire at the time bore the image of the Sun, or more exactly, equal-armed sun crosses, Signs of the Sun. And Constantine himself was generally known as the Sun cult follower. Was it right?

What is more, Turkic, dubbed "soldiery", was spoken in the Byzantine army for a long time afterward. Thousands of Kipchak families were induced to settle on Greek lands. They were given the best lands and their relocation costs were paid by the Byzantine treasury in gold to the khans of Desht-i-Kipchak. Their relocation was, of course, part of the Great Migration of the Peoples. Actually, though, it was not a free movement of free people—the Kipchaks' services were bought for gold.

In real fact, the Kipchaks were behind the rise of the Byzantine Empire, a major presence in Eastern Europe for a millennium. Three generations past, a Byzantine culture sprouted in the new country, a product of cooperation between two nations admitted to this day. According to experts, its eastern component played a predominant role.

Nothing to wonder about. Europe offered a replay of the Kushan Khanate scenario, with the only difference that the Byzantine Empire was ruled by a Greek rather than a Turki. Whatever the case, it was a close fusion of two cultures. (Doesn't it strike you how cheaply and smartly the Greeks bought the Kipchaks?)

Constantine had no enemies now, keeping a tight rein on the gullible Kipchaks. He played generous with them and spared no efforts to have them on his side. Unless he did, no one would have heard of the Byzantine Empire, ever.

In 324 Constantine laid a new capital, Constantinople, for his empire. And again he turned to Turkic architects, so they could build it in their own way, as a challenge to Rome, with churches erected in the name of Tengri. A foxy trickster, that what he was.

Anyway, the Byzantine Empire was born.

Rome's colony of yesteryear, the new empire was gaining strength with each passing year and turning, with Kipchaks' helping hand, into a prosperous country. Alliance with the Turkis gave it the weight to dictate its will to Egypt,

Syria, Palestine and Rome itself. Constantine's appetite was growing, however.

In 325 he summoned all Christian priests to Nicaea (modern Iznik, Turkey) for the First Ecumenical Council of the Christian Church (General Council) that went down in history as the Council of Nicaea.

The Council set a sole objective no one cared to disguise. The emperor told the Council to establish a Christian church on a Greek, not Turkic, pattern. He had toyed with that idea for years, stinting no efforts or money to achieve his aim.

Under Constantine's design, Tengri and Christ were to become one person, or rather a sole God. The Greeks thought that the name of Tengri they usurped would give them divine power. And they needed the Council of Nicaea and the church itself for this purpose.

By appropriating Tengri for the needs of their church, they encroached upon Turkic prayers, rites and churches, upon Turkic culture as a whole. The treasures the Turkis had spent centuries to amass were now taken over by the Byzantine Empire and its Church. A real crime against the Turkic people, isn't it carefully concealed to this day?

The priests gathered at the Council of Nicaea failed to see through Emperor Constantine's design. When they finally realised what was behind it, they got indignant. Making God and man one-could there be a sillier thing? A sacrilege?

The first to speak out in defence of Tengri was Bishop Arius of Alexandria, Egypt. You could not, he said, equate man and God, for God was spirit and man was flesh, or God's creation to be born and die by the will of God.

Arius was a very enlightened man, confident in his power of persuasion. He was supported by bishops of the Armenian, Albanian (Caucasus), Syrian and several other churches. Not one of them, of course, rejected Christ, and no one wanted to equate him with God, for fear of divine punishment.

The argument ended abruptly and pathetically. Emperor Constantine, an unbaptised neophyte, who presided at the Council, interrupted Arius rudely, saying he was not there to be contradicted.

My comment: Arius was not a Greek as so many historians say. He was a Turk or Aryan as indicated by his name. At one time, the Greeks and the Turks were the same people, but they both separated. In the time of Arius, no self-respecting Greek would have even thought of calling himself Arius (Ari).

The dissident bishops remained unconvinced. They defied Constantine's will and did not equate God and Christ. Which signified that they retained loyalty to the faith they had been taught by Turkic clerics at Derbent.

Tengri remained the true God in the Christian churches of Armenia, Albania (Caucasus), Iveria, Syria, Egypt and Ethiopia, and congregations in those countries continued to pray to Him alone. His images were portrayed on icons and churches were dedicated to Him.

Surprisingly, the Turkic khans seemed to overlook the Council of Nicaea, as though they lived in a different world, in which "there is no god but God."

Again, the Greeks got away with impunity. To vindicate themselves, they came up with a New Testament, a book of Christ's deeds and genealogy, which, they claimed, were records left by Christ's disciples. It was a brazen lie.

How and where could they find those records, if Christ's name was first mentioned in the 2nd century (by the Greeks themselves)?

A situation, of which the Turkis say, "Spit at the Sky and get the spittle in your face."

Anyway, the New Testament compilers did not bother much about niceties. When they learned about Gheser (Tengri's son), the Greeks attributed some of his deeds to Christ and borrowed some other details from Buddha's life story. In the end, the politicians, little concerned about religion, succeeded in composing a sacred book for the Christian world, which was reviewed and rewritten time and again by none other than politicians. The whole thing has nothing to do with true faith.

My comment: When I was planning this book, I was at first attempted to omit totally Adji's evidence that our New Testament was compiled from Turkic, Buddhist, Hindu, Jewish, and other sources. Take Catholic rituals as an example. They are in no way similar to Jewish rituals and ceremonies. Yet, anyone having knowledge of Buddhism and Hinduism knows exactly the origins of those rituals. The architecture of our Christian churches is modeled after the old pagan Armenian churches, for the Armenians were the first to accept Christianity. Adji even wrote more about this reality, which I did leave out. However, this fact can bother and anger only those who mistakenly "believe" that "scriptures make the religion," just as clothes supposedly "make the man." Since each human thinks uniquely, and since all mankind's concepts are constantly changing, our understanding of the holy books never remains frozen. If we could go back into the past, we would be shocked to see that, ss far as the scriptures and tales about Jesus are concerned, these are in a contant state of change. Essentially, the origins of our scriptures are unimportant. We read scriptures for inspiration and guidance, no matter what their origins. The only requirement of true religious practice is knowledge of Duality, the Cross, and the Holy Trinity (Logos). All else is water under the bridge. All the writings and thoughts of mankind are just Babel, even the words that I write in this book.

Constantine was a politician with a deep sense of what he wanted. He picked the right time to set up his own church. Tensions boiled over between the Kipchaks and their neighbours, the Alans, so the Kipchaks' concerns were very far from Greek intrigues.

"When two men fight one of them dies," runs an Oriental saying.

I would like to comment that even Flavius Josephus, in his *Antiquities of the Jews,* complained that the Greeks were notorious copycats wanting even to sequester Judaism as their own invention. According to what little we know of ancient history, the Greeks and the Kuruks (Turks) were once Phoenicians. Even today, they are famous sailors. The *Gr* and the *Kr* in their names indicate this possibility. Later on, they separated. They have been inimical to each other ever since. Many Greeks argue that their civilization preceded that of the Turks. This is not true, for they all originated from the same Aryan Phoenician Krishtayas. They're the same people. For most of my life, I thought that Anatolia belonged to Greece. I needed most of my life to understand that the Anatolians were Turks; not Greeks. The squabble between the Greeks and Turks is like two siblings born of the same mother and father, each calling the other a bastard.

I can't speak for any of my readers, but I have always felt that the Aryanists and the Nicene supporters were just splitting hairs. In their own way, both were correct. God and his Son are one and the same. The Son is flesh and blood man. The Father is the divine energy coursing through the brain and spinal column of mankind. Mankind is just a microcosm of the macrocosm which is Creation itself. In reality, The Holy Trinity just describes the totality of a single body or thing, whether physical or spiritual: *Infinite or Finite Volume = Infinite or Finite (Length x Width x Height).*

We must also accept the fact that we are too ignorant and stupid to decide in favor of one or the other group. Something seems to be playing a not-so-funny game with us. Are some strange beings in Outer Space laughing at the fun they're having with us? Are they saying, "How can they expect to rise to our spiritual status? They cannot understand that the world is for all the five Krishtaya or Manu races, not for any particular manmade religious sect. Ha! Ha! The joke is not only on them, they *are* the joke."

If we practice consistency and faithfully the doctrine of the Holy Trinity, sooner or later our minds will expand sufficiently to know exactly what is right, wrong, or in between. Also, as I have stated before, it really makes no difference whether we accept the reality of reincarnation or not. What will happen, will happen, regardless of what we "believe" or "don't believe." Keeping that in mind, I ask: What can possibly be wrong with admitting the Gospel of Thomas, which contains Christ's original teachings of Christianity, back to the Bible? And what can possibly be wrong with admitting that nearly all of our ideas about Christianity we inherited from the Kipchaks? Let's give Christianity back to the Christians and Tengri back to the Turks.

In the past few years, the Vatican has come to realize that its basic teachings are entirely scientific. Right now, as the first Catholic fathers did in using the ancient Turkish sign of the Cross, duality, the Sacred Directions, etc., all taken from the Tengri religion, the Church is realizing that after all's said and done, it originally incorporated in its doctrines a powerful, simple and universally effective science that anyone can understand and apply in minutes. Church leaders and thinkers are additionally studying other religions, to find out what else they can add in order to increase Catholicism's effectiveness. But things were not always this way. For example, in the 1200s, the Church and its militaristic followers killed an estimated one million Aryanist *Catharis* (Kedaris) because they were getting too competitive. Yet, the Catharis had made discoveries which even today would seem miraculous. The persecution of the Catharis initiated the Inquisition. The good news is all that has ended forever. The Church is back on tract. The bad news is that many of its prelates appear to have no faith in their priestly duties. They're trying politics on for size. They must remember that they weren't educated to be politicians. They were educated in the ways and science of the Cross.

The time has arrived to bring this book to a close. I pray that what I have written will find acceptance. I still have much more to say, but what I have said up to this point must be digested before I can present new information to the world. I do have much more evidence than what is in this book. Christianity is the first religion ever to appear on earth. This is a truth beyond any kind of contradiction. Here is another original name of Christianity: *Krishtiyoni* (The Original Source of all Mankind). Again, I repeat: Don't accept what I say blindly. Investigate for yourself.

I promised at the beginning of this book that I would give the Atheists and skeptics a few welcome rays of hope. After all, they, too, should get what they really want out of life or the lack of it. Christ said:

> …Whoever blasphemes against the Father will be forgiven, and whoever blasphemes against the Son will be forgiven, but whoever blasphemes against the Holy Spirit will not be forgiven either in earth or in heaven. (Thomas Saying 44.)

What is the Holy Spirit? It is your unseen body that accompanies you until your physical carcass is ready to turn back to earth.

What is Heaven and Earth? It is the here and now. It is in no other place.

What is Hell? Hell is what the world becomes when we deny our duality as humans.

Where is Christ? Not only is he in your heart but he is constantly staring at you from the sky. Just go outside on a sunny day and see for yourself.

Now for the "treat" I promised my atheistic and "scientific" readers. If you are absolutely convinced that all I have written and all that Christ said, are just a conglomeration of lies and lunatic ravings, why don't you put your money where your mouth is? All you have to do is deny the reality of your own spirit and curse it. I guarantee: if you'll do that, you'll be in business. Or would it be more accurate to say, "out of business?" Do it now!

About the References Used
in the Book

Each person has his own idiosyncrasies, and I am no exception. One of my pet peeves is footnoting quotes and references and then listing the cited works at the end of a page, chapter, or book. I prefer to give credit immediately after commenting on or quoting a source. Additionally, I see no need for a bibliography at the end of a book if the references were cited within the book itself.

The perennially popular *Plain English Handbook,* by J. Martin Walsh and Anna Kathleen Walsh, states: "If the source is clear, you may mention it briefly in a sentence within your paragraph…but usually a footnote is best for complete reference to your source. (p. 121.)

In the past, providing footnotes for references and sources was necessary, for most people had to go to a library to find out more about the sources they were investigating. Local libraries had limited resources. Therefore, dedicated researchers generally had to travel many miles to do research in a university or large city library-or pay someone to do the research for them.

Fortunately for all mankind, the worldwide web and personal computers have brought the libraries of the world into our homes. We can now corroborate or study source materials on almost any subject, and to any depth, without leaving our homes. We who are passionately addicted to researching our respective fields of interest are too impatient to procrastinate in investigating the sources quoted in books and magazines. After reading a quote from or comment about a certain author's field of interest, we get to work immediately, stopping only when our hunger for more information has been satisfied. Having done that, we move on until we come upon another quote or comment that interests us. For that reason, I know that people seriously researching the subjects mentioned in my book may have already satisfied their curiosity by the time they finish it. They won't need to refer to a bibliography, either. There will be scribbled notes in a nearby notebook; passages and references highlighted in bright yellow or some other color.

The margins of the book will also have notations and comments. They will also have found pertinent material that not even I have found. In this way, authors and their readers interact with each other. Readers often send me information that will add to my own knowledge.

Most people read for information or general interest only. They don't wish to pursue a subject further. Therefore, by naming my sources in the book itself, I satisfy the intellectual needs and requirements of general readers and researchers alike.

Another of my pet peeves is some author's bothersome habit of using footnotes to inter- and extrapolate. I have read books in which the inter- and extrapolations delivered more vital information than the book itself. This made it necessary for me to read two books at once. If a person is going to write a book, let him write only one book at a time; not two in one.

Recommended References

Although I don't like footnotes and bibliographies, I do favor recommending certain references to my readers, as follows:

Pagan Sun Worship and Catholicism-La Verita-The Truth, at www.aloha.net~mikesch/verita.htm, produced by Michael Scheifler's Bible Light Homepage. Mr. Scheifler's outstanding essay and accompanying graphics about the abundance of solar symbols and rituals in Catholicism is a masterpiece. Whatever Mr. Scheifler's opinions, good or bad, about Catholicism's alleged perpetuation of "pagan sun worship," valid or not, does not concern me in the slightest. Evidently, I favor the "sun worshiping" approach as evidenced by my book. There is one thing I do know for sure: Regardless of what one may think of Catholicism's spiritual proximity to the pagan sun cults. Anyone who takes the sun seriously will improve all aspects of his material and spiritual life.

The World's Sixteen Crucified Saviors, by Kersey Graves. Don't be afraid to read the works of atheists. They, too, have a vital part to play in mankind's spiritual and secular history.

The Healing Sun, by Richard Hobday.

Jesus Christ, Sun of God-Ancient Cosmology and Early Christian Symbolism, by David Fideler.

Bible Myths and Their Parallels in Other Religions, by T. E. Doane.

The Bible in India-Hindoo Origin of Hebrew and Christian Reveleation, by Louis Jacolliot.

Suns of God-Krishna, Buddha, and Christ, by Acharya S.

¡Mariolatría! El Enigma de la Virgen, by Martín Careaga Montaño. This enlightening book will tell us anything we have ever wanted to know about the impor-

tance of "The Mother Goddess" in human religions. It's a shame that this all-important book has not yet been translated into English.

Jung on Christianity, Selected and Introduced by Murray Stein.

Christianity-Mankind's First Worldwide Religion! by Gene D. Matlock.

We humans have now arrived at a critical crossroads. We have just two roads open to us now. Shall we take the road to the left, or the one to the right? One of those roads will more than likely lead us to the destruction of this world and everything in it. The other one may save us and put us back on the right path. I quote often from Turkic author Murad Adji's writings in this book. I now urge anyone who takes what I say in this book seriously to read Mr. Adji's online books, especially his *Asia's Europe, Volume 1 (Europa, Turkic, the Great Steppe);* www.adji.ru/book 10 2.html.

Although I'm not in agreement with everything he says, especially the part where he shows partiality to Attila the Hun, he certainly lets all humans know who and what our origins were. After reading his writings, you'll never again see the world and human history in the same way.

978-0-595-39446-3
0-595-39446-9

www.ingramcontent.com/pod-product-compliance
Lightning Source LLC
Chambersburg PA
CBHW030323290526
45785CB00001B/482